Th

# Contents

## Dear Student,

The private schools you'll find in books and on television may be interesting, but the real world of private schools is even more amazing. You're reading this guide because you think that a private school might be right for you, and you're ready for one of the first steps—taking the SSAT.

This book will introduce you to the SSAT, the test format, and what to expect on test day. It contains practice tests that resemble the one you'll be taking, plus preparation tips to help you do your best on the SSAT and the Character Skills Snapshot.

*The Official Study Guide for the SSAT* gives you:

- The definition of an admission test
- Descriptions of the test sections
- Test-taking strategies
- An introduction to the Character Skills Snapshot
- Plenty of sample questions to practice
- Full-length practice tests
- Information about how to interpret scores
- Registration and test day checklists

What won't you find here? Shortcuts, tricks, or gimmicks. This is the only book that contains sample questions and practice tests written by the SSAT assessment developers and the test-taking strategies to help you to do your best. There are some valuable hints that can help you stay on track and maximize your time. But when it comes down to it, getting familiar with the test format and scoring, studying specific content types covered on the test, and solving practice questions is the best way to prepare for the SSAT. In addition to this guide, we offer an online practice program (see page 6) that provides even more sample questions, subject quizzes, and practice tests.

The path ahead will be exciting, and you'll probably learn a lot about yourself on the way. We wish you the best as you prepare for this journey, which will help you apply to a school that can change your life.

**The SSAT Assessment and Research Team**

# Dear Parent/Guardian,

Congratulations on your decision to explore a private school education for your child! For more than 50 years, the SSAT has been the gold standard in admission testing for the world's best private schools. We know that the process of taking the SSAT can be fraught with concern and distress, but it needn't be. The SSAT is one important step on the road to a private school education—one that should be taken seriously but should not cause undue anxiety.

The results of admission testing, while integral to an application, are just one of many factors considered by admission officers when determining if your child and their school make a great match. The degree of emphasis placed on scores depends on the school and on other information, such as transcripts and teacher recommendations. For the vast majority of schools, students with a wide range of SSAT scores are admitted.

Here are a few questions that admission officers contemplate when reviewing an applicant's scores:

• Are the scores consistent with the student's academic record?

• Do the scores highlight areas of academic strength or weakness?

• How do these scores compare with those of other students in the applicant pool?

• How do these scores compare with students who have enrolled over the last few years?

As a parent, you have a central role to play in helping your child to succeed in the school application process by reminding them to keep the SSAT in perspective. Schools are most interested in finding out who your child is.

There are a multitude of sources, both on- and offline, that promise to prepare your child for the SSAT and increase their test score. This guide was created by our assessment development team to support your child's preparation efforts with legitimate information, test-taking strategies, and practice tests. We encourage you to use this guide as your official source for SSAT preparation and the Character Skills Snapshot information. On page 73, we share tips to help you support your student during this important preparation for taking the SSAT.

Finally, we urge you to use the ssat.org website not only to register your child for the test but also to access information about the private school application process, search for schools that are the right fit for your child and your family, and take advantage of our online practice program.

We hope *The Official Study Guide for the Upper Level SSAT* will help to make your family's experience of testing and applying to private school a successful and enjoyable one.

Good luck!

Heather Hoerle, Executive Director & CEO, The Enrollment Management Association

# Chapter One: What Is the SSAT?

## What Is the Purpose of the SSAT?

The SSAT is designed for students who are seeking entrance to private schools worldwide. The purpose of the SSAT is to measure the verbal, quantitative, and reading skills students develop over time and that are needed for successful performance in private schools. The SSAT provides private school admission professionals with meaningful information about the possible academic success of students at their institutions, regardless of background or experience.

The SSAT is not an achievement test, although knowledge of a certain amount of mathematical content is necessary in order to do well on the quantitative sections of the test. Your most recent classroom math test, for example, was probably an achievement test: Your teacher designed it to evaluate how much you know about what was covered in class. The SSAT, on the other hand, is designed to measure the overall verbal, quantitative, and reading skills you have acquired, instead of focusing on your mastery of particular course materials.

SSAT tests are not designed to measure other characteristics, such as initiative, resilience, or teamwork, that may contribute to your success in school. As a complement to the SSAT's assessment of cognitive skills, we also offer the Character Skills Snapshot, which was designed expressly to measure character skills valued by private schools. To learn more about the Snapshot, visit ssat.org/snapshot.

## How Is the SSAT Designed?

The SSAT measures three constructs: verbal, quantitative, and reading skills that students develop over time, both in and out of school. It emphasizes critical thinking and problem-solving skills that are essential for academic success.

The overall difficulty level of the SSAT is built to be at 50%–60%. This means that on average, 50%–60% of the test takers can answer the questions correctly. The distribution of question difficulties is set so that the test will effectively differentiate among test takers, who vary in their level of abilities.

To develop the SSAT, The Enrollment Management Association convenes content committees composed of content experts and independent school teachers. The committees write and review items, and reach consensus regarding the appropriateness of the questions. Questions judged to be acceptable after the committee review are then pretested and analyzed. Those that are statistically sound are selected and assembled into test forms.

## The SSAT Is Reliable

The SSAT is a highly reliable test. A test is said to have a high reliability if it produces similar results under consistent conditions. Reliability coefficients range between 0.00 (no reliability) and 1.00 (perfect reliability). On the SSAT, the scaled-score reliability is higher than 0.90 for both the verbal and quantitative sections, and is approaching 0.90 for the reading section.

## The SSAT Is a Norm-Referenced Test

A norm-referenced test interprets an individual tester's score relative to the distribution of scores for a comparison group, referred to as the norm group. The SSAT norm groups consist of all the test takers (same grade) who have taken the test for the first time on one of the Standard SSAT administrations in the United States and Canada typically within the past three years.

The SSAT reports percentile ranks, which are referenced to the performance of the norm group. For example, if you are in the eighth grade, and your percentile rank on the March 2019 verbal section is 90%, it means that verbal scores for 90% of all the other eighth-grade students (who have taken the test for one of the SSAT administrations in the United States and Canada typically using the most recent three years of data) fall below your scaled score. The same scaled score on the SSAT may have a slightly different percentile rank from year to year, and the SSAT percentile ranks should not be compared to those of other standardized tests because each test is taken by a different group of students.

In contrast, a criterion-referenced test interprets a test taker's performance without reference to the performance of other test takers. For example, you would receive a 90% on a classroom test if you answered 90% of the questions correctly. Your score is not referenced to the performance of anyone else in your class.

It is important to remember that the SSAT norm group is highly competitive. You are being compared to all the other students (same grade) who are taking this test for admission into private schools, some of which are the most selective in the country. Most important to remember is that the SSAT is just one piece of information considered by schools when making admission decisions, and for the vast majority of schools, students with a wide range of SSAT scores are admitted.

# The SSAT Is a Standardized Test

The SSAT is scored in a consistent (or standard) manner. It adheres to standard administration processes and practices, based on the testing mode. The reported (or scaled) scores are comparable and can be used interchangeably, regardless of which test form was taken. A scaled score of 710 on the June 2018 Upper Level verbal section, for example, has the same meaning as the scaled score of 710 from the December 2016 Upper Level verbal section, although the forms are different. This score interchangeability is achieved through a statistical procedure referred to as *score equating*. Score equating is used to adjust for minor form difficulty differences, so that the resulting scores can be compared directly.

Standard also refers to the way in which tests are developed and administered. A standard process for writing, testing, and analyzing questions—before they ever appear on a live test—is used. The Enrollment Management Association provides precise instructions to be followed by qualified and experienced test administrators from the moment students are admitted to the test center until the time of dismissal. Any deviations from the uniform testing conditions are reported by the test administrator in writing. Of course, a student may apply for testing accommodations, but the processes and procedures for the test's administration remain the same.

# Should I Guess on the SSAT?

The answer is: It depends. You must first understand how the test is scored.

When your test is scored, you will receive one point for each correct answer. One quarter of a point is deducted for each incorrect answer. You will not receive or lose points for questions that are not answered. If you guess, try guessing only when you can eliminate at least one (but optimally more than one) answer choice.

A few things to keep in mind:

**Keep moving.** Do not waste time on a question that is hard for you. If you cannot answer it, make a note of it, skip over it, and move on. If you have time left in the section, go back to it then.

**Take care with each question.** You receive one point for each correct answer, no matter how hard or easy the questions are. Approach all questions with equal consideration; don't risk losing points to careless errors on seemingly easy questions.

**Check your answer sheet.** If taking the test on paper, mark your answers in the correct row on the answer sheet. Be especially careful if you skip questions.

# SSAT Practice Online

A perfect complement to this study guide, our online practice program is another official source for SSAT practice. SSAT Practice Online helps you prepare by providing practice questions similar to those appearing on the SSAT, and identification of exactly which topics you should focus on before you test. Other key features include: section tests that target quantitative, reading, or verbal practice; SSAT topic quizzes with tips on how to answer each question; and study tools. Visit ssat.org/practice or access the program via your SSAT account.

## ssat.org/practice

*Students who use a fee waiver for the SSAT registration are also provided free access to the online practice program for both the Middle and Upper Level SSAT, as well as free access to the Admission Academy, a resource to help families navigate the K–12 private school admission process.*

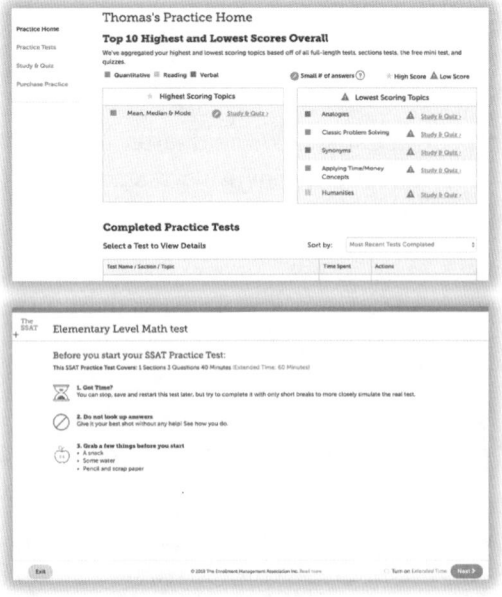

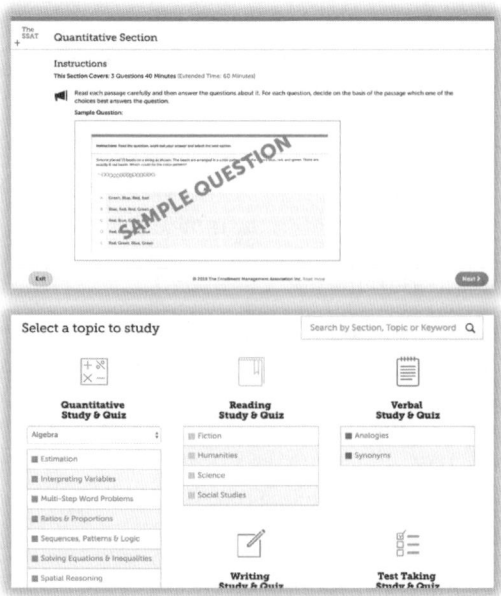

# Chapter Two:
# About the Upper Level SSAT

The SSAT is a multiple-choice test that consists of verbal, quantitative (math), and reading comprehension sections. The Upper Level SSAT is for students in grades 8–11 and provides admission officers with an idea of your academic ability and "fit" in their schools. The best way to ensure that you perform as well as you possibly can on the SSAT is to familiarize yourself with the test. Understanding the format of the test and reviewing practice questions will make your test-taking experience easier. You'll feel more comfortable with the test and be able to anticipate the types of questions you'll encounter.

This chapter will introduce you to the kinds of questions you'll see on SSAT and the best ways to approach them. The sample questions that accompany each section will give you some practice before you tackle the practice tests that appear later in the book. In this chapter, we also will provide test-taking strategies that students should know when they take the SSAT. The bonus of these test-taking strategies is that they may also help you perform better on the tests you take in school!

# The Upper Level Test Consists of FIVE Sections:

## 1. Writing Sample

**Number of questions:** You will have a choice between two prompts.

**What it measures:** Your ability to think insightfully, organize your ideas, and write clearly

**Scored section:** Your writing sample is not scored, but it is provided to the schools you have selected to receive your score reports.

**Time allotted:** 25 minutes

**Topics covered:** Students are given a choice between two essay prompts: one personal and one general. You choose one of them and write an essay.

> The best way to make sure you perform as well as you can on the SSAT is to become familiar with the test.

## 2. Quantitative (Math) Section

**Number of questions:** 50, divided into two parts

**What it measures:** Your ability to solve problems involving the topics below

**Scored section:** Yes

**Time allotted:** 30 minutes for the first 25 questions, and 30 minutes for the final 25 questions

**Topics covered:**

**Algebra**
- Algebraic Word Problems
- Exponential Expressions
- Factoring
- Functions
- Graphs
- Linear Equations/Systems of Equations
- Inequalities
- Quadratic Equations
- Polynomial Expressions/Equations
- Radical Expressions/Equations
- Ratio/Proportion/Percent/Rates
- Rational Expressions/Equations
- Slope

*Continued on next page*

## 2. Quantitative (Math) Section *(continued)*

### Geometry
- Angles
- Area
- Coordinate
- Length/Perimeter/Circumference
- Pythagorean Theorem
- Transformations: Reflections/Translations/ Rotations
- 3D: Volume/Surface Area
- Visual/Spatial Reasoning

### Data Analysis
- Counting
- Mean/Median/Mode/Range
- Probability
- Set Theory
- Tables/Graphs

### Number Concepts and Operations
- Arithmetic Computations/Word Problems
- Converting Units
- Estimation
- Number Sense/Number Theory
- Order of Operations
- Logical Reasoning/Puzzle Problems
- Sequences and Patterns

## 3. Reading Comprehension Section

**Number of questions:** 40

**What it measures:** Your ability to understand and interpret what you read

**Scored section:** Yes

**Time allotted:** 40 minutes

**Topics covered:** Questions about reading passages. There are 7–8 reading passages, each 150–350 words in length. Passages are either literary or expository. Literary passages are drawn from works of fiction or poetry. Expository passages examine topics in the fields of science, social science, history, or the humanities.

### Literary passages:
- Fiction
- Poetry

### Expository passages:
- Science
- Social Science
- History
- Humanities (art, music, etc.)

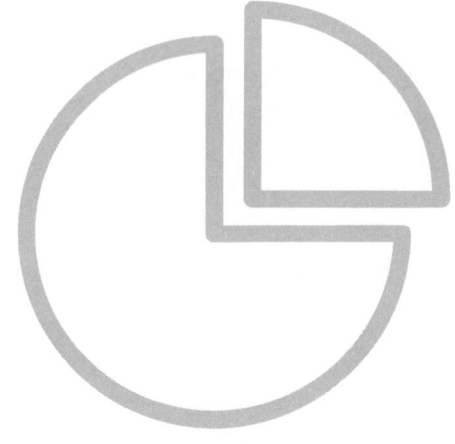

# 4. Verbal Section

**Number of questions:** 60 (30 synonyms and 30 analogies)

**What it measures:** Your ability to understand the meanings of words and to recognize relationships between words with different meanings

**Scored section:** Yes

**Time allotted:** 30 minutes

**Topics covered:** Questions asking you to identify words that have similar meanings (synonyms) and questions asking you to identify word pairs that have similar relationships (analogies). The words tested are nouns, adjectives, or verbs.

# 5. Experimental Section

**Number of questions:** 16

**What it measures:** Verbal, reading comprehension, and quantitative skills

**Scored section:** No

**Time allotted:** 15 minutes

**Topics covered:** This section contains six verbal, five reading, and five quantitative questions.

*Students utilizing the 1.5x time accommodation do not complete the experimental section.*

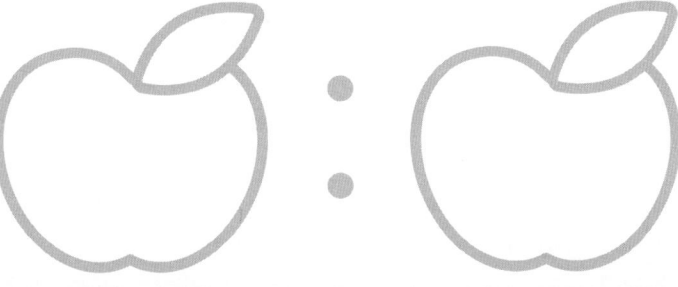

| Test Overview | | |
|---|---|---|
| **Section** | **Number of Questions** | **Time Allotted to Administer Each Section** |
| **Writing Sample** | 1 | 25 minutes |
| **Break** | | 10 minutes |
| **Section 1 (Quantitative)** | 25 | 30 minutes |
| **Section 2 (Reading)** | 40 | 40 minutes |
| **Break** | | 10 minutes |
| **Section 3 (Verbal)** | 60 | 30 minutes |
| **Section 4 (Quantitative)** | 25 | 30 minutes |
| **Section 5 (Experimental)** | 16 | 15 minutes |
| **Totals** | **167[1]** | **3 hours, 10 minutes** |

[1]Of the 167 items including the writing sample, 150 questions are scored.

# 1. The Writing Sample

At the beginning of the test, you will be asked to write an essay in 25 minutes. You'll have a choice between a personal and a general essay prompt. Your writing sample will be sent to the admission officers at the schools to which you're applying to help them assess your writing skills. This section is not scored. You will not receive a copy of the writing sample unless you choose to purchase it separately.

## What Are the Directions for the Writing Sample Section of the Test?

Schools would like to get to know you better through an essay you write. If you choose to write a personal essay, base your essay on the topic presented in A. If you choose to write a general essay, base your essay on the topic presented in B. Please fill in the circle next to your choice.

## How Are the Writing Prompts Presented?

| **EXAMPLE:** | (A) Who is a person from history you would like to get to know and why? <br> *or* <br> (B) What are the qualities of an effective leader? Support your answer with reasons and examples. |
|---|---|

## Just the Facts
### The Writing Sample

**Number of questions:**
You will have a choice between two writing prompts

**What this measures:**
This gives admission officers a feel for how you write

**Scored section:**
No, but it is provided to the schools you have selected to receive your score reports

**Time allotted:**
25 minutes

## Tips for Getting Your Writing Sample Started

Read the prompts carefully. Take a few minutes to think about them and choose the one you prefer. Then, organize your thoughts before you begin writing (scrap paper for organizing your thoughts will be provided when you test). Be sure that you use a pencil, that your handwriting is legible, and that you stay within the lines and margins. Remember to be yourself and let your ideas flow!

If you want to change what you have written, erase or neatly cross out the words you want to eliminate and add the new words so they are legible. Two line-ruled pages are provided. Don't feel as if you have to fill both pages—just do your best to provide a well-written essay.

Remember: Your writing sample will not be scored. Schools use it to get to know you better through your writing.

## Practice Writing Samples

This book includes practice writing sample prompts, which can be found at the beginning of the practice tests. Each sample includes directions, two prompts, and an answer sheet similar to the one you'll receive during the test.

## Writing Sample Test-Taking Strategies

1. While creativity is encouraged, remember that the admission officers in the schools to which you are applying will read your writing sample. Be sure that your essay is one that you would not hesitate to turn in for a school assignment.

2. Read both prompts. Take a couple of minutes to think about what you're going to write. You can use your scrap paper to organize your thoughts.

3. Choose a working title for your essay. The Upper Level SSAT doesn't require a title, but creating one might help keep you on track.

4. If you choose to write a personal essay, be sure to provide interesting details to illustrate your thoughts and feelings.

5. If you choose to write a general essay, be sure to organize your ideas and provide plenty of reasons and examples to support your point of view.

6. If there's time, check your writing for spelling, punctuation, and grammatical errors.

# 2. The Quantitative Section

The two quantitative (math) sections of the Upper Level SSAT measures your knowledge of algebra, geometry, data analysis, and number concepts and operations. The words used in SSAT problems refer to mathematical operations with which you are already familiar.

## What Are the Directions for the Quantitative Section on the Test?

Following each problem in this section, there are five suggested answers. Work each problem in your head, in the blank space at the right of the page if taking the test on paper, or on scrap paper if taking the test on the computer. Then, look at the five suggested answers and decide which one is best.

## How Are the Quantitative Problems Presented?

Many of the problems that appear in the quantitative section of the Upper Level SSAT are structured in mathematical terms that directly state the operation you need to perform to determine the best answer choice.

| **EXAMPLE:** | 1. What is the slope of the line that is perpendicular to $2x + 3y = 6$ ? <br> (A) $-\frac{3}{2}$ <br> (B) $-\frac{2}{3}$ <br> (C) $-\frac{1}{2}$ <br> (D) $\frac{2}{3}$ <br> (E) $\frac{3}{2}$ <br> **The correct answer is (E).** |
| --- | --- |

Other problems are structured as word problems. A word problem often does not specifically state the mathematical operation or operations that you will need to perform in order to determine the answer. In these problems, your task is to carefully consider how the question is worded and the way the information is presented to determine what operations you will need to perform.

| **EXAMPLE:** | 2. A group went to a restaurant for lunch. The total bill for the meal was $70. Not including a $15 service charge, the cost per person was $5.50. How many people were in the group? <br> (A) 10 <br> (B) 11 <br> (C) 13 <br> (D) 14 <br> (E) 15 <br> **The correct answer is (A).** |
| --- | --- |

## Just the Facts
### The Quantitative Section

**Number of questions:** 50, divided into two parts

**What it measures:** Your ability to solve problems involving algebra, geometry, data analysis, and number concepts and operations

**Scored section:** Yes

**Time allotted:** 30 minutes for the first 25 problems and 30 minutes for the final 25 problems

# Quantitative Test-Taking Strategies

1. Read each problem carefully.

2. Pace yourself. Try not to spend too much time on one problem.

3. Be sure to use the "Use This Space for Figuring" area of your test book to do the scratch work. If taking the computer-based test at a Prometric test center, you will receive a white board.

4. Always check to see if you have answered the question asked in the problem. Circling what's being asked can be helpful, so you don't mistakenly choose the wrong answer.

5. Watch for units of measure. Be sure you know and understand in which unit of measure the answer is supposed to be given.

6. Draw pictures. If you find that a problem is complicated, you can draw a graph, diagram—anything that will allow you to understand what the problem is asking.

7. Remember to mark your answers on the answer sheet if taking the test on paper! If your problem is solved in the test book but not marked on the answer sheet, it will not be counted.

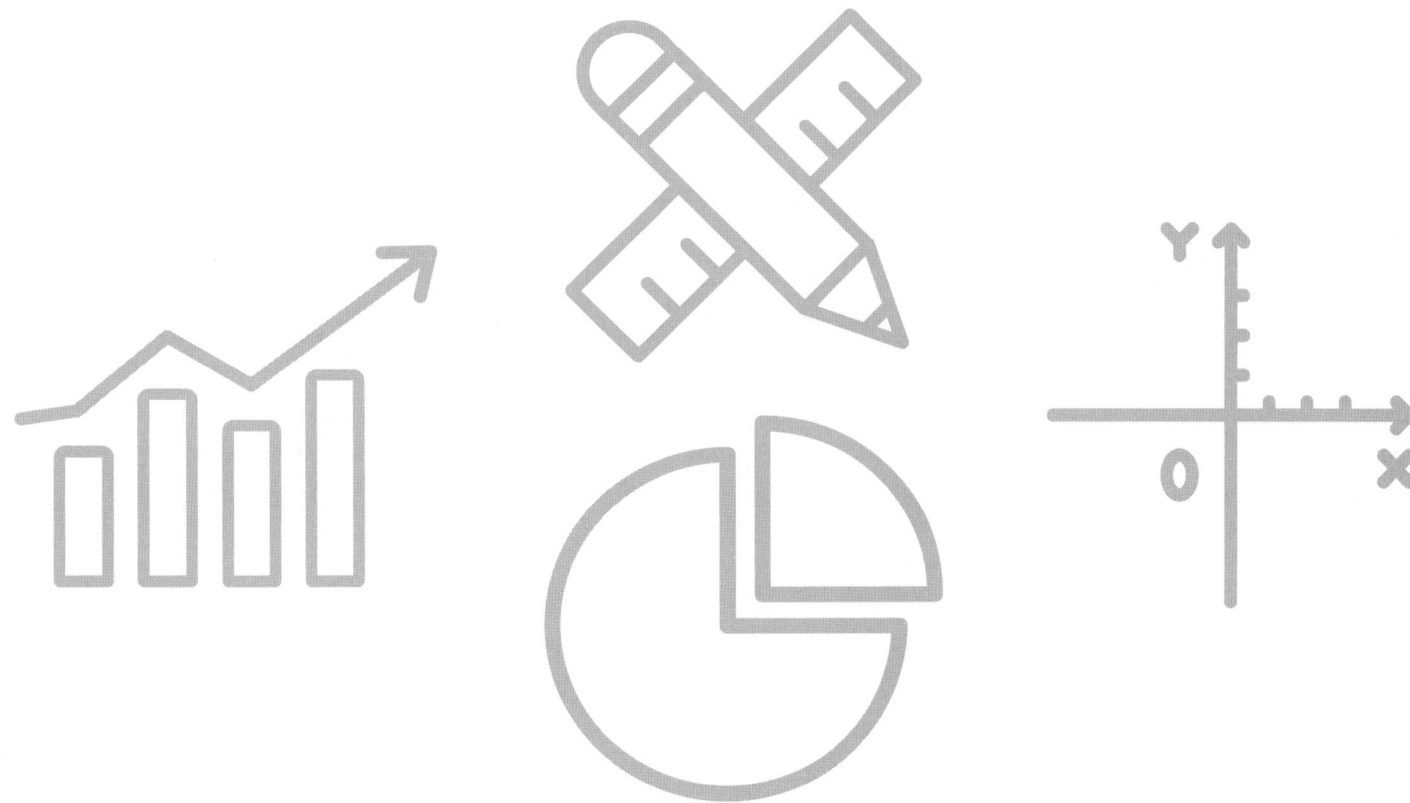

# Sample Questions: Quantitative

On the following pages, you'll find sample problems from these topics: algebra, geometry, data analysis, and number concepts and operations. Each topic will also include a brief overview of related content. Review each sample problem description and then work the problems that illustrate the concept.

## Section I: Algebra

In this section, you will find 20 sample problems and related overviews of mathematical concepts in algebra. The answers are located at the end of this section.

## Algebraic Word Problems

> An algebraic word problem can be presented in either a real-life or an abstract setting. Some word problems will require you to set up and solve an equation or inequality to arrive at the final answer. Other word problems will require you to translate words into an expression, equation, or inequality, which will be the final answer.

1.  Kyle has three times as much money in his savings account as Hayden. Hayden has twice as much money in his savings account as Jeremy. Combined Kyle, Hayden, and Jeremy have a total of $612.  How much money does Kyle have in his account?

    (A)   $68
    (B)   $136
    (C)   $204
    (D)   $306
    (E)   $408

---

> 3 less than twice the value of a quantity is greater than 5.

2.  Which of the following inequalities is equivalent to the statement above?

    (A)   $2x - 3 > 5$
    (B)   $2x - 3 < 5$
    (C)   $3 - 2x > 5$
    (D)   $3 - 2x < 5$
    (E)   $2(3 - x) > 5$

## Exponential Expressions

You will need to know the properties for manipulating algebraic expressions that involve exponents. For example, when multiplying expressions that have the same base, you add the exponents: $a^n a^r = a^{n+r}$ and when dividing expressions that have the same base, you subtract the exponents: $\dfrac{a^n}{a^r} = a^{n-r}$. When raising an expression to a power, you multiply exponents: $(a^n)^r = a^{nr}$. When raising an expression to a negative power, you raise the reciprocal of the expression to the positive power: $a^{-n} = \dfrac{1}{a^n}$. When raising a product to a power, you raise each of the variables in the product to that power: $(ab)^n = a^n b^n$ and when raising a fraction to a power, you raise both the numerator and the denominator to the power: $\left(\dfrac{a}{b}\right)^n = \dfrac{a^n}{b^n}$.

3. If $ab \neq 0$, which of the following is equivalent to $\left(\dfrac{3a}{b}\right)^3 \left(\dfrac{a^2 b}{3a^5}\right)$?

   (A) $\dfrac{1}{b^2}$

   (B) $\dfrac{3}{b^2}$

   (C) $\dfrac{9}{b^2}$

   (D) $\dfrac{a}{b^2}$

   (E) $\dfrac{9a}{b^2}$

# Factoring

Factoring on the test will involve simple factoring, factoring trinomials, or factoring the difference of two squares.

For simple factoring, you will need to find the common factor for two or more algebraic expressions. For example, $3xy$ is the common factor of $6xy$ and $9xy^2$. So, an expression such as $6xy + 9xy^2$ can be factored as $3xy(2 + 3y)$.

For factoring trinomials, you will need to factor the trinomial into two binomial factors. For example, the expression $x^2 + 2x - 15$ can be factored into $(x - 3)(x + 5)$.

For factoring the difference of two squares, you will need to factor the difference of two squares into two binomial factors. For example, the expression $9x^2 - 16y^2$ can be factored into $(3x - 4y)(3x + 4y)$.

4. What is the greatest common factor of $12x^2y$ and $10xy^2$ ?

(A) $2xy$

(B) $12xy$

(C) $12x^2y^2$

(D) $120x^2y^2$

(E) $120x^3y^3$

5. Which of the following is a factor of $x^2 + 2x - 8$ ?

(A) $x - 2$

(B) $x - 4$

(C) $x - 8$

(D) $x + 2$

(E) $x + 8$

# Functions

Functions can be represented by an algebraic equation, a graph, or a table. All three representations of a function may be included on the test. Finding a value of a function that is defined by an algebraic equation, such as $f(x) = 10 - 5(x - 3)$ involves substituting a value of $x$ into the expression. For example, $f(6) = 10 - 5(6 - 3) = 10 - 15 = -5$. Finding a value of a function that is represented by a graph involves finding a corresponding $y$ value on the graph for a given $x$ value, or vice versa. Finding a value of a function defined by a table involves finding the $f(x)$ or $y$ value in the table that corresponds to a given $x$ value, or vice versa.

6. Let the function $f$ be defined as $f(x) = 2x + 7$. For what value of $a$ is $f(a)$ equal to 11 ?

   (A)   2
   (B)   9
   (C)   15
   (D)   18
   (E)   29

---

| $x$ | 0 | 1 | 2 | 3 | 4 |
|-----|---|---|---|---|---|
| $f(x)$ | 4 | 8 | 5 | 1 | 3 |

7. The function $f$ is defined by the values in the table above. What is the value of $f(1) + f(3)$ ?

   (A)  0
   (B)  3
   (C)  5
   (D)  7
   (E)  9

# Graphs

You may be asked to determine a graph for a given equation, or you may be given a graph and asked for the equation that defines the graph. You may also be asked to identify properties of a graph. For example, you may be asked to identify a graph that has a given slope, $x$-intercept, or $y$-intercept.

8.  Which of the following could be the graph of $y = mx + b$, where $m > 0$ and $b < 0$ ?

(A)
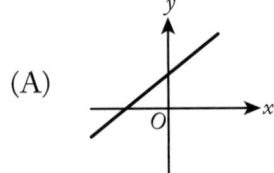

(B)
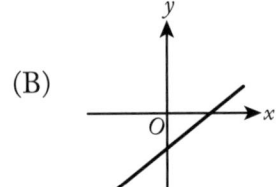

(C)
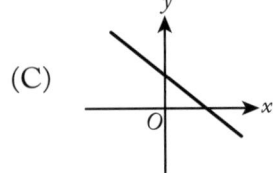

(D)
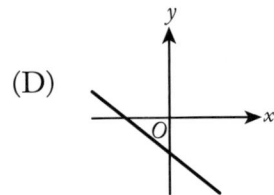

(E)
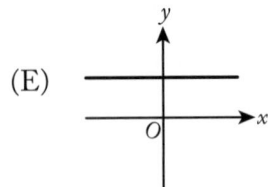

# Linear Equations/Systems of Equations

You may be asked to solve linear equations and/or systems of equations. Various techniques can be used to solve a system of equations.

9. What is the solution to the equation $4x + 2 - 2x = 7(x - 2)$ ?

(A) $-\dfrac{16}{5}$

(B) $-\dfrac{12}{5}$

(C) $-\dfrac{4}{5}$

(D) $\dfrac{4}{5}$

(E) $\dfrac{16}{5}$

---

$$3x + 2y = 15$$
$$4x - 2y = 13$$

10. If $(x, y)$ is the solution to the system of equations above, what is the value of $y$ ?

(A) 1

(B) $\dfrac{3}{2}$

(C) 2

(D) 4

(E) $\dfrac{27}{2}$

## Inequalities

You may be asked to solve an inequality or work through a problem that involves inequalities.

11. If $x$ is a point in the darkened region on the number line shown, which of the following intervals describes all possible values of $x$ ?

    (A) $x > -2$
    (B) $x \leq 3$
    (C) $-2 \leq x < 3$
    (D) $-2 < x \leq 3$
    (E) $x < -2$ or $x \geq 3$

## Quadratic Equations

The quadratic equations on the test may be given in a factored form or in a form that you will need to factor in order to solve the equation. Some equations will be set equal to 0, and for others you will need to manipulate the equation to set it equal to 0. None of the quadratic equations on the test will require you to know the quadratic formula.

$$3(x - 2)(x + 1) = 0$$

12. Which of the following values of $x$ satisfies the equation above?

    (A) 3
    (B) 1
    (C) 0
    (D) $-1$
    (E) $-2$

## Polynomial Expressions/Equations

You may be asked to add, subtract, multiply, or divide polynomial expressions or solve equations that use polynomial expressions. When adding or subtracting polynomial expressions, you may need to use the distributive property and group like terms. You can use various techniques to multiply or divide polynomial expressions. For some polynomial expression problems, you may be asked to evaluate a polynomial expression for given values of the variables in the expression.

13. Simplify: $(3x^3 + 2x^2 - x - 1) + (2x - 1)$

(A) $3x^3 + 2x^2$

(B) $3x^3 + 2x^2 + x$

(C) $3x^3 + 2x^2 + x - 2$

(D) $5x^4 + 4x^3 - 2x^2$

(E) $5x^4 + 4x^3 - 2x^2 - 2$

14. Which of the following is equivalent to $(x - 1)(x^2 + 2)$ ?

(A) $x^3 + 1$

(B) $x^3 - 2$

(C) $x^3 + x^2 + 2x - 2$

(D) $x^3 - x^2 + 2x - 2$

(E) $x^3 + x^2 - 2x - 2$

## Radical Expressions/Equations

You may be asked to simplify radical expressions, add or subtract radical expressions, or multiply or divide radical expressions. The radical expressions on the test will mostly involve algebraic expressions.

15. Which of the following is equivalent to $\sqrt{12x^2} + \sqrt{27x^2}$ for positive values of $x$ ?

(A) $15x$

(B) $18x$

(C) $x\sqrt{39}$

(D) $5x\sqrt{3}$

(E) $6x\sqrt{3}$

## Ratio/Proportion/Percentages/Rates

This category involves several topics, so there will be more than one of these topics covered on the test. Ratio and proportion problems, any problems that involve percents, and word problems that test rates may be tested.

16. A fruit basket contains 5 apples, 6 bananas, 7 pears, and no other fruit. What is the ratio of the number of bananas in the basket to the total number of fruit in the basket?

(A) $\frac{5}{18}$

(B) $\frac{3}{10}$

(C) $\frac{1}{3}$

(D) $\frac{7}{18}$

(E) $\frac{1}{2}$

Coupon 1: 20% off a purchase
Coupon 2: $10 off a purchase of $40 or more

17. Ingrid has the above coupons that can be used at a grocery store. She can only use one coupon for each purchase. She plans to make a purchase of $60 at the grocery store. Which of the following statements is true?

(A) Ingrid will save $10 if she uses coupon 1.
(B) Ingrid will save $12 if she uses coupon 1.
(C) Ingrid will save $20 if she uses coupon 1.
(D) Ingrid will save $15 if she uses coupon 2.
(E) Ingrid will save $20 if she uses coupon 2.

---

18. Machine $A$ and Machine $B$ work at constant rates to produce billing envelopes. To produce 20 billing envelopes, it takes Machine $A$ 4 minutes and Machine $B$ 5 minutes. At these rates, what is the total number of envelopes that Machine $A$ and Machine $B$ can produce in 40 minutes?

(A) 90
(B) 180
(C) 360
(D) 380
(E) 400

# Rational Expressions/Equations

Rational expressions and equations contain algebraic expressions in the numerator, denominator, or in both.

19. What are possible solutions of $\dfrac{1}{x^4} = \dfrac{1}{x^2}$ ?

(A) 0 only

(B) 1 only

(C) –1 and 1 only

(D) 0 and 1 only

(E) –1, 0, and 1

## Slope

> You should know how to find the slope of a line given two points. The slope between two points $(a, b)$ and $(t, u)$ is $\dfrac{u - b}{t - a}$. You should also know how to identify the slope of a line from its linear equation. For the linear equation of the line $y = mx + b$, the slope of the line is $m$ and the $y$-intercept is $b$. When two lines have equal slopes, the lines are parallel. When two lines have slopes that are negative reciprocals of each other, the lines are perpendicular. For example, a line with slope 2 is perpendicular to a line with slope $-\dfrac{1}{2}$.

20. In the $xy$-coordinate plane, if the slope of the line passing through the points $(5, 6)$ and $(a, b)$ is 0, which of the following could be the point $(a, b)$ ?

    (A) $(-5, -6)$
    (B) $(0, 0)$
    (C) $(0, 6)$
    (D) $(5, 0)$
    (E) $(6, 5)$

# Answer Key
## Section I: Algebra

1.  **Answer (E) $408**

    Let $K$, $H$, and $J$ represent the amount of money for Kyle, Hayden, and Jeremy, respectively.

    So, $K + H + J = 612$, $K = 3H$, and $H = 2J$. Since $J = \dfrac{H}{2}$ then $K + H + J = 3H + H + \dfrac{H}{2} = 612$,

    and solving the equation for $H$ yields $H = 136$;

    Therefore, $K = 3(136) = 408$.

2.  **Answer (A) $2x - 3 > 5$**

3.  **Answer (C) $\dfrac{9}{b^2}$**

    $$\left(\frac{3a}{b}\right)^3 \left(\frac{a^2 b}{3a^5}\right) = \left(\frac{27a^3}{b^3}\right)\left(\frac{a^2 b}{3a^5}\right) = \frac{27a^5 b}{3a^5 b^3} = 9b^{-2} = \frac{9}{b^2}$$

4.  **Answer (A) $2xy$**

5.  **Answer (A) $x - 2$**

    The factored form of $x^2 + 2x - 8$ is $(x + 4)(x - 2)$. Since only one of these factors is listed in the answer choices, the answer is $x - 2$.

6.  **Answer (A) 2**

    Since $f(a) = 2a + 7 = 11$, then $2a = 4$, and $a = 2$.

7.  **Answer (E) 9**

    According to the table, $f(1) = 8$ and $f(3) = 1$. Therefore, $f(1) + f(3) = 8 + 1 = 9$

8.  **Answer (B)**

    In the equation $y = mx + b$, the letter $m$ represents the slope, and the letter $b$ represents the $y$-intercept. The line graph in (B) has a positive slope and a negative $y$-intercept.

9.  **Answer (E) $\dfrac{16}{5}$**

    $4x + 2 - 2x = 7(x - 2)$
    $+ 2 = 7x - 14$
    $16 = 5x$, so $x = \dfrac{16}{5}$

10. **Answer (B) $\dfrac{3}{2}$**

    Adding the two expressions $3x + 2y = 15$ and $4x - 2y = 13$ yields $7x = 28$, so $x = 4$. Substituting $x = 4$ in the first equation yields $3(4) + 2y = 15$, or $12 + 2y = 15$. Solving the equation further yields $2y = 3$ or $y = \dfrac{3}{2}$

# Answer Key
## Section I: Algebra *(continued)*

11.   **Answer (D)  $-2 < x \le 3$**
      The darkened region is between $-2$ and 3. Since there is an open circle at $-2$ and
      a closed circle at 3, the inequality $-2 < x \le 3$ describes all possible values of $x$.

12.   **Answer (D)  $-1$**
      The expression $3(x - 2)(x + 1)$ equals 0 when $x = 2$ or $x = -1$. Since only one of these values of
      $x$ is listed in the answer choices, the answer is $-1$.

13.   **Answer (C)  $3x^3 + 2x^2 + x - 2$**
      Combining terms in the given problem yields the correct answer.

14.   **Answer (D)  $x^3 - x^2 + 2x - 2$**
      $(x - 1)(x^2 + 2) = x^3 + 2x - x^2 - 2$ and ordering the expressions by their degree values
      yields the answer.

15.   **Answer (D)  $5x\sqrt{3}$**
      $\sqrt{12x^2} = \sqrt{4 \cdot 3x^2} = 2x\sqrt{3}$ and $\sqrt{27x^2} = \sqrt{9 \cdot 3x^2} = 3x\sqrt{3}$, so $2x\sqrt{3} + 3x\sqrt{3} = 5x\sqrt{3}$

16.   **Answer (C)  $\frac{1}{3}$**

      $$\frac{Number\ of\ bananas}{Total\ number\ of\ fruit} = \frac{6}{18} = \frac{1}{3}$$

17.   **Answer (B)  Ingrid will save \$12 if she uses coupon 1.**
      If Ingrid uses coupon 1, she will get 20% of \$60 or $(0.2)(60)$ or \$12

18.   **Answer (C)  360**
      Since Machine $A$ produces 20 billing envelopes in 4 minutes, it will produce 200 billing envelopes
      in 40 minutes.
      Since Machine $B$ produces 20 billing envelopes in 5 minutes, it will produce 160 billing envelopes
      in 40 minutes.
      $200 + 160 = 360$

# Answer Key
## Section I: Algebra *(continued)*

19.  **Answer (C) –1 and 1 only**

To solve the equation $\dfrac{1}{x^4} = \dfrac{1}{x^2}$, cross multiply to get $x^4 = x^2$ or $x^4 - x^2 = 0$. Factoring the left side of the equation yields $x^2(x^2 - 1)$ or $x^2(x - 1)(x + 1) = 0$. The solutions to this equation are $x = 0, 1$, and $-1$. However, when $x = 0$, the expressions in the original equation are undefined, so the solutions to the original equation are $-1$ and $1$ only. The $0$ is an extraneous solution.

20.  **Answer (C) $(0, 6)$**

The slope between the two points $(5, 6)$ and $(a, b)$ is $\dfrac{b - 6}{a - 5}$. For this expression to equal $0$, $b$ must equal $6$. A line with a slope of $0$ is a horizontal line, so $a$ can equal any number except $5$. The only answer choice with a $y$-coordinate of $6$ is $(0, 6)$, so this is the answer.

# Section II: Geometry

In this section, you will find 14 sample problems and related overviews of mathematical concepts in geometry. The answers are located at the end of this section.

Some of the geometry items on the test will have figures, and others will not have figures. For a geometry item without a figure, it may be helpful to sketch a figure and label it with the information given.

## Angles

> Angle relationships that will be tested involve angles in triangles, in quadrilaterals, and in other polygons. For example, you should know that the sum of the measures of the interior angles of a triangle is 180 degrees. Angle relationships between vertical angles, complementary angles, supplementary angles, angles about a point, and angles formed by parallel lines and a transversal are some of the topics that will also be tested. You should also know that the base angles of an isosceles triangle are equal and that the interior angles of an equilateral triangle each measure 60°.

21. In the figure, lines $m$, $k$, and $p$ intersect at one point. Which of the following must be true?

    (A) $x = y$

    (B) $x = 2y$

    (C) $x + y = 90$

    (D) $x - y = 90$

    (E) $x + y = 180$

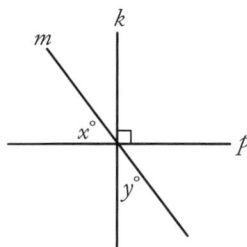

Figure is not drawn to scale.

22. In the figure, side $\overline{AC}$ of $\triangle ABC$ is extended through point $D$. What is the value of $x$ ?

    (A) 50
    (B) 55
    (C) 60
    (D) 65
    (E) 70

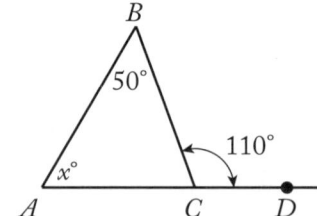

# Area

> You should know the formulas for finding the area of triangles $\left(A = \frac{1}{2}bh\right)$, the area of squares and rectangles $(A = lw)$, the area of trapezoids $\left(A = \frac{1}{2}h(b_1 + b_2)\right)$, and the area of circles $(A = \pi r^2)$.

23. What is the area of the semicircle shown?
    (A)  $4\pi$
    (B)  $8\pi$
    (C)  $16\pi$
    (D)  $32\pi$
    (E)  $64\pi$

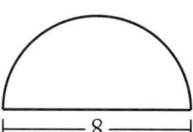

24. In the rectangle shown, the length is 3 times the width. What is the area of the rectangle?
    (A)  $9\ cm^2$
    (B)  $18\ cm^2$
    (C)  $24\ cm^2$
    (D)  $27\ cm^2$
    (E)  $36\ cm^2$

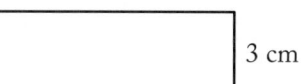

3 cm

# Coordinate

> Coordinate geometry problems on the test involve points in the $xy$-coordinate plane. You will need to identify points with certain properties. You may be asked to find the distance or the midpoint between two points.

25. In the $xy$-coordinate plane, segment $\overline{AB}$ has a length of 2 units. If the coordinates of point $A$ are $(x, y)$, which of the following could be the coordinates of point $B$?

    (A)  $(x - 2, y - 2)$

    (B)  $(x - 1, y - 1)$

    (C)  $(x, 2y)$

    (D)  $(x, y + 2)$

    (E)  $(x + 1, y + 1)$

# Length/Perimeter/Circumference

Finding the length of segments, side lengths of geometric figures, the perimeter of figures, and the circumference of circles may be tested.

26. Points $A$, $B$, $C$, and $D$ are on a line in that order. Point $B$ is the midpoint of $\overline{AC}$, and $\overline{CD}$ is twice as long as $\overline{BC}$. If $CD = 10$, what is the length of $\overline{AD}$ ?
    (A)  15
    (B)  20
    (C)  25
    (D)  40
    (E)  50

---

27. What is the perimeter of the figure shown?
    (A)  16
    (B)  20
    (C)  24
    (D)  28
    (E)  32

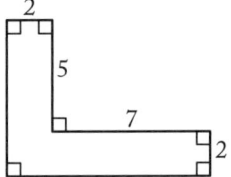

---

28. The circle shown has center $O$. If the area of the shaded region is $6\pi$ square meters, what is the circumference of the circle, in meters?
    (A)   $6\pi$
    (B)  $12\pi$
    (C)  $18\pi$
    (D)  $24\pi$
    (E)  $36\pi$

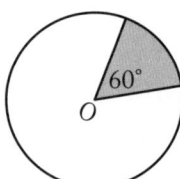

# Pythagorean Theorem

> You will need to know how to find the hypotenuse or the side lengths of a right triangle using the Pythagorean Theorem ($a^2 + b^2 = c^2$).

29. In the figure, $AB = 3$, $AD = 4$, and $CD = 5$. What is the length of $\overline{BC}$?

    (A)  5
    (B)  10
    (C)  25
    (D)  $5\sqrt{2}$
    (E)  $10\sqrt{2}$

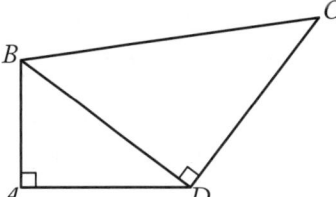

# Transformations: Reflections/Translations/Rotations

> You will need to know how to reflect points and figures across the $x$- and $y$-axes and across other lines in the $xy$-coordinate plane. You will also need to know how to translate and rotate points and figures in the $xy$-coordinate plane.

30. In the $xy$-coordinate plane, segment $\overline{AB}$ is to be shifted 2 units up and 1 unit right. What will be the new coordinates of point $B$?

    (A)  $(-4, 0)$
    (B)  $(-2, -2)$
    (C)  $(-1, 1)$
    (D)  $(0, 0)$
    (E)  $(0, 3)$

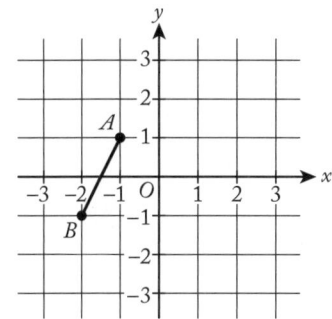

31. In the $xy$-coordinate plane, a line segment with endpoints $P(-2, 2)$ and $Q(2, 2)$ is reflected over the $x$-axis and then rotated $90°$ clockwise about its new midpoint. What will be the resulting coordinates of point $P$ after these transformations?

    (A)  $(-2, -2)$
    (B)  $(-2, 0)$
    (C)  $(0, 0)$
    (D)  $(0, -2)$
    (E)  $(0, -4)$

# 3D: Volume/Surface Area

> You will need to know how to find the volume of a cube and rectangular solid ($V = lwh$), and the volume of a cylinder ($V = \pi r^2 h$). You will also need to know how to find the surface area of a cube and rectangular solid ($SA = 2lw + 2lh + 2hw$) and the surface area of a cylinder ($SA = 2\pi r^2 + 2\pi rh$). If you are asked to find the volume or surface area of other figures, those formulas may be given in the problem.

32. The volume, in cubic centimeters, of a right circular cylinder is $45\pi$. If the radius of the base is 3 centimeters, what is the height of the cylinder?

    (A)  5 cm
    (B)  7.5 cm
    (C)  10 cm
    (D)  15 cm
    (E)  18 cm

---

33. The figure shown consists of two squares and represents the base of a prism with height 2 inches. What is the surface area of the prism, in square inches?

    (A)  30
    (B)  52
    (C)  58
    (D)  60
    (E)  62

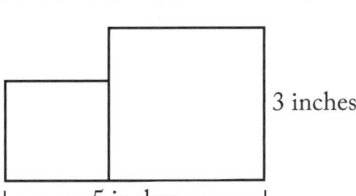

3 inches

5 inches

## Visual/Spatial Reasoning

Problems that test visual/spatial reasoning are all different. Examples of some of the types of problems that may be tested include visualizing different faces of a cube as the cube is turned and rotating a figure about a point.

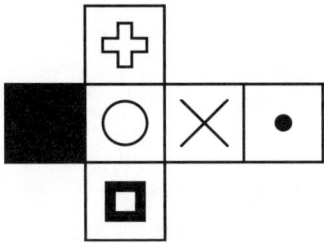

34. The figure shown is to be folded so that each square is a different face of a cube. Which of the following shows a view of this cube?

(A)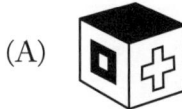

(B)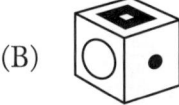

(C)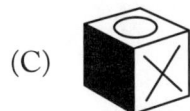

(D)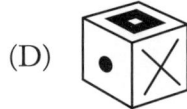

(E)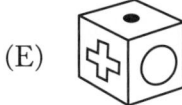

EMA
SSAT

# Answer Key
## Section II: Geometry

**21.** **Answer (C)** $x + y = 90$

**22.** **Answer (C) 60**

**23.** **Answer (B) $8\pi$**
The area of the semicircle is $\frac{1}{2}\pi r^2$ or $\frac{1}{2}\pi(4)^2 = \frac{1}{2}\pi(16) = 8\pi$

**24.** **Answer (D) 27 cm²**
The length of the rectangle is 3(3cm) = 9cm, so the area of the rectangle is (9cm)(3cm) = 27 cm².

**25.** **Answer (D) $(x, y + 2)$**
Point $(x, y + 2)$ is located 2 units directly above point $A$ $(x, y)$, making the length of $\overline{AB}$ equal to 2.

**26.** **Answer (B) 20**
Let $x$ be the length of $\overline{AB}$. Then $AB = x$, $BC = x$, and $CD = 2x$. $CD = 2x = 10$, so $x = 5$. $AD = AB + BC + CD = 5 + 5 + 10 = 20$. It may be helpful in solving the problem to draw the four points on a line and mark the figure.

**27.** **Answer (E) 32**
The perimeter of the figure is the sum of all the side lengths. Starting at the top of the figure, this is $2 + 5 + 7 + 2 + 9 + 7 = 32$.

**28.** **Answer (B) $12\,\pi$**
The area of the shaded region can be represented by the equation $\frac{60}{360}(\pi r^2) = 6\pi$,

so $r^2 = 36$ or $r = 6$. So the circumference of the circle is $2\pi r$ or $12\pi$.

**29.** **Answer (D) $5\sqrt{2}$**
In right triangle $ABD$, the two legs equal 3 and 4. So, by the Pythagorean Theorem, $3^2 + 4^2 = BD^2$ or $BD = 5$. In right triangle $DBC$, the two legs are both equal to 5. By the Pythagorean Theorem, $5^2 + 5^2 = BC^2$, so $BC = \sqrt{50} = 5\sqrt{2}$.

**30.** **Answer (C) (–1, 1)**
The coordinates of point $B$ in the figure are $(-2, -1)$, so shifting point $B$ up 2 units and to the right 1 unit results in $(-2 + 1, -1 + 2)$, which is $(-1, 1)$.

# Answer Key
## Section II: Geometry *(continued)*

**31.** **Answer (C) (0, 0)**

When the line segment with endpoints $P(-2, 2)$ and $Q(2, 2)$ is reflected over the $x$-axis, the endpoints of the new line segments will have coordinates $(-2, -2)$ and $(2, -2)$, respectively. The midpoint of the reflected segment is $(0, -2)$. When the new line segment is rotated 90° clockwise about point $(0, -2)$, the resulting coordinates of point $P$ will be $(0, 0)$.

**32.** **Answer (A) 5 cm**

The formula for the area of a right circular cylinder is $\pi r^2 h$. So when $\pi r^2 h = 45\pi$ and $r = 3$, then $\pi(3)^2 h = 45\pi$, so $9h = 45$ or $h = 5$.

**33.** **Answer (C) 58**

The area of each base is $(2 \times 2) + (3 \times 3) = 4 + 9 = 13$, so 26 is the total area of the two bases. The total area of the faces is $3(2 \times 2) + 3(3 \times 2) + 1(2) = 12 + 18 + 2 = 32$.

Therefore, $SA = 26 + 32 = 58$.

**34.** **Answer (D)**

The other four answer choices are not possible views of the cube.

# Section III: Data Analysis

In this section, you will find 10 sample problems and related overviews of mathematical concepts in data analysis. The answers are located at the end of this section.

## Counting

> Counting problems on the test may involve determining the number of paths to get from one point to another, determining the number of combinations or permutations that are possible in certain situations, and may include other counting situations.

35. In the figure shown, how many paths in the direction of the arrows exist from point $A$ to point $F$?

    (A) Three
    (B) Four
    (C) Five
    (D) Seven
    (E) Twelve

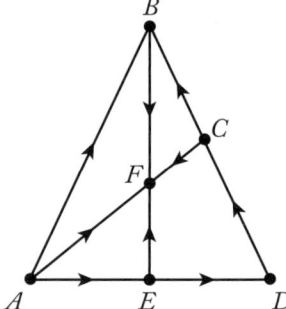

## Mean/Median/Mode/Range

> You will need to know how to find the mean, median, mode, and range of a list of numbers. To find the mean, you add the numbers in the list together and divide by the number of numbers in the list. To find the median, you arrange the numbers in increasing or decreasing order, and find the middle number. To find the mode, you determine which number appears the most times in the list. To find the range, you subtract the least number from the greatest number.

36. What is the mean of the numbers in the set $\{2,5,6,6,8,15\}$?

    (A)  6
    (B)  6.5
    (C)  7
    (D)  14
    (E)  21

$$4, 6, 2, 5, 12, 8, x$$

37. The median of the list of numbers above is 6. Which of the following could be the value of $x$ ?

    (A)  0
    (B)  3
    (C)  4
    (D)  5
    (E)  8

---

$$6, 2, 3, 2, 2, 8, 5$$

38. What is the mode of the numbers above?

    (A)  1
    (B)  2
    (C)  3
    (D)  4
    (E)  6

---

$$19, 16, x, 10, 7, 9, 17$$

39. If $x$ represents the least number in the list above, and the range of the seven numbers is 15, what number does $x$ represent?

    (A)  1
    (B)  2
    (C)  3
    (D)  4
    (E)  5

# Probability

Probability problems may be presented in either a real-life or an abstract setting. Geometric probability may also be included on the test.

40. In a parking lot, there are 60 white cars, 50 gray cars, 20 blue cars, 10 red cars, and no other cars. If a car is to be selected at random from the parking lot, what is the probability that the selected car will <u>not</u> be white?

(A) $\frac{1}{4}$

(B) $\frac{3}{7}$

(C) $\frac{1}{2}$

(D) $\frac{4}{7}$

(E) $\frac{3}{4}$

# Set Theory

Set theory problems can be presented in either a real-life or an abstract setting. Problems in a real-life setting can be solved more easily if you draw a Venn diagram to display the information given in the problem. For some problems, a Venn diagram may be given. Some questions may ask you to find the intersection or union of sets, but set notation for these terms will not be used.

$$P = \{1, 3, 5, 7, 9\}$$
$$Q = \{2, 4, 5, 6, 7\}$$
$$R = \{3, 7, 8, 9\}$$

41. Sets $P$, $Q$, and $R$ are defined above. If $x$ is a number in both sets $P$ and $Q$, but not in set $R$, what is the number $x$ ?
(A) 2
(B) 3
(C) 4
(D) 5
(E) 7

42. Each student in a group of 34 students participates in either chorus or band. If 20 students participate in chorus and 22 students participate in band, how many students participate in chorus but <u>not</u> in band?

    (A)   8
    (B)  10
    (C)  12
    (D)  14
    (E)  16

# Tables/Graphs

You will be asked to read information from a data graph and work with this information to solve problems. Tables, bar graphs, histograms, line graphs, scatterplots, dot plots, and circle graphs may be on the test.

43. In a survey, adults were asked which TV genres they liked most and the gender they identified with. The results of the survey are shown in the bar graph. Based on the graph, which genre is preferred by 50% more males than females?

    (A)  Comedy
    (B)  Drama
    (C)  Mystery
    (D)  News
    (E)  Fantasy

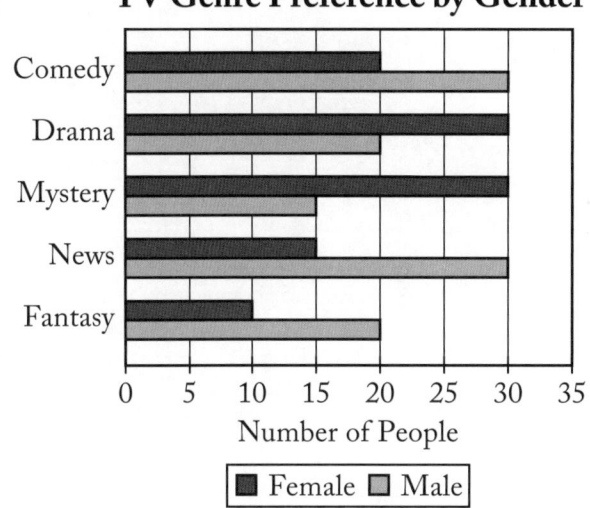

**TV Genre Preference by Gender**

44. The 20 students in Ms. Wei's class were surveyed as to which subject they enjoyed most. The results of the survey are displayed in the circle graph. How many students in Ms. Wei's class chose either math or science?

(A)   2
(B)   6
(C)   8
(D)  12
(E)  40

**Ms. Wei's Class Survey Results**

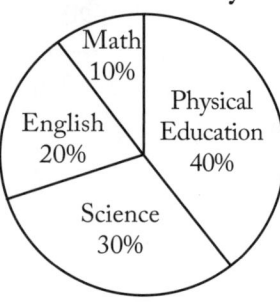

# Answer Key
## Section III: Data Analysis

35. **Answer (C) Five**

36. **Answer (C) 7**
The mean equals $\dfrac{2 + 5 + 6 + 6 + 8 + 15}{6} = \dfrac{42}{6} = 7$

37. **Answer (E) 8**
Putting the six numbers in increasing order yields 2, 4, 5, 6, 8, 12. Since 6 is the median, 6 must be the middle number in the list. So $x$ must be greater than or equal to 6. Of the answer choices, 8 is the only number with this property, so $x = 8$.

38. **Answer (B) 2**
The mode is 2 since it is the number that appears the most times in the list.

39. **Answer (D) 4**
Since the range is the least number subtracted from the greatest number, $19 - x = 15$, or $x = 4$.

40. **Answer (D) $\dfrac{4}{7}$**
The probability that a car selected <u>is</u> white is $\dfrac{60}{140}$ or $\dfrac{3}{7}$. So the probability that a car selected is <u>not</u> white is $1 - \dfrac{3}{7} = \dfrac{4}{7}$.

41. **Answer (D) 5**
Since $x$ is in both sets $P$ and $Q$, then $x$ may be 5 or 7. Of these two numbers, 5 is the only number that is not in set $R$.

42. **Answer (C) 12**
It is probably helpful to draw a Venn Diagram to solve this problem:
From the Venn diagram, it follows that

chorus   band

$$x + y + z = 34$$
$$x + y = 20$$
$$y + z = 22$$

The number of students who participate in chorus but <u>not</u> band is $x$. Therefore, substituting $y + z = 22$ into the first equation yields $x + (22) = 34$, so $x = 12$.

43. **Answer (A) Comedy**
For Comedy, $\dfrac{30 - 20}{20} = \dfrac{10}{20} = \dfrac{1}{2}$, which is equivalent to 50%.

44. **Answer (C) 8**
Math and science make up 10% + 30% = 40% of the circle graph. Since $(0.4)(20) = 8$, there are 8 students who chose either math or science.

# Section IV: Number Concepts and Operations

In this section, you will find 11 sample problems and related overviews of mathematical concepts in number concepts and operations. The answers are located at the end of this section.

## Arithmetic Computations/Word Problems

Problems in this category may be presented in either a real-life or an abstract setting. Arithmetic word problems may be included. These are word problems that do not require using algebra to solve. There may be some straight computation on the test, but testing computation is not a primary emphasis of this test.

45. Which of the following is equivalent to $(3 \times 10^8) \times (6 \times 10^7)$ ?
   (A)  $1.8 \times 10^8$
   (B)  $1.8 \times 10^{15}$
   (C)  $1.8 \times 10^{16}$
   (D)  $1.8 \times 10^{55}$
   (E)  $1.8 \times 10^{56}$

## Converting Units

For problems in this category, most conversions will be given. However, you will be expected to know metric conversions. For example, you will need to know conversions such as 1 meter equals 100 centimeters and 1 liter equals 1,000 milliliters.

| |
|---|
| 1 foot = 12 inches |
| 1 yard = 3 feet |
| 1 rod = 5.5 yards |

46. Based on the information above, how many <u>inches</u> are there in 2 rods?
   (A)  2.75
   (B)  27.5
   (C)  33
   (D)  198
   (E)  396

# Estimation

Estimation problems can be presented in either a real-life or an abstract setting. When solving an estimation problem, round the numbers as close to the given number as possible. It may be to your advantage to look at the answer choices first before you begin to round numbers.

47. For Olympic National Park, the average annual high temperature is 59.9°F, and the average annual low temperature is 43.3°F. Of the following, which is closest to how much greater the average annual high temperature is than the average annual low temperature?

(A) 15°F
(B) 16°F
(C) 17°F
(D) 18°F
(E) 19°F

# Number Sense/Number Theory

Problems in this category may include testing multiples, divisibility, properties of even and odd integers, prime numbers, place value, and factors.

48. If $n = 2^3 \times 3 \times 5^3 \times 7$ and $p = 2^2 \times 3^2 \times 5 \times 11$, which of the following is the least common multiple of $n$ and $p$ ?

(A) $2 \times 3 \times 5$
(B) $2 \times 3 \times 5 \times 7 \times 11$
(C) $2^2 \times 3 \times 5$
(D) $2^3 \times 3^2 \times 5^3$
(E) $2^3 \times 3^2 \times 5^3 \times 7 \times 11$

49. If $n + 1$ represents an even integer, which of the following is also an even integer?

(A) $3n$
(B) $2n + 3$
(C) $4n + 1$
(D) $5(n + 2)$
(E) $7n + 7$

50. If $2A$ and $3B$ represent 2-digit prime numbers, where $A$ and $B$ are digits, what is the greatest possible value of $3B - 2A$ ?

(A) 8
(B) 10
(C) 14
(D) 16
(E) 18

# Order of Operations

When simplifying numeric expressions, you must follow this order:

1. Perform all operations that are included within grouping symbols or in fractions.

2. Simplify indicated powers in order from left to right.

3. Perform indicated multiplications and divisions in order from left to right.

4. Perform indicated additions and subtractions in order from left to right.

51. Simplify: $5 + 3 - 6 \div 2(9 - 6)$

   (A) $-1$

   (B) $\frac{1}{3}$

   (C) $3$

   (D) $7$

   (E) $8$

# Logical Reasoning/Puzzle Problems

Problems in this category involve using logical reasoning to solve a problem. For example, you may need to put students in order by height or by certain characteristics. Newly defined operations may also be included in this category.

| Statement 1: | Cara is the youngest, and Amy is the oldest. |
| Statement 2: | Bob is the youngest, and Cara is the oldest. |

52. Three students, Amy, Bob, and Cara, are in a classroom. The teacher made the two statements above. If only half of each of the statements is true, which of the following lists the students from youngest to oldest?

   (A) Amy, Bob, Cara
   (B) Bob, Amy, Cara
   (C) Bob, Cara, Amy
   (D) Cara, Amy, Bob
   (E) Cara, Bob, Amy

53. Let $\square$ be defined as $a \square b = 2a + 4b$, where $a$ and $b$ are nonzero numbers. If $3 \square x = 16$, what is the value of $x$ ?

    (A)  2

    (B)  $\frac{5}{2}$

    (C)  $\frac{11}{4}$

    (D)  $\frac{13}{14}$

    (E)  $\frac{9}{2}$

# Sequences and Patterns

For sequence problems, the pattern for generating the sequence will be stated. You may be asked to find a number or a figure in the pattern or be given a number in the sequence and asked which term it is.

54. In a sequence, the first term is 16. Each term after the first is $\frac{1}{4}$ of the preceding term. What is the seventh term of the sequence?

    (A)  $\frac{1}{32}$

    (B)  $\frac{1}{48}$

    (C)  $\frac{1}{64}$

    (D)  $\frac{1}{128}$

    (E)  $\frac{1}{256}$

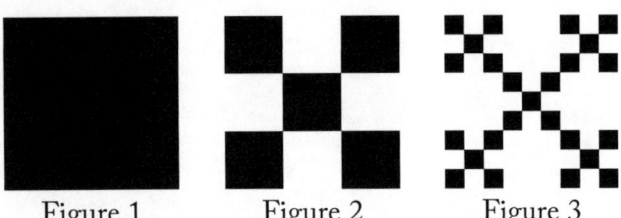

| Figure 1 | Figure 2 | Figure 3 |

55. Three figures of a pattern are shown above, and Figure 1 is the first figure in the pattern. The number of squares in each figure after the first is 5 times the number of squares in the preceding figure. Which of the following represents the number of squares in Figure 6 ?

(A)  $5 \times 6$

(B)  $3 \times 5 \times 6$

(C)  $3 \times 5 \times 5 \times 5$

(D)  $5 \times 5 \times 5 \times 5 \times 5$

(E)  $5 \times 5 \times 5 \times 5 \times 5 \times 5$

# Answer Key
## Section IV: Number Concepts and Operations

45. **Answer (C) $1.8 \times 10^{16}$**
$(3 \times 10^8) \times (6 \times 10^7) = 18 \times 10^{15} = 1.8 \times 10^{16}$

46. **Answer (E) 396**
Since 1 rod = 5.5 yards, then 2 rods = 11 yards.
Since 1 yard = 3 feet, then 11 yards = 33 feet.
Since 1 foot = 12 inches, then 33 feet = $12 \times 33$ = 396 inches.

47. **Answer (C) 17°F**
Using rounded value 60°F for 59.9°F and rounded value 43°F for 43.3°F yields the answer 60°F – 43°F = 17°F.

48. **Answer (E) $2^3 \times 3^2 \times 5^3 \times 7 \times 11$**

49. **Answer (E) $7n + 7$**
Since $7n + 7 = 7(n + 1)$ and $(n + 1)$ represents an even integer, the product $7(n + 1)$ will also be an even integer.

50. **Answer (C) 14**
The greatest prime number represented by $3B$ is 37. The least prime number represented by $2A$ is 23. Subtracting the least prime number, 23, from the greatest prime number, 37, yields 14, which is the greatest possible value of $3B - 2A$.

51. **Answer (A) –1**
First $5 + 3 - 6 \div 2(3)$, then $5 + 3 - 3(3) = 8 - 9 = -1$.

52. **Answer (C) Bob, Cara, Amy**

Statement 1 $\begin{cases} \text{C true and A not true} & \cancel{\text{C}} \text{ A B} \\ \text{C not true and A true} & \cancel{\text{B}} \text{ C A} \end{cases}$

Statement 2 $\begin{cases} \text{B true and C not true} & \cancel{\text{B}} \text{ C A} \\ \text{B not true and C true} & \cancel{\text{A}} \text{ B C} \end{cases}$

Since BCA follows from both Statement 1 and Statement 2 under the given conditions, this is the correct order for the students.

53. **Answer (B) $\frac{5}{2}$**
If $3 \square x = 16$, then $2(3) + 4x = 16$. Solving this equation yields $4x = 10$ or $x = \frac{10}{4}$, which reduces to $\frac{5}{2}$.

54. **Answer (E) $\frac{1}{256}$**
According to the pattern described, the sequence is $16, 4, 1, \frac{1}{4}, \frac{1}{16}, \frac{1}{64}, \frac{1}{256}, \cdots$

55. **Answer (D) $5 \times 5 \times 5 \times 5 \times 5$**
The pattern described yields the following: Figure 1 has 1 square, Figure 2 has 5 squares, Figure 3 has $5 \times 5$ squares, Figure 4 has $5 \times 5 \times 5$ squares, Figure 5 has $5 \times 5 \times 5 \times 5$ squares, Figure 6 has $5 \times 5 \times 5 \times 5 \times 5$ squares.

# 3. The Reading Comprehension Section

The reading comprehension section presents several reading passages, each followed by a series of questions designed to measure how well you understand what you have read. The questions ask not only about the ideas presented in the passage but also about the ways in which the author expresses those ideas. Passages are of two kinds: **literary** and **expository**. Literary passages are excerpts from works of fiction or poetry. They generally tell part of a story or develop a certain theme. Expository passages explore topics related to the humanities (art, music, etc.), history, science (biology, astronomy, technology, etc.), or social science (psychology, anthropology, etc.).

> **Just the Facts**
> Reading Comprehension
>
> **Number of questions:** 40
>
> **What it measures:** Your ability to understand and interpret what you read
>
> **Scored section:** Yes
>
> **Time allotted:** 40 minutes

## What Are the Directions for the Reading Comprehension Section on the Test?

Read each passage carefully and then answer the questions about it. For each question, decide on the basis of the passage which one of the choices best answers the question.

## What Types of Questions Are Presented in the Reading Comprehension Section?

Most of the questions in the reading comprehension section focus on the following:

### 1. Basic information

*Understanding what is directly stated in the passage*

**Examples:**
- According to the passage, the elephant's diet consists mainly of...
- In the second stanza, the poet indicates that she is...
- According to the passage, what accounts for the enduring popularity of Bach's music?
- What is the main idea of the passage?
- In the final paragraph, the author argues for...

### 2. Inference

*Understanding what is implied but not directly stated in the passage*

**Examples:**
- It can be inferred from the passage that the "old cabin" (line 8) was...
- The author's description of his childhood suggests that he...
- The author assumes that her readers are...
- The "grave concerns" mentioned in line 6 were most likely...
- The description of the "office" (line 10) implies that it was...

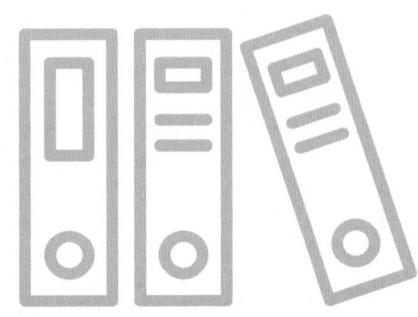

## 3. Language

*Interpreting the author's use of specific words and phrases*

**Examples:**

- As used in line 16, the word "fair" most nearly means...
- In line 7, the expression "safety net" refers to...
- In line 10, the pronoun "they" refers to...
- To describe the effects of the storm, the author makes use of which literary device?
- In the third stanza, the poet develops a metaphor drawn from the realm of...
- Throughout the poem, the "candle" serves as a symbol of...
- The rhyme scheme of the poem's last stanza is...

## 4. Purpose

*Understanding the author's writing strategy: how the writing is structured and why it is structured that way*

**Examples:**

- The main purpose of the final paragraph is to...
- The author mentions "fairy tales" (line 1) in order to...
- The narrator repeats the word "paper" (lines 6–7) in order to...
- Why is the detective's sentence left unfinished in line 17?
- The list in the third paragraph serves to...
- The examples cited in the second paragraph are intended to...
- How does the third paragraph relate to the second paragraph?

## 5. Tone

*Recognizing the tone, mood, or style of the passage or the attitude of the author, speaker, or character*

**Examples:**

- In the second paragraph, the author adopts a tone of...
- In the second stanza, the poet sounds a note of...
- In the first paragraph, the narrator creates an atmosphere of...
- The style of the passage is best described as...
- As indicated in the quotation (lines 9–10), Lawry's attitude toward modern art is one of...

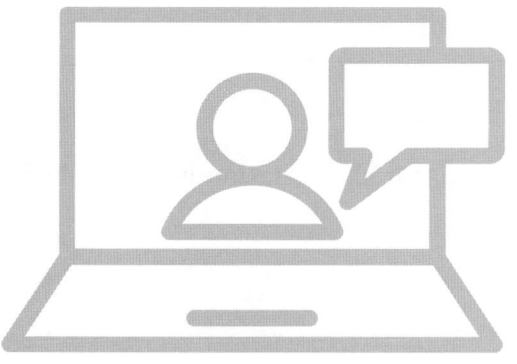

# How Are the Reading Comprehension Questions Presented?

The SSAT presents each passage (or poem) with a corresponding group of three to eight questions. The directions instruct you to read each passage and answer the questions about it.

---

We had a consuming desire to see a pony rider, but somehow or other all that passed us streaked by in the night, and so we heard only a whiz and a hail, and the swift phantom was gone. But now the driver exclaims: "Here he comes!" Every neck is stretched and every eye strained.

Away across the endless dead level of the prairie a black speck appears. Soon it becomes a horse

*Line 5* and rider, rising and falling, sweeping nearer and nearer, and the flutter of hoofs comes faintly to the ear. Another instant a whoop and hurrah from our upper deck, a wave of the rider's hand, but no reply, and man and horse burst past our excited faces and go winging away like a belated fragment of a storm!

---

1.  The narrator's description of "every eye" (line 3) suggests that the people were

    (A) eager
    (B) puzzled
    (C) hysterical
    (D) frightened
    (E) disappointed

**The correct answer is (A). The narrator says that the people had a "consuming desire" (line 1) to see a pony rider, and this eagerness is reflected in the fact that every eye was "strained" (line 3) in an attempt to see the rider as he approached from a great distance.**

2.  The narrator uses the word "becomes" (line 4) to indicate a change in

    (A) speed
    (B) direction
    (C) appearance
    (D) attitude
    (E) behavior

**The correct answer is (C). The narrator indicates that what at first appeared to be only "a black speck" now appears more clearly to be a horse and rider.**

3.  The last sentence of the passage ends with which of the following literary devices?

    (A) simile
    (B) personification
    (C) onomatopoeia
    (D) alliteration
    (E) oxymoron

**The correct answer is (A). A simile is a literary device in which one thing is likened to another. Here the horse and rider are likened to a storm.**

## How Do You Answer the Reading Comprehension Questions?

As you read, determine the main idea of the passage or poem. Identify the important details that move the narrative along or create a mood or tone. In an expository passage, identify the details that support the writer's argument or illustrate the ideas being presented. The first sentence of each paragraph will give you a general sense of the topic. Identify the topic of each paragraph and underline or make note of key facts. Try to figure out the writer's intention or purpose of the passage. Notice the writer's attitude, tone, and general style.

These habits can help you understand what you read, whether you are taking the SSAT, preparing for a history test, or getting ready to write an essay for your English class.

# Reading Comprehension Test-Taking Strategies

1. Take time to read and understand the first sentence of each paragraph. This will provide you with a general sense of the topic.

2. Scan the answer choices, since they are generally short and provide excellent clues. If an answer choice refers you to a specific line in the passage, underline or make note of that line for reference.

3. Read each passage carefully. Follow the author's reasoning. Notice attitude, tone, and general style.

4. Pay attention to words such as always, never, every, and none. They may play an important role in the answer.

5. Identify the topic of each paragraph, key facts, and the author's purpose for writing. Underline or make note of the key facts for quick reference.

6. Read all answer choices carefully before you choose. When you find an answer choice that fails to satisfy the requirements of the question or statement, cross it out.

# Sample Questions: Reading Comprehension

Directions: Read each passage carefully and then answer the questions about it. For each question, decide on the basis of the passage which one of the choices best answers the question.

> There is probably no part of the world that stimulates more curiosity in an archeologist or even in a casual traveler than that part of South America which was once inhabited by the Incas of Peru. Tiahuanaco's finely carved gateway and its ponderous stone platforms, Sacsahuaman's gigantic walls, Ollantaytambo's monolithic
> *Line 5* fortress, and Machu Picchu's picturesque grandeur fill one with an admiration for their builders which is equaled only by the sorrow that today, over three centuries after the advent of Pizarro and his *conquistadores*, we can do little more than make conjectures concerning the ancient Peruvians. And, furthermore, it is doubtful if we can ever go very far in solving the problem of man in the Andes. Although they made
> *10* great progress in architecture, agriculture, engineering, and the science of government, the ancient Peruvians did not achieve the art of writing, nor did they even reach the stage of hieroglyphics. Their records were kept on *quipus*, variously colored strings with many different kinds of knots. These seem, however, to have been used only for accounting purposes. Thus far, the *quipus* in possession of our archeologists have been of
> *15* no particular aid in deciphering the history of their makers. Accordingly, what we know of the Incas consists of traditions gathered together by early Spaniards, and the work of present-day students who, by modern archeological methods, are slowly bringing some light to bear on this apparently insolvable problem.

1. It can be inferred from the passage that Tiahuanaco, Sacsahuaman, and Ollantaytambo (lines 3-4) are
   (A) Incan rulers
   (B) Incan cities
   (C) Incan gods
   (D) *conquistadores*
   (E) mountains

2. The cause of the author's "sorrow" (line 6) is
   (A) the tragic collapse of Incan civilization
   (B) the arrival of Pizarro and the *conquistadores*
   (C) a lack of reliable historical information about the Incas
   (D) the deterioration of ancient Incan monuments
   (E) disputes between rival archeologists

3. In line 9, the author uses the word "Although" to acknowledge
   (A) the major achievements of the Incas
   (B) the weakness of scholarly conjectures
   (C) the complexity of Incan hieroglyphics
   (D) the crimes of the *conquistadores*
   (E) the influence of Spanish culture

4. In line 15, "Accordingly" most nearly means
   (A) Because Incan sites are difficult to reach
   (B) Because the Spaniards conquered the Incas
   (C) Because the *quipus* are undecipherable
   (D) Because Incan legends are greatly exaggerated
   (E) Because the Incas had no system of writing

Simon Wheeler backed me into a corner and blockaded me there with his chair, and then sat down and reeled off the monotonous narrative which follows this paragraph. He never smiled, he never frowned, he never changed his voice from the gentle-flowing key to which he tuned his initial sentence, he never betrayed the slightest
*Line 5* suspicion of enthusiasm; but all through the interminable narrative there ran a vein of impressive earnestness and sincerity which showed me plainly that, so far from his imagining that there was anything ridiculous or funny about his story, he regarded it as a really important matter, and admired its two heroes as men of transcendent genius in finesse. I let him go on in his own way, and never interrupted him once.

5. To describe Simon's "voice" (line 3), the narrator develops a metaphor drawn from the realm of

   (A) drama
   (B) music
   (C) dance
   (D) painting
   (E) architecture

6. As it is used in line 5, the word "ran" most nearly means

   (A) fled
   (B) managed
   (C) campaigned
   (D) stretched
   (E) sprinted

7. The narrator implies that Simon

   (A) lacked a sense of humor
   (B) was not to be trusted
   (C) wanted to write a novel
   (D) was a man of genius
   (E) considered himself a hero

8. The narrator's attitude toward Simon is best described as

   (A) envious
   (B) reverential
   (C) indulgent
   (D) hostile
   (E) grateful

## Answer Key: Reading Comprehension

1.  **(B)** Of the fives choices, cities are the only things that can plausibly be said to have a "carved gateway," "stone platforms," "gigantic walls," or a "fortress" (lines 3-5) and to be the works of "builders" (line 6).

2.  **(C)** The words "that today . . . we can do little more than make conjectures concerning the ancient Peruvians" (lines 6-8) indicate that the author is unhappy having to rely on guesswork rather than firm evidence in trying to learn about the Incas.

3.  **(A)** The author uses "Although" to begin a contrast between the "great progress" (line 10) the Incas made in architecture, etc. and their failure to develop a system of writing.

4.  **(E)** The author uses "Accordingly" to sum up the main point made in the immediately preceding part of the passage, i.e., that the Incas "did not achieve the art of writing" (line 11). This lack of written texts, the author explains, is why archeologists must rely on the unwritten oral traditions recorded by the Spaniards.

5.  **(B)** The narrator uses the musical terms "key" (line 4) and "tuned" (line 4) to describe Simon's manner of speaking.

6.  **(D)** Of the five answer choices, "stretched" is the only word that makes sense when substituted for "ran" in the passage: ". . . all through the interminable narrative there stretched a vein of impressive earnestness and sincerity." A vein can be said to "run" only in the sense that it extends or stretches from one point to another.

7.  **(A)** The narrator's words "so far from his imagining that there was anything ridiculous or funny about his story, he regarded it as a really important matter" (lines 6-8) imply that Simon is unable to appreciate the humor in the story he is telling.

8.  **(C)** Though the narrator found Simon's story to be "monotonous" (line 2) and "interminable" (line 5), he nonetheless "let him go on in his own way, and never interrupted him once" (line 9), thus showing his indulgence.

# 4. The Verbal Section

The verbal section of the Upper Level SSAT presents two types of questions: **synonyms** and **analogies**. The synonym questions primarily test the strength of your vocabulary. The analogy questions test not only your knowledge of individual words but also your ability to recognize logical relationships between pairs of words.

## Synonyms

Synonyms are words that have the same or nearly the same meaning as each other. For example, *fortunate* is a synonym for *lucky; hoist* is a synonym for *raise*; and *melody* is a synonym for *tune*. Synonym questions on the SSAT ask you to choose a word that has a meaning similar to that of a given word.

### What Are the Directions for the Synonym Section on the Test?

Each of the following questions consists of one word followed by five words or phrases. You are to select the one word or phrase whose meaning is closest to that of the word in capital letters.

### How Are the Synonym Questions Presented?

Synonym questions present a single word in capital letters followed by five answer choices in lowercase letters.

| **EXAMPLE:** | 1. LACKLUSTER:<br>(A) harsh<br>(B) smug<br>(C) soggy<br>(D) parched<br>(E) dull<br>**The correct answer is (E).** |
|---|---|

---

### Just the Facts
#### The Verbal Section

**Number of questions:**
60 (30 synonyms and 30 analogies)

**What it measures:**
Your ability to understand the meanings of words and to recognize relationships between words with different meanings

**Scored section:**
Yes

**Time allotted:**
30 minutes

## How Do You Answer Synonym Questions?

There is only one correct response, so make sure you consider all of the choices carefully and select the one that is closest in meaning to the capitalized word. Don't just pick the first word that seems approximately right. If you're having difficulty deciding between two word choices, try making up a short sentence using the capitalized word and then ask yourself which choice would be the best substitute for the capitalized word in that sentence.

## How Can You Prepare?

The best way to prepare is to read as much as you can to build your vocabulary. If you encounter an unfamiliar word in your reading, make sure you look it up. Keep track of the word and its meaning on an index card, notepad, or in notes on your smartphone. Keeping a list of new words that you review from time to time is a great way to build a tremendous vocabulary.

Another way to prepare is to learn the meaning of the word parts that make up many English words. These word parts consist of **prefixes, suffixes,** and **roots**. If you encounter an unfamiliar word, you could take apart the word and think about the parts.

> The greater your vocabulary, the greater your chance of getting the correct answer.

## Prefixes

| Prefix | Meaning | Example |
|---|---|---|
| a-, an- | not, without | amoral, anonymous |
| ab- | from | abnormal |
| ad- | to, toward | advance, adhere |
| ante- | before | antebellum |
| anti- | against, opposite | antibacterial, antithesis |
| auto- | self | autobiography, automobile |
| bi- | two | bicycle, binary |
| circu(m)- | around | circumference, circulate |
| de- | away from | derail, defend |
| dia- | through, across | diagonal |
| dis- | away from, not | disappear, disloyal |
| en- | put in, into | encircle, enlist |
| ex- | out of | exit, exhale |
| extra- | outside of, beyond | extraordinary |
| hyper- | over, more | hyperactive, hyperbole |
| in-, ill-, im- | not | inanimate, illicit, impossible |
| in-, ill-, im- | in, into | insert, illuminate, impose |
| inter- | between | interact |
| intra- | within | intrastate |
| macro- | large | macroeconomics |
| mal- | bad, wrong | malady, malpractice |
| micro- | small | microscope |
| mono- | one | monopoly, monotonous |
| multi- | many | multicolor, multiply |
| non- | without, not | nonsense |
| peri- | around | perimeter, periscope |
| post- | after | postscript |
| pre-, pro- | before, forward | preview, prologue |
| semi- (also hemi-) | half | semicircle, hemisphere |
| sub- | under | subway, submarine |
| syn-, sym- | same | synonym, sympathy |
| trans- | across | transport, transit |
| tri- | three | triangle, triple |
| un- | not | unkind |
| uni- | one, together | unity, unique |

# Suffixes

| Suffix | Meaning | Example |
| --- | --- | --- |
| -able, -ible | able to be | habitable, edible |
| -acy | state or quality | privacy, literacy |
| -al | relating to, belonging to | theatrical |
| -an (-ian) | relating to, belonging to | equestrian |
| -ance, -ence | state or quality | brilliance, patience |
| -ant | a person | informant, participant |
| -arian | a person | librarian, vegetarian |
| -cide | act of killing | genocide |
| -cracy | rule, government, power | aristocracy |
| -dom | state or quality | wisdom, freedom |
| -dox | belief | orthodox |
| -en | make a certain way | sharpen, sadden |
| -er, -or | person doing something | lover, actor |
| -ese | relating to a place | Japanese |
| -esque | in the style of/like | arabesque, grotesque |
| -fy | make a certain way | beautify, terrify, magnify |
| -ful | full of | graceful |
| -gam/-gamy | marriage, union | monogamous |
| -gon | angle | decagon, trigonometry |
| -hood | state, condition, or quality | parenthood |
| -ile | relating to, capable of | juvenile, mobile |
| -ious, -ous | characterized by | contagious, studious |
| -ish | having the quality of | childish |
| -ism | doctrine, belief | socialism |
| -ist | person doing or advocating | dramatist, communist |
| -ity, -ty | quality of | ferocity |
| -ive | having a tendency | talkative, divisive |
| -ize | make a certain way | prioritize, advertize |
| -log(ue) | word, speech | analogy, dialogue |
| -ment | condition or action | ailment, assessment |
| -ness | state or quality | happiness, kindness |
| -phile | one who loves | bibliophile |
| -phobia | abnormal fear of | acrophobia |
| -ship | quality or position of | craftsmanship, dictatorship |
| -sion, -tion | action or condition | tension, destruction |

## Word Roots     G = Greek     L = Latin

| Root | Meaning | Example |
|---|---|---|
| ann, enn (L) | year | anniversary, perennial |
| anthrop (G) | man | anthropomorphism |
| ast(er) (G) | star | astrology, asterisk |
| audi (L) | hear | audible, audience |
| auto (G) | self | autobiography |
| bene (L) | good | beneficial |
| bio (G) | life | biography, biology |
| chron (G) | time | chronology, chronicle |
| civ (L) | citizen | civilization, civilian |
| cred (L) | believe | credential, incredible |
| dem(o) (G) | people | democracy, epidemic |
| dict (L) | say | predict, dictator |
| duc (L) | lead, make | conduct, reduce |
| gen (G & L) | give birth | genesis, generation |
| geo (G) | earth | geometry |
| graph (G) | write | autograph, graphic |
| jur, jus (L) | law | juror, justice, injure |
| log, logue (G) | thought, word | logical, prologue |
| luc (L) | light | lucid, translucent |
| man(u) (L) | hand | manual, manufacture |
| mand (L) | order | command, mandate |
| min (L) | small | minimal, diminish |
| mis, mit (L) | send | missile, transmit |
| nov (L) | new | novel, innovate |
| omni (L) | all | omnivore, omniscient |
| pan (G) | all | panorama, panacea |
| pater, patr (G & L) | father | paternal, patriarchy |
| path (G) | feel | sympathy |
| phil (G) | love | philosophy, philanthropist |
| phon (G) | sound | phonetic, telephone |
| photo (G) | light | photosynthesis |
| poli (G) | city | political, metropolis |
| port (L) | carry | deport, report |
| scrib, script (L) | write | prescribe, inscription |
| sens, sent (L) | feel | sentiment, resent |
| sol (L) | sun | solar, parasol |

# Word Roots    G = Greek    L = Latin

| Root | Meaning | Example |
| --- | --- | --- |
| tele (G) | far off | television |
| terr (L) | earth | terrestrial |
| tract (L) | drag, draw | detract, traction |
| vac (L) | empty | evacuation, vacant |
| vid, vis (L) | see | invisible, video |
| vit (L) | life | vitality, vitamin |
| zo (G) | life | zoology |

# Sample Questions: Synonyms

Directions: Each of the following questions consists of a word followed by five words or phrases. You are to select the one word or phrase whose meaning is closest to the word in capital letters.

1. DISHEVELED:
   (A) weak
   (B) unkempt
   (C) doubtful
   (D) vulnerable
   (E) worthless

2. LAMENT:
   (A) mourn
   (B) cover
   (C) argue
   (D) sicken
   (E) adhere

3. CONSPIRE:
   (A) trick
   (B) hide
   (C) plot
   (D) guess
   (E) gasp

4. NOXIOUS:
   (A) angry
   (B) stubborn
   (C) obscure
   (D) harmful
   (E) nightly

5. AMNESTY:
   (A) truce
   (B) ransom
   (C) contract
   (D) pardon
   (E) guarantee

6. CAPITULATE:
   (A) repeat
   (B) profit
   (C) punish
   (D) confess
   (E) surrender

7. ACUMEN:
   (A) despair
   (B) excess
   (C) shrewdness
   (D) arrogance
   (E) charisma

8. FLAMBOYANT:
   (A) showy
   (B) petulant
   (C) combustible
   (D) reckless
   (E) feverish

## Answer Key: Synonyms

1. **(B) unkempt**
2. **(A) mourn**
3. **(C) plot**
4. **(D) harmful**
5. **(D) pardon**
6. **(E) surrender**
7. **(C) shrewdness**
8. **(A) showy**

# Verbal Analogies

An **analogy**, very generally, is a statement saying that one thing is similar to another thing. A simple example would be "Life is like a roller-coaster ride." The analogy questions in the verbal section of the SSAT ask you to compose a special kind of analogy, called a verbal analogy because it has to do with the meanings of words. A verbal analogy is a statement saying that the relationship between one pair of words is similar to the relationship between another pair of words. For example, the verbal analogy *"Swim is to water as fly is to air"* says that the verb "swim" is related to the noun "water" in the same way that the verb "fly" is related to the noun "air." To swim is to move through water, just as to fly is to move through the air.

> The analogy portion of the SSAT asks you to identify the answer that best matches the relationship between two words.

## What Are the Directions for the Verbal Analogies Section on the Test?

The following questions ask you to find relationships between words. For each question, select the answer choice that best completes the meaning of the sentence.

## What Are the Things to Remember When Doing Analogies?

### Parts of Speech

The parts of speech in the first word pair must match the parts of speech in the second word pair. If, for example, the words in the first pair are noun/adjective, then the words in the second pair must also be noun/adjective.

### Word Order

If the first pair expresses a particular relationship, the second pair must express the same relationship in the same order.

### Exactness

Sometimes two or more of the given choices would make sense. When this happens, choose the answer that most exactly fits the relationship between the words in the stem of the question.

## How Are Verbal Analogies Presented?

The SSAT analogy questions present a **stem** followed by five **options**. The stem is an incomplete sentence, and each option offers a different way of finishing the sentence. The stem has the form A is to B as, (with A and B representing the first word pair), and the options have the form C is to D (with C and D representing the second word pair). When the stem and an option are put together, the result is a sentence of the form A is to B as C is to D.

| **EXAMPLE:** | 1. Loud is to hear as<br>(A) sad is to cry<br>(B) bright is to see<br>(C) rude is to speak<br>(D) angry is to feel<br>(E) bland is to taste<br>**The correct answer is (B).** |
| --- | --- |

# What Are Verbal Analogy Relationships?

Below are examples of some of the most common types of analogical relationships that you will find on the SSAT. This list is not complete; there are other types of verbal relationships not represented here.

1. **Antonyms**: X is the opposite of Y.
   EXAMPLE: Success is to failure as joy is to sadness.

2. **Degree:** To be X is to be extremely Y.
   EXAMPLE: Furious is to angry as enormous is to large.

3. **Type:** An X is a kind of Y.
   EXAMPLE: Sonnet is to poem as elm is to tree.

4. **Specific Type:** An X is a [gender] Y.
   EXAMPLE: Father is to parent as brother is to sibling.

5. **Specific Manner:** To X is to Y quickly.
   EXAMPLE: Glance is to look as jot is to write.

6. **Part:** An X is part of a Y.
   EXAMPLE: Chapter is to book as singer is to chorus.

7. **Specific Part:** An X is the outer part of a Y.
   EXAMPLE: Shell is to egg as rind is to orange.

8. **Specific Part:** An X is a unit of Y.
   EXAMPLE: Blade is to grass as grain is to sand.

9. **Associated Characteristic:** An X is Y.
   EXAMPLE: Liar is to dishonest as genius is to intelligent.

10. **Associated Characteristic:** Someone who Xes is Y.
    EXAMPLE: Attack is to aggressive as donate is to generous.

11. **Associated Characteristic:**
    Something X pertains to a Y.
    EXAMPLE: Solar is to sun as nautical is to ship.

12. **Associated Action:** An X Ys.
    EXAMPLE: Fugitive is to flee as arbiter is to decide.

13. **Associated Action:**
    Something that is X is easily Yed.
    EXAMPLE: Obvious is to see as weak is to overpower.

14. **Negative Association:**
    Someone who is X is NOT Ying.
    EXAMPLE: Awake is to sleep as silent is to talk.

15. **Negative Association:** Someone who is X lacks Y.
    EXAMPLE: Foolish is to wisdom as dauntless is to fear.

16. **Negative Association:**
    Something that is X cannot Y.
    EXAMPLE: Numb is to feel as immobile is to move.

17. **Associated Tool:** An X typically uses a Y.
    EXAMPLE: Farmer is to plow as navigator is to compass.

18. **Associated Material:** An X typically works with Y.
    EXAMPLE: Carpenter is to wood as tailor is to fabric.

19. **Associated Location:** An X is kept in a Y.
    EXAMPLE: Book is to library as artwork is to museum.

20. **Associated Location:** One Xes in a Y.
    EXAMPLE: Prosecute is to courtroom as compete is to arena.

21. **Purpose:** An X is used to Y.
    EXAMPLE: Pen is to write as shovel is to dig.

22. **Specific Purpose:** An X is used to measure Y.
    EXAMPLE: Yardstick is to length as scale is to weight.

23. **Purpose:** An X provides Y.
    EXAMPLE: Shield is to protection as blanket is to warmth.

24. **Specific Purpose:** An X protects a Y.
    EXAMPLE: Helmet is to head as glove is to hand.

25. **Product:** An X produces Y.
    EXAMPLE: Cow is to milk as bee is to honey.

26. **Result:** Something that Xes increases in Y.
    EXAMPLE: Expand is to size as accelerate is to speed.

27. **Result:** One becomes an X by Ying.
    EXAMPLE: Student is to enroll as soldier is to enlist.

28. **Result:** What has Xed is Y.
    EXAMPLE: Perish is to dead as depart is to absent.

29. **Result:** Something X elicits Y.
    EXAMPLE: Humorous is to laughter as pathetic is to pity.

30. **Expression:** An X expresses Y.
    EXAMPLE: Smile is to pleasure as sneer is to contempt.

# How Do You Solve Verbal Analogy Questions?

A useful strategy for solving analogies is to use a **bridge sentence**. A bridge sentence is a sentence that defines the relationship between two words using the letters **X** and **Y** in place of the words themselves. For instance, the bridge sentence **An X is not Y** defines the relationship between the words **coward** and **brave**.

When those words are substituted for **X** and **Y**, the result is a true sentence: "A coward is not brave." Of course, there are other word pairs that fit the same bridge sentence—for example, **fool** and **wise**. What this tells you is that the relationship between **coward** and **brave** is the same as the relationship between **fool** and **wise**. The two word pairs are analogous.

When answering an analogy question, the first thing to do is figure out the relationship between the two key words in the stem and then try to represent that relationship in a bridge sentence. So, for instance, if the words in the stem are **tulip** and **flower**, you'll probably recognize that a tulip is a kind of flower, and so you'll then formulate the bridge sentence **An X is a kind of Y**. Now that you have your bridge sentence, you can try out each of the word pairs in the options and see which pair fits the bridge sentence. For instance, if **stick** and **stone** are the words in one of the options, then you substitute these words for **X** and **Y** in the bridge sentence to produce the sentence "A stick is a kind of stone." But this sentence is obviously not true, and that tells you that the option with **stick** and **stone** is not the correct answer choice. If another option contains the words **apple** and **fruit**, then you substitute these words for **X** and **Y** to get the sentence "An apple is a kind of fruit." Since this sentence is true, the option that produced it must be the correct answer. You've solved the analogy!

Try this strategy out on the sample questions that follow.

> Be careful of the order of the words when you're determining the corresponding relationships.

## Verbal Test-Taking Strategies

1. The best way to improve your vocabulary is to read, read, and read some more.

2. Take note of unfamiliar words and look up their meanings.

3. Review the words you don't know.

4. Practice your vocabulary by taking the practice tests in this book. If you missed any of the verbal questions, read the questions and answers again, so you'll understand why you answered those questions incorrectly. Look them up and write them down.

## Sample Questions: Analogies

Directions: The following questions ask you to find relationships between words. For each question, select the answer choice that best completes the meaning of the sentence.

1.  Devastate is to damage as
    (A) listen is to hear
    (B) transform is to alter
    (C) design is to implement
    (D) conceal is to disclose
    (E) condemn is to judge

2.  Canoe is to boat as
    (A) room is to house
    (B) wheat is to oat
    (C) sedan is to car
    (D) pint is to gallon
    (E) shark is to whale

3.  Awkward is to graceful as
    (A) smart is to brilliant
    (B) normal is to regular
    (C) guilty is to suspicious
    (D) greedy is to poor
    (E) trivial is to important

4.  Crest is to wave as
    (A) river is to stream
    (B) trunk is to tree
    (C) boulder is to pebble
    (D) peak is to mountain
    (E) ceiling is to floor

5.  Liter is to volume as
    (A) pound is to weight
    (B) radius is to circle
    (C) cup is to beverage
    (D) mile is to speed
    (E) inch is to ruler

6.  Remind is to memory as
    (A) disguise is to identity
    (B) believe is to truth
    (C) inspire is to creativity
    (D) assure is to fear
    (E) criticize is to fault

7.  Slacken is to loose as
    (A) accelerate is to fast
    (B) betray is to trustworthy
    (C) pity is to compassionate
    (D) verify is to obvious
    (E) diminish is to large

8.  Satellite is to orbit as
    (A) spacecraft is to planet
    (B) ship is to course
    (C) train is to station
    (D) automobile is to map
    (E) bicycle is to wheel

9.  Shrug is to uncertainty as
    (A) think is to knowledge
    (B) sigh is to exhalation
    (C) argue is to agreement
    (D) dream is to fantasy
    (E) groan is to distress

10. Weak is to strength as
    (A) foolish is to error
    (B) lazy is to pride
    (C) clumsy is to grace
    (D) hungry is to thirst
    (E) reckless is to risk

## Answer Key: Analogies

1. **(B) transform is to alter**
   To X something is to Y it on a large scale.

2. **(C) sedan is to car**
   An X is a kind of Y.

3. **(E) trivial is to important**
   Being X is the opposite of being Y.

4. **(D) peak is to mountain**
   An X is the highest part of a Y.

5. **(A) pound is to weight**
   An X is a unit of measure for Y.

6. **(C) inspire is to creativity**
   To X is to activate Y.

7. **(A) accelerate is to fast**
   To X something is to make it more Y.

8. **(B) ship is to course**
   A Y is the path of an X.

9. **(E) groan is to distress**
   Xing expresses Y.

10. **(C) clumsy is to grace**
    Someone who is X lacks Y.

# Summing It Up

**Here are a few things to keep in mind when you take the Upper Level SSAT:**

- Make sure that you understand the directions before you start to work on any section. If there is anything that you do not understand, read the directions again.

- You don't need to answer every question on the test to score well. Some of the questions will be very easy and others will be difficult. Most students find that they do not know the answer to every question in every section. By working as quickly as you can without rushing, you should be able to read and think about every question.

- If you are not sure of an answer to a question, make note of it and move on. Make sure you also skip that question. If taking the test on paper, skip filling in that question's answer bubble on your answer sheet. If you have time left in that section, you can come back to questions you have not answered.

- If taking the test on paper, you may make as many marks on the test booklet as you need. Just be sure to mark your answers on the answer sheet!

- Answers written in the test book will not count toward your score. Space is provided in the book for scratch work in the quantitative sections. Check often to make sure that you are marking your answer in the correct row on the answer sheet.

- If you decide to change an answer, be sure to erase your first mark on the answer sheet completely. If taking the computer-based SSAT, make sure you change your answer before completing the section.

THIS PAGE INTENTIONALLY LEFT BLANK.

# Chapter Three: Scores

## What Your Scores Mean

If you're like most people, you'll quickly scan the score report trying to find **the** magic number that will tell you whether the scores are "good." With an admission test like the SSAT, this is not an easy thing to do. Remember that the purpose of an admission test is to offer a common measure of academic ability that can be used to compare all applicants. The SSAT test-taker population is composed only of students applying to college-preparatory private schools. It is important to keep in mind that your scores are being compared just to students in this highly competitive group.

As described in Chapter 1, admission tests differ from other tests such as classroom and achievement tests in significant ways. Achievement and classroom tests both assess a specific body of knowledge. If all students perform well, the teacher and school system have fulfilled their objective. If all students performed well on an admission test, it would lose its value in helping differentiate between and among candidates.

## Formula Scoring

The SSAT uses a method of scoring known in the testing industry as "formula scoring." Students earn one point for every correct answer, receive no points for omitted questions, and lose one quarter of a point for each incorrect answer. This is different from "right scoring," which computes the total score by counting the number of correct answers with no penalty for incorrect answers. Formula scoring is used to eliminate the test taker's gain from random guessing.

Test takers are instructed to omit questions for which they cannot make an educated guess. Since most students have not encountered this kind of test before, it is an important concept to understand and experience prior to taking the SSAT. SSAT score reports provide detailed information by section on the number of questions answered correctly, answered incorrectly, and not answered to aid families and schools in understanding the student's test-taking strategies and scores.

# The Score Report

It cannot be said often enough: *admission test scores are only one piece of the application.* The degree of emphasis placed on scores in a school's admission process depends on that school and on other information, such as transcripts, applicants' statements, and teacher recommendations.

The descriptions indicated by the letters below correspond to the lettered sections on the sample score report on page 71.

## Ⓐ About You

Parents and students should review this section carefully. Is the student's name spelled correctly? Is the date of birth listed correctly? And—very important—the student should be listed in his/her current grade. The student's current grade is used to determine which test form he/she will take and also dictates the comparison or norm groups. If the grade to which the student is applying was mistakenly used, he/she may get the wrong form and his/her SSAT scaled score will be compared with students a year (or grade) older. If any of this information is incorrect, contact The Enrollment Management Association immediately.

## Ⓑ About the Test You Took

Again, parents and students should review this information for accuracy. For Test Level, the student should have taken the Upper Level SSAT, because he/she is applying for admission to grades 9–12. The Middle Level SSAT is meant for students applying to grades 6–8. There is a different score scale for each of these levels.

## Ⓒ About Your Scores

SSAT scores are listed by section so you can understand the student's performance on each of the three scored sections: verbal, quantitative/math, and reading comprehension. A total score (a sum of the three sections) is also reported. For the Upper Level SSAT, the lowest number on the scale (500) is the lowest possible score a student can earn, and the highest number (800) is the highest possible score a student can earn.

Scores are first calculated by awarding one point for each correct answer and subtracting one quarter of one point for each incorrect answer. These scores are called raw scores. Raw scores can vary from one edition of the test to another due to differences in difficulty among different editions. A statistical procedure called *score equating* is used to adjust for these differences. After equating, the reported scores or scaled scores (e.g., the scores on the 500–800 scale for the Upper Level test) can be compared to each other across forms.

### Score Range

Even after equating adjustments are made, no single test score provides a perfectly accurate estimate of proficiency. Many factors can affect a student's score. We provide a scaled-score range to suggest where a student's scores might fall if taking a different version of the test. Assuming the student's ability remains the same, there is a high likelihood that the scores would fall within the range indicated.

*Continued on page 72*

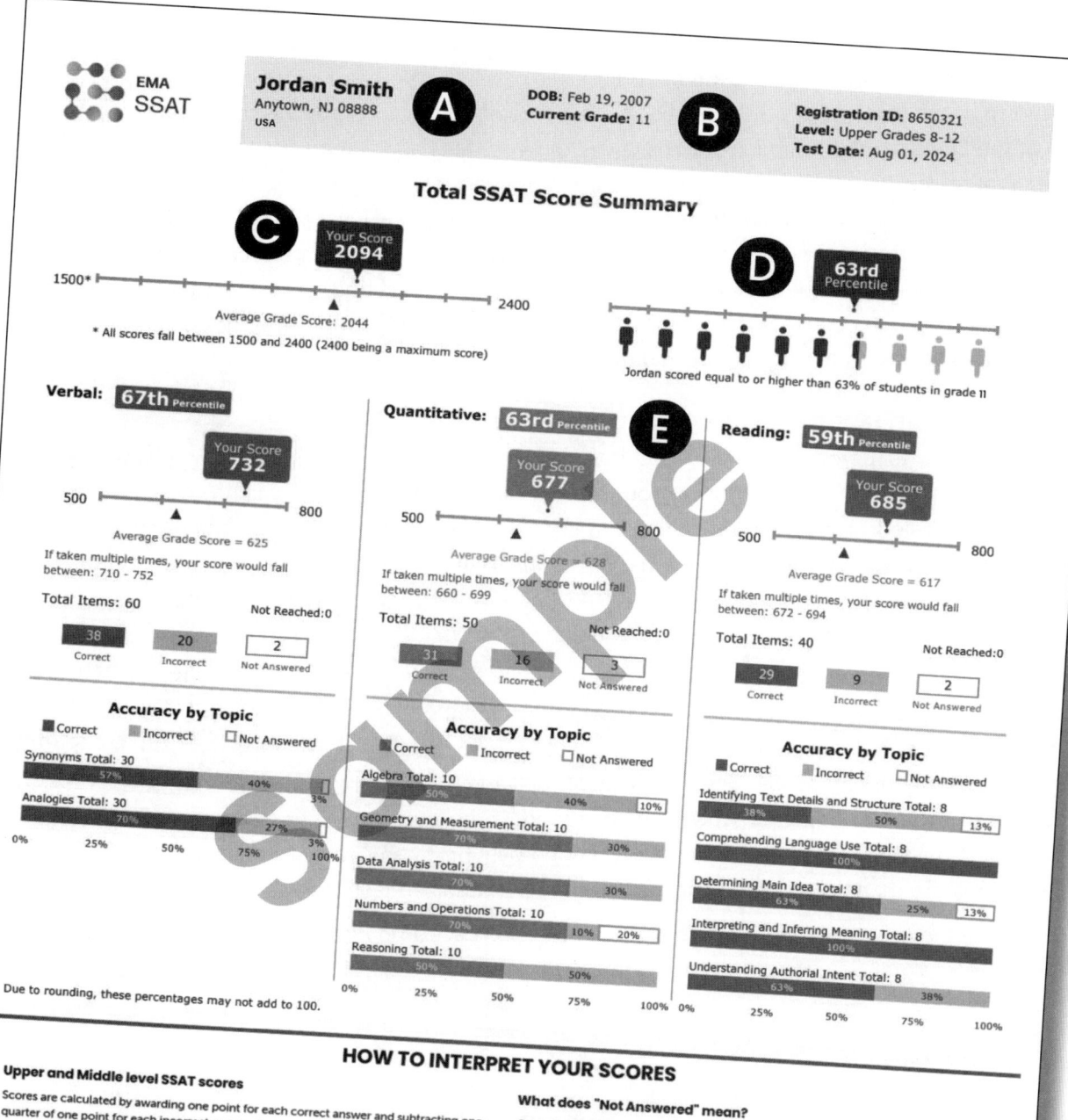

**EMA SSAT**

**Jordan Smith**
Anytown, NJ 08888
USA

A

DOB: Feb 19, 2007
Current Grade: 11

B

Registration ID: 8650321
Level: Upper Grades 8-12
Test Date: Aug 01, 2024

## Total SSAT Score Summary

C

Your Score
**2094**

1500* ———————————— 2400
Average Grade Score: 2044

* All scores fall between 1500 and 2400 (2400 being a maximum score)

D

**63rd** Percentile

Jordan scored equal to or higher than 63% of students in grade 11

**Verbal:** **67th** Percentile

Your Score
**732**

500 ———————————— 800
Average Grade Score = 625

If taken multiple times, your score would fall between: 710 - 752

Total Items: 60          Not Reached:0

| 38 | 20 | 2 |
| Correct | Incorrect | Not Answered |

### Accuracy by Topic

■ Correct   ■ Incorrect   □ Not Answered

Synonyms Total: 30
57%   40%   3%

Analogies Total: 30
70%   27%   3%

0%   25%   50%   75%   100%

**Quantitative:** **63rd** Percentile

E

Your Score
**677**

500 ———————————— 800
Average Grade Score = 628

If taken multiple times, your score would fall between: 660 - 699

Total Items: 50          Not Reached:0

| 31 | 16 | 3 |
| Correct | Incorrect | Not Answered |

### Accuracy by Topic

■ Correct   ■ Incorrect   □ Not Answered

Algebra Total: 10
50%   40%   10%

Geometry and Measurement Total: 10
70%   30%

Data Analysis Total: 10
70%   30%

Numbers and Operations Total: 10
70%   10%   20%

Reasoning Total: 10
50%   50%

0%   25%   50%   75%   100%

**Reading:** **59th** Percentile

Your Score
**685**

500 ———————————— 800
Average Grade Score = 617

If taken multiple times, your score would fall between: 672 - 694

Total Items: 40          Not Reached:0

| 29 | 9 | 2 |
| Correct | Incorrect | Not Answered |

### Accuracy by Topic

■ Correct   ■ Incorrect   □ Not Answered

Identifying Text Details and Structure Total: 8
38%   50%   13%

Comprehending Language Use Total: 8
100%

Determining Main Idea Total: 8
63%   25%   13%

Interpreting and Inferring Meaning Total: 8
100%

Understanding Authorial Intent Total: 8
63%   38%

0%   25%   50%   75%   100%

Due to rounding, these percentages may not add to 100.

## HOW TO INTERPRET YOUR SCORES

**Upper and Middle level SSAT scores**

Scores are calculated by awarding one point for each correct answer and subtracting one-quarter of one point for each incorrect answer. Points are neither awarded nor subtracted for questions left unanswered.

**How are my scores calculated?**

We provide score ranges to emphasize the possibility of small score differences if you had taken a different edition of the test instead of the one you took, accounting for changes in difficulty and different editions of the test.

A statistical approach called "equating" is used to adjust for these differences. Even after these adjustments, no single test score provides a perfectly accurate estimate of your proficiency.

For more information about the SSAT and to take a free practice test, please visit our website: www.ssat.org/practice.

**What does "Not Answered" mean?**

Questions not answered include both skipped questions and questions not reached. The number of correct, incorrect, not answered or not reached questions should not be compared between different test takers. These not only depend on the test takers ability but also on the difficulty of questions.

**What do percentiles mean?**

SSAT percentiles have range from 1 to 99, indicating that your scaled score was equal to or higher than the percentage of other test takers shown. If you are concerned that your percentile is lower than other scores, that may be because the SSAT test takers are a small & highly competitive group of students who plan to go the world's best independent schools

# ⒟ SSAT Score Information

Beginning with the 2021–2022 academic year, SSAT provides reference information based on one norm group. The norm group, such as all students in grade 8, contains all test takers in the same grade level who have taken one of the Standard SSAT administrations in the United States and Canada typically within the past three years. If a test taker completed the SSAT in previous years, a second norm group, such as female students in grade 8, would have been displayed, indicating test takers of the same grade level and gender who have taken one of the Standard administrations in the United States and Canada within the past three years. The difference between the two norm groups is that the total norm group contains both male and female test takers, whereas the second norm group is gender specific. You will only see the grade-specific norm group going forward. You will also see the average scaled score attained by the group.

## SSAT Percentile

The SSAT reports percentile ranks. The percentile rank is the percentage of students in the norm group whose scores fall below your scaled score. For example, if an eighth-grade student's verbal scaled score is 698 and the percentile rank is 70 on the verbal section in the total group, 70% of all eighth-grade students in the norm group had a verbal score lower than 698.

Many parents/guardians express concern that their student's SSAT percentiles are lower than those they have earned on other tests. Remember that SSAT test takers are a small and highly competitive group of students who plan to attend some of the world's best private schools. Do not be discouraged by what seems to be a lower score than the student usually attains on standardized testing.

> It is important to remember that SSAT test takers are members of a small and highly competitive group of students who plan to attend some of the world's best private schools. Being in the middle of this group is still impressive!

International and Flex test scores are not included in the comparison norm group. However, international and Flex test takers' scaled scores are compared to the domestic/Standard/first-time test-taker norm group described above.

## SSAT Average Score

SSAT average scores provide additional context information for your SSAT scaled score on each of the three scored sections (verbal, quantitative/math, and reading). These average scores are based on the same norm group used to provide the SSAT percentiles.

The average score is the average performance of all other students in the total norm group.

# ⒠ Test Question Breakdown

This section provides useful and detailed information about the test's content and the student's test-taking strategies. Look carefully at the ratio of wrong answers to unanswered questions. If the student had many wrong answers but omitted few or no questions, meaning that they were guessing quite a bit instead of skipping questions they couldn't answer, that could have an adverse effect on scores.

# Supporting the Test Taker

Here are a few simple things you can do to help your student perform as well as possible on the Upper Level SSAT.

**Practice! Practice! Practice!** Help your student structure time to take the practice tests in the next chapter. Act as the proctor—administer the timed practice tests while approximating testing conditions as closely as possible.

**Review and encourage!** Review any incorrect answers. Which sections or types of questions proved most difficult? Focus, encourage, and help your student sharpen those skills. Examine your student's guessing strategy. Try to determine the cause of the errors so that your student can develop a strategy for avoiding similar mistakes on the actual test.

**Some common pitfalls:**
- Accidentally marking the wrong circle on the answer sheet when the student knows the correct answer
- Making simple arithmetic mistakes

Double-checking answers and not rushing can help with this.

**Extra help!** If taking the practice tests reveals that your student lacks a particular skill that is necessary for success, seeking extra help for your student may be useful. If you would rather self-direct this process, consider signing up for SSAT Practice Online. With diagnostic tools, progress indicators, and study tools, it provides a full year of help and feedback.

**Perspective is everything!** Keep the importance of the SSAT in perspective and help your student do the same. The SSAT is an important and valuable part of the application package and students should prepare for it. But remember that the SSAT is just *one* part of the entire package. Schools will weigh your student's test scores along with other information.

**Retaking the test?** Scheduling options are available at ssat.org should your student want to retake the SSAT. In general, the lower the initial scores, the more likely the scores will increase the second time.

**Rest up and eat well!** Make sure your student gets enough sleep on the days leading up to the test and that he or she eats a healthy breakfast on the day it is administered.

**Be prepared for the unexpected!** If your student panics, freezes, or gets sick during the administration of the SSAT, she or he has the option to leave the test. It's important for you to know that if your child does leave the test, the results will be canceled. It's your responsibility, however, to alert The Enrollment Management Association immediately so that the scores are voided and not sent to schools. Please note that your fee for the canceled test will not be refunded, but for a service charge, you may reschedule for a new test date.

THIS PAGE INTENTIONALLY LEFT BLANK.

# Chapter Four:
# The Character Skills Snapshot

## What Is the Character Skills Snapshot?

The Character Skills Snapshot is an online assessment tool designed for students in grades 5 to 11 who are seeking entrance to private schools for grades 6 to 12. The purpose of the Snapshot is to measure essential character skills deemed important by private schools. The Snapshot is considered one new and important piece of the student admissions process, but it should not be used independently of other pieces of information to make admissions decisions.

## What Is the Purpose of the Snapshot?

We know that schools care about students and how they grow—not just in cognitive skills such as writing and math, but also growing into good citizens with initiative, resilience, and social awareness—those skills that carry them forward into a successful adult life.

While character education is a hallmark of a private school education and is a salient piece of every school's mission, gaining insight into an applying student's current character skill development has been largely a matter of intuition and an investigative screening of the application. While many schools assess character in some way (e.g., via student interviews or teacher recommendations), reliance on unstandardized or inconsistent methods to assess character skills can introduce bias and subjectivity into the admissions process. This highlights the need for a standardized and empirically supported approach.

The Snapshot is meant to provide a snapshot in time of a student's character skills—it is not a fixed, absolute measure. It provides a way for schools to get to know a student better and an opportunity for them to enumerate the ways in which their communities can enrich and develop a student's developing skills.

## How Was the Snapshot Designed?

The development of the Snapshot was research- and data-driven. Over the last six years, The Enrollment Management Association has put considerable time and resources toward developing the Snapshot. Spearheaded by the recommendation of the Think Tank on the Future of Assessment, EMA worked with 56 private and independent schools, and Educational Testing Service, to conceptualize, build, pilot, and launch the Character Skills Snapshot. The Snapshot, a revolutionary new tool for the admissions process, enables member schools to include a standardized measure of character into their admissions process.

Prior to launching the Snapshot, multiple pretesting and field trials were conducted with more than 12,000 students completing the assessment. Additionally, user testing was conducted with parents to gain feedback on the design and content elements of the results reports, as well as the assessment itself.

# What Does the Snapshot Measure?

The Snapshot measures seven character skills.

| Character Skill | Definition | Example Preferences |
|---|---|---|
| Initiative | This skill describes the student's inclination to work on assignments in a timely manner and emphasizes the point at which a student chooses to start work rather than when the student finishes work. | Starts working on assignments early<br><br>Does not do things at the last minute |
| Intellectual Engagement | This skill focuses on the student's enjoyment of and willingness to pursue learning opportunities, regardless of how much difficulty they might present. | Enjoys challenging assignments and tasks<br><br>Likes to learn more about topics of interest |
| Open-Mindedness | This skill describes the student's willingness to try new things. | Is open to trying new and unfamiliar approaches<br><br>Does not avoid trying new activities, experiences, music and/or food |
| Resilience | This skill highlights the student's ability to adjust to unexpected situations and changing circumstances. | Readily adapts when plans change<br><br>Is comfortable in stressful situations |
| Self-Control | This skill focuses on the student's ability to monitor and control his or her thoughts and actions, and what he or she says to others. | Thinks carefully about what he or she says<br><br>Thinks things through before making a decision |
| Social Awareness | This skill describes a student's ability to recognize the appropriate ways to interact with others. | Adapts behavior based on the particular context<br><br>Attempts to resolve conflicts and act appropriately |
| Teamwork | This skill highlights the student's ability to engage in supportive behaviors and emphasizes empathetic qualities that enable productive collaboration with others. | Attempts to comfort friends when they are upset<br><br>Tries to resolve conflicts between people in a group |

# The Character Skills Snapshot Consists of TWO Sections

The first section has 20–30 forced-choice questions, depending on the form. A forced-choice question presents three short statements and asks you to select the response that is MOST like you and the response that is LEAST like you. One option will always be left blank. (See Sample Questions at the end of this chapter.)

The second section has 10 situational judgment scenarios. You are asked to read each scenario then read the four corresponding responses. You are asked to rate the appropriateness of each response using a scale of 1 (not appropriate) to 4 (very appropriate). You can use the same ratings for each response. For example, if you think each response is very appropriate, you can use a rating of 4 for each option.

# How Is the Snapshot Administered?

The Snapshot is administered online. After parents consent for their student(s) to take the Snapshot and respond to an integrity statement, the student can then log into their Student Access Portal and begin the Snapshot.

The tool is untimed, but usually takes about 30 minutes to complete.

# Is the Snapshot Reliable?

Yes, the Snapshot is reliable. Reliability is a measure of consistency. Think of it this way: If you weigh yourself every day for a week and the scale registers the same weight, you can say that the scale is reliable. In statistics, reliability is measured on a scale from 0–1: "0" means no reliability at all and "1" means perfect reliability, which is rarely achieved in reality. Depending on the purpose of the test, the desired range of reliability can vary. For a noncognitive assessment like the Snapshot, a reliability of 0.7 or higher is preferable. The Snapshot has achieved this target reliability.

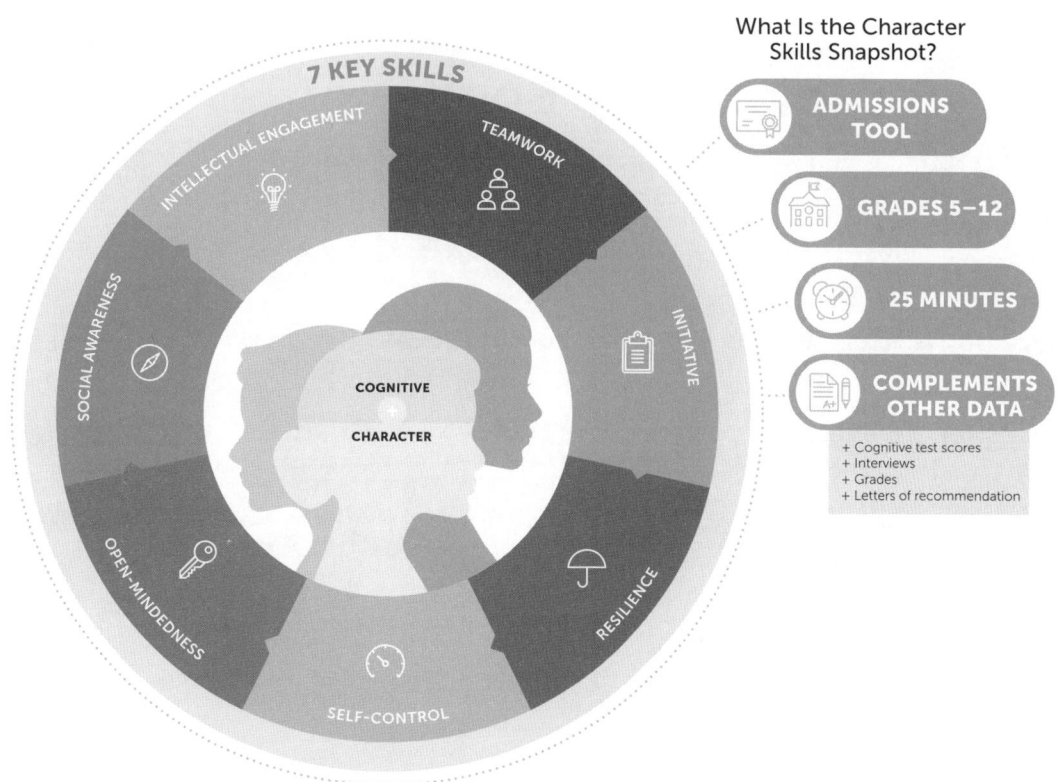

# The Snapshot Is a Norm-Referenced Assessment

A norm-referenced assessment interprets an individual's results compared to the results distribution of a comparison group, referred to as the norm group. The Snapshot norm groups are based on a group of approximately 5,000 students who took the Snapshot during a given academic year. There are two norm groups for the Snapshot, determined by grade band. The middle-level norm group consists of all students in grades 5–7 applying to grades 6–8. The upper-level norm group consists of all students in grades 8–11 applying to grades 9–12.

The Snapshot reports results for each of the seven skills in three performance categories: Emerging, Developing, and Demonstrating.

| Emerging | Developing | Demonstrating |
|---|---|---|
| The student's result fell into the lowest 25% (0–25th percentile) of scores in the comparison sample. | The student's result fell into the middle 50% (above 25th and below 75th percentile) of scores in the comparison sample. | The student's results fell in the upper 25% (at or above 75th percentile) of scores in the comparison sample. |
| The student is starting to show signs of this skill. Note that emerging does not imply a student does not have any of this skill. | The student displays the skill but is continuing to develop it. | The student displays a clear understanding and use of this skill. Note that demonstrating a skill does not imply that a student has mastered the skill. There is still room to grow. |

# Strategies for Taking the Snapshot

**Relax.** The Snapshot provides you with an opportunity to share more about yourself and your preferences as they relate to the seven character skills with schools. Remember, it is only one piece of the application.

**Answer honestly.** Remember this is the way you see yourself—not how your parents, your friends, your teacher, or your coach would describe you.

**Select the choice that is MOST like you or the choice that is LEAST like you.** You are sometimes going to have to make a difficult choice. You may see multiple options that are all like you or not like you at all.

**Consider your answers carefully.** The assessment will not allow you to go back and change your answers. Once a selection is made, it is final.

**Do not misrepresent yourself.** Trying to answer questions in such a way as to make yourself look good on any one skill may have an adverse effect on some of the other skills. Don't over think your answers, just be yourself!

## Sample Questions

### Forced-Choice

*Select the statement that describes you most accurately and the statement that describes you least accurately. There will always be one statement in each set of three that will not be dragged into the "most" and "least" boxes.*

| I say the first thing that comes to my mind. | I get bored when trying to solve difficult problems. | I avoid being emotionally involved in other people's problems. |
| --- | --- | --- |

Most like me

Least like me

| I am open to trying new things. | I like to research topics that are interesting to me. | I am willing to help people whenever they ask for my help. |
| --- | --- | --- |

Most like me

Least like me

| I do not like to change the way something is done if the current way still works. | Before doing something, I first think carefully about it. | It is easy for me to find something else to do if someone cancels at the last minute. |
| --- | --- | --- |

Most like me

Least like me

## Situational Judgment

*Please rate the appropriateness of each possible response from 1 (not appropriate at all) to 4 (very appropriate). You can apply the same rating to more than one response. If, for example, you believe that two of the possible responses would be 1 (not appropriate at all), you may mark them both with a 1.*

After two weeks of late nights, Sarah feels overwhelmed by the demands of her Spanish class and the upcoming assessment. Sarah has been an attentive student, but Spanish does not come easy to her. She wants to meet with her Spanish teacher, but he has been ill during the week and will not return to school tomorrow. Unfortunately, this is the day before the test.

| Possible Responses | 1 (not appropriate at all) | 2 | 3 | 4 (very appropriate) |
|---|---|---|---|---|
| Meet with the Spanish teacher and suggest that giving the test this week is not fair since he has been absent. | | | | |
| Meet with the Spanish teacher and ask him if there is a way he can give her a few more days to prepare for the test. | | | | |
| Speak to her parents and ask them to call the Spanish teacher to voice their concern about giving students a test immediately after the teacher was unavailable to students for so long. | | | | |
| Meet with the Spanish teacher when he returns to discuss her recent progress and develop a long-term plan to improve. | | | | |

As a member of the student council, Caroline is on a committee that plans themes for school dances. While Caroline proposes a 1960's theme for the winter formal, the other members of the committee propose a "night at the movies" theme.

| Possible Responses | 1 (not appropriate at all) | 2 | 3 | 4 (very appropriate) |
|---|---|---|---|---|
| Accept the proposal of the majority of committee members. | | | | |
| Accept the proposal of the majority of committee members, but demand that she can choose the theme for the next dance. | | | | |
| Resign from student council because she did not get her way. | | | | |
| Accept the proposal of the majority of committee members, but quietly convince as many students as she can not to attend the dance. | | | | |

# Upper Level
# Practice Tests

# Trying Out the Upper Level SSAT

Now it's time to find out what it's actually like to take the Upper Level SSAT. Ask a parent or other adult to help you set up a simulation — a re-creation of the experience that is as close as possible to actually taking the SSAT. Think of it as a dress rehearsal for the real thing. Simulating the SSAT experience can help you gain confidence and clarity about what to expect.

Remove (or photocopy) the answer sheet and use it to complete each practice test.

You can choose to do your simulation section by section or by taking an entire test from start to finish.

Here are the rules you'll need to follow to make your SSAT simulation as realistic as possible:

+ Ask your "test proctor" to keep time and tell you when to begin and end each section.
+ No talking or music is allowed during the SSAT; so, make sure the room in which you are taking the test is quiet and turn off anything that makes noise, such as your phone, iPod, or TV.
+ You will not be allowed to use any research material while taking the SSAT; so, put away your phone, laptop, books, dictionary, calculator, ruler, and notes.
+ Work only on one section during the time allotted. Do not go back to another section to finish unanswered questions.
+ Use sharpened #2 pencils and an eraser.
+ Fill in the answer sheet (located before each test in the book) just as you would during a regular test.

# Simulating the Test: Section by Section

If your goal is to sharpen your test-taking techniques in a specific area, use the individual sections for the simulation. Review the exercises in Chapter 2 before beginning, and be sure to follow the instructions for each section carefully. Schedule the allotted time for each section, and ask the person supervising your simulation to time you, or set a timer for yourself.

As you will when you actually take the SSAT, mark your answer choices on the answer sheet.

# Simulating the Test: Start to Finish

If your goal is to practice taking the entire SSAT (minus the experimental section), here's how to schedule your time blocks, including breaks:

| Test Overview | | |
|---|---|---|
| **Section** | **Number of Questions** | **Time Allotted to Administer Each Section** |
| Writing Sample | 1 | 25 minutes |
| Break | | 10 minutes |
| Section 1 (Quantitative) | 25 | 30 minutes |
| Section 2 (Reading) | 40 | 40 minutes |
| Break | | 10 minutes |
| Section 3 (Verbal) | 60 | 30 minutes |
| Section 4 (Quantitative) | 25 | 30 minutes |
| **Totals** | **151** | **2 hours, 55 minutes** |

When you add this all up, you'll see that the total testing time is 2 hours and 35 minutes. When you add in the two breaks, the total time is 2 hours and 55 minutes (these practice tests do not include an experimental section). Be sure to use your breaks for stretching, getting a drink of water, and focusing your eyes on something other than a test paper. This will help clear your mind and get you ready for the next section.

A note about special timing: Some students are granted "time and a half" accommodations, and are given 1.5 times the minutes available for each test section, including the writing sample. Students who are granted 1.5x time do not take the experimental section.

THIS PAGE INTENTIONALLY LEFT BLANK.

# Practice Test I: Upper Level Answer Sheet

**Be sure each mark completely fills the circle.**
Start with number 1 for each new section of the test.

## Section 1

| | | | | |
|---|---|---|---|---|
| 1 ⒶⒷⒸⒹⒺ | 6 ⒶⒷⒸⒹⒺ | 11 ⒶⒷⒸⒹⒺ | 16 ⒶⒷⒸⒹⒺ | 21 ⒶⒷⒸⒹⒺ |
| 2 ⒶⒷⒸⒹⒺ | 7 ⒶⒷⒸⒹⒺ | 12 ⒶⒷⒸⒹⒺ | 17 ⒶⒷⒸⒹⒺ | 22 ⒶⒷⒸⒹⒺ |
| 3 ⒶⒷⒸⒹⒺ | 8 ⒶⒷⒸⒹⒺ | 13 ⒶⒷⒸⒹⒺ | 18 ⒶⒷⒸⒹⒺ | 23 ⒶⒷⒸⒹⒺ |
| 4 ⒶⒷⒸⒹⒺ | 9 ⒶⒷⒸⒹⒺ | 14 ⒶⒷⒸⒹⒺ | 19 ⒶⒷⒸⒹⒺ | 24 ⒶⒷⒸⒹⒺ |
| 5 ⒶⒷⒸⒹⒺ | 10 ⒶⒷⒸⒹⒺ | 15 ⒶⒷⒸⒹⒺ | 20 ⒶⒷⒸⒹⒺ | 25 ⒶⒷⒸⒹⒺ |

## Section 2

| | | | | |
|---|---|---|---|---|
| 1 ⒶⒷⒸⒹⒺ | 9 ⒶⒷⒸⒹⒺ | 17 ⒶⒷⒸⒹⒺ | 25 ⒶⒷⒸⒹⒺ | 33 ⒶⒷⒸⒹⒺ |
| 2 ⒶⒷⒸⒹⒺ | 10 ⒶⒷⒸⒹⒺ | 18 ⒶⒷⒸⒹⒺ | 26 ⒶⒷⒸⒹⒺ | 34 ⒶⒷⒸⒹⒺ |
| 3 ⒶⒷⒸⒹⒺ | 11 ⒶⒷⒸⒹⒺ | 19 ⒶⒷⒸⒹⒺ | 27 ⒶⒷⒸⒹⒺ | 35 ⒶⒷⒸⒹⒺ |
| 4 ⒶⒷⒸⒹⒺ | 12 ⒶⒷⒸⒹⒺ | 20 ⒶⒷⒸⒹⒺ | 28 ⒶⒷⒸⒹⒺ | 36 ⒶⒷⒸⒹⒺ |
| 5 ⒶⒷⒸⒹⒺ | 13 ⒶⒷⒸⒹⒺ | 21 ⒶⒷⒸⒹⒺ | 29 ⒶⒷⒸⒹⒺ | 37 ⒶⒷⒸⒹⒺ |
| 6 ⒶⒷⒸⒹⒺ | 14 ⒶⒷⒸⒹⒺ | 22 ⒶⒷⒸⒹⒺ | 30 ⒶⒷⒸⒹⒺ | 38 ⒶⒷⒸⒹⒺ |
| 7 ⒶⒷⒸⒹⒺ | 15 ⒶⒷⒸⒹⒺ | 23 ⒶⒷⒸⒹⒺ | 31 ⒶⒷⒸⒹⒺ | 39 ⒶⒷⒸⒹⒺ |
| 8 ⒶⒷⒸⒹⒺ | 16 ⒶⒷⒸⒹⒺ | 24 ⒶⒷⒸⒹⒺ | 32 ⒶⒷⒸⒹⒺ | 40 ⒶⒷⒸⒹⒺ |

## Section 3

| | | | | |
|---|---|---|---|---|
| 1 ⒶⒷⒸⒹⒺ | 13 ⒶⒷⒸⒹⒺ | 25 ⒶⒷⒸⒹⒺ | 37 ⒶⒷⒸⒹⒺ | 49 ⒶⒷⒸⒹⒺ |
| 2 ⒶⒷⒸⒹⒺ | 14 ⒶⒷⒸⒹⒺ | 26 ⒶⒷⒸⒹⒺ | 38 ⒶⒷⒸⒹⒺ | 50 ⒶⒷⒸⒹⒺ |
| 3 ⒶⒷⒸⒹⒺ | 15 ⒶⒷⒸⒹⒺ | 27 ⒶⒷⒸⒹⒺ | 39 ⒶⒷⒸⒹⒺ | 51 ⒶⒷⒸⒹⒺ |
| 4 ⒶⒷⒸⒹⒺ | 16 ⒶⒷⒸⒹⒺ | 28 ⒶⒷⒸⒹⒺ | 40 ⒶⒷⒸⒹⒺ | 52 ⒶⒷⒸⒹⒺ |
| 5 ⒶⒷⒸⒹⒺ | 17 ⒶⒷⒸⒹⒺ | 29 ⒶⒷⒸⒹⒺ | 41 ⒶⒷⒸⒹⒺ | 53 ⒶⒷⒸⒹⒺ |
| 6 ⒶⒷⒸⒹⒺ | 18 ⒶⒷⒸⒹⒺ | 30 ⒶⒷⒸⒹⒺ | 42 ⒶⒷⒸⒹⒺ | 54 ⒶⒷⒸⒹⒺ |
| 7 ⒶⒷⒸⒹⒺ | 19 ⒶⒷⒸⒹⒺ | 31 ⒶⒷⒸⒹⒺ | 43 ⒶⒷⒸⒹⒺ | 55 ⒶⒷⒸⒹⒺ |
| 8 ⒶⒷⒸⒹⒺ | 20 ⒶⒷⒸⒹⒺ | 32 ⒶⒷⒸⒹⒺ | 44 ⒶⒷⒸⒹⒺ | 56 ⒶⒷⒸⒹⒺ |
| 9 ⒶⒷⒸⒹⒺ | 21 ⒶⒷⒸⒹⒺ | 33 ⒶⒷⒸⒹⒺ | 45 ⒶⒷⒸⒹⒺ | 57 ⒶⒷⒸⒹⒺ |
| 10 ⒶⒷⒸⒹⒺ | 22 ⒶⒷⒸⒹⒺ | 34 ⒶⒷⒸⒹⒺ | 46 ⒶⒷⒸⒹⒺ | 58 ⒶⒷⒸⒹⒺ |
| 11 ⒶⒷⒸⒹⒺ | 23 ⒶⒷⒸⒹⒺ | 35 ⒶⒷⒸⒹⒺ | 47 ⒶⒷⒸⒹⒺ | 59 ⒶⒷⒸⒹⒺ |
| 12 ⒶⒷⒸⒹⒺ | 24 ⒶⒷⒸⒹⒺ | 36 ⒶⒷⒸⒹⒺ | 48 ⒶⒷⒸⒹⒺ | 60 ⒶⒷⒸⒹⒺ |

## Section 4

| | | | | |
|---|---|---|---|---|
| 1 ⒶⒷⒸⒹⒺ | 6 ⒶⒷⒸⒹⒺ | 11 ⒶⒷⒸⒹⒺ | 16 ⒶⒷⒸⒹⒺ | 21 ⒶⒷⒸⒹⒺ |
| 2 ⒶⒷⒸⒹⒺ | 7 ⒶⒷⒸⒹⒺ | 12 ⒶⒷⒸⒹⒺ | 17 ⒶⒷⒸⒹⒺ | 22 ⒶⒷⒸⒹⒺ |
| 3 ⒶⒷⒸⒹⒺ | 8 ⒶⒷⒸⒹⒺ | 13 ⒶⒷⒸⒹⒺ | 18 ⒶⒷⒸⒹⒺ | 23 ⒶⒷⒸⒹⒺ |
| 4 ⒶⒷⒸⒹⒺ | 9 ⒶⒷⒸⒹⒺ | 14 ⒶⒷⒸⒹⒺ | 19 ⒶⒷⒸⒹⒺ | 24 ⒶⒷⒸⒹⒺ |
| 5 ⒶⒷⒸⒹⒺ | 10 ⒶⒷⒸⒹⒺ | 15 ⒶⒷⒸⒹⒺ | 20 ⒶⒷⒸⒹⒺ | 25 ⒶⒷⒸⒹⒺ |

## Section 5

| | | | |
|---|---|---|---|
| 1 ⒶⒷⒸⒹⒺ | 5 ⒶⒷⒸⒹⒺ | 9 ⒶⒷⒸⒹⒺ | 13 ⒶⒷⒸⒹⒺ |
| 2 ⒶⒷⒸⒹⒺ | 6 ⒶⒷⒸⒹⒺ | 10 ⒶⒷⒸⒹⒺ | 14 ⒶⒷⒸⒹⒺ |
| 3 ⒶⒷⒸⒹⒺ | 7 ⒶⒷⒸⒹⒺ | 11 ⒶⒷⒸⒹⒺ | 15 ⒶⒷⒸⒹⒺ |
| 4 ⒶⒷⒸⒹⒺ | 8 ⒶⒷⒸⒹⒺ | 12 ⒶⒷⒸⒹⒺ | 16 ⒶⒷⒸⒹⒺ |

**Experimental Section – See page 9 for details.**

THIS PAGE INTENTIONALLY LEFT BLANK.

**Writing Sample**

Schools would like to get to know you better through an essay you write. If you choose to write a personal essay, base your essay on the topic presented in A. If you choose to write a general essay, base your essay on the topic presented in B. Please fill in the circle next to your choice.

Ⓐ Which three literary characters would you invite to dinner and why? What would you want to talk about with them?

Ⓑ What book do you think students should be required to read and why?

**Use this page and the next page to complete your writing sample.**

*Continue on next page*

THIS PAGE INTENTIONALLY LEFT BLANK.

## SECTION 1
## 25 Questions

Following each problem in this section, there are five suggested answers. Work each problem in your head or in the blank space provided at the right of the page. Then look at the five suggested answers and decide which one is best.

<u>Note</u>: Figures that accompany problems in this section are drawn as accurately as possible EXCEPT when it is stated in a specific problem that its figure is not drawn to scale.

Sample Problem:

| | | |
|---|---|---|
| 5,413 | (A) | 586 |
| - 4,827 | (B) | 596 |
| | (C) | 696 |
| | (D) | 1,586 |
| | (E) | 1,686 |

● Ⓑ Ⓒ Ⓓ Ⓔ

---

1. Which point shown in the *xy*-coordinate plane has the coordinates (2, –3) ?

    (A)  *A*
    (B)  *B*
    (C)  *C*
    (D)  *D*
    (E)  *E*

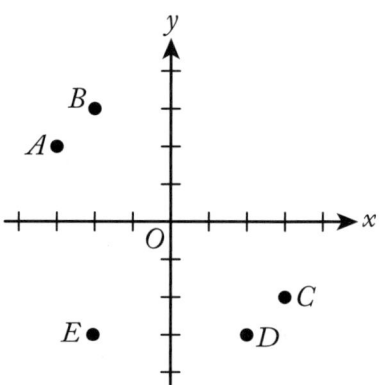

---

2. Franz has *k* fewer points in a game than Annie. Annie has 7 points in the game. How many points does Franz have, in terms of *k* ?

    (A)  $\dfrac{k}{7}$

    (B)  $\dfrac{7}{k}$

    (C)  $k - 7$

    (D)  $7 - k$

    (E)  $7 + k$

**GO ON TO THE NEXT PAGE.**

**USE THIS SPACE FOR FIGURING.**

3.  A rectangular prism has a volume of 288 cubic meters. Which of the following could be its dimensions?

    (A)  4m by 7m by 9m
    (B)  8m by 8m by 4m
    (C)  8m by 9m by 4m
    (D)  12m by 6m by 2m
    (E)  12m by 12m by 4m

---

$$\frac{87,412}{3,024}$$

4.  Which of the following numbers is closest in value to the fraction above?

    (A)        30
    (B)     2,900
    (C)   30,000
    (D)   85,000
    (E)   90,000

---

5.  Which of the following figures can be drawn without lifting a pencil or retracing any line segments or curves in the figure?

    (A)

    (B)

    (C)

    (D)

    (E)

**GO ON TO THE NEXT PAGE.**

**USE THIS SPACE FOR FIGURING.**

6. If the mean of five consecutive whole numbers is 18, what is the smallest of these five numbers?

   (A)  8
   (B) 12
   (C) 16
   (D) 17
   (E) 18

---

$8x$

7. If the perimeter of the square shown is 640, what is the value of $x$?

   (A)  10
   (B)  20
   (C)  40
   (D)  80
   (E) 160

---

8. A truck driver took between 5.5 and 6 hours to make a 350-mile trip. The average speed, in miles per hour, must have been between which of the following two numbers?

   (A) 48 and 50
   (B) 50 and 55
   (C) 55 and 58
   (D) 58 and 64
   (E) 64 and 100

---

9. When $r + s = 13$ and $2t + s = 13$, what is the value of $t$?

   (A) 13
   (B)  5
   (C) −5
   (D) −7
   (E) It cannot be determined from the information given.

**GO ON TO THE NEXT PAGE.**

**USE THIS SPACE FOR FIGURING.**

10. In the figure, segment $\overline{PQ}$ is 45 centimeters long. How long is segment $\overline{RQ}$ ?

(A) 15 cm
(B) 18 cm
(C) 24 cm
(D) 27 cm
(E) 30 cm

11. One staple weighs 31 milligrams. If a box of staples holds 250 staples, how many <u>grams</u> of staples does the box hold?

(A)  6.75
(B)  7.75
(C)  67.5
(D)  77.5
(E)  7,750

12. If $\dfrac{x + 1}{x - 1} = 3$, what is the value of $x$ ?

(A)  –2
(B)  –1
(C)   0
(D)   1
(E)   2

13. What is the probability that an integer selected at random from the interval $1 < x < 12$ will be divisible by 3 but <u>not</u> divisible by 2 ?

(A)  $\dfrac{1}{6}$

(B)  $\dfrac{1}{5}$

(C)  $\dfrac{3}{10}$

(D)  $\dfrac{1}{3}$

(E)  $\dfrac{7}{10}$

**GO ON TO THE NEXT PAGE.**

**USE THIS SPACE FOR FIGURING.**

14. In a survey, each of 500 people was found to have a checking account, a savings account, or both. If 300 of these people have checking accounts and 300 have savings accounts, how many people have both a checking account and a savings account?

    (A)   50

    (B)  100

    (C)  150

    (D)  250

    (E)  300

15. Two numbers whose difference is 8 add up to 50. What is the smaller of these two numbers?

    (A)  21

    (B)  22

    (C)  23

    (D)  28

    (E)  29

16. If $g$, $v$, and $z$ are positive numbers, which of the following expressions is equivalent to $\dfrac{15g^2 v^3 z}{35 g v^2 z}$ ?

    (A)  $\dfrac{gv}{3}$

    (B)  $\dfrac{3}{7gv}$

    (C)  $\dfrac{3gv}{7}$

    (D)  $\dfrac{3g^3 v^5 z^2}{7}$

    (E)  $\dfrac{5gv}{7z}$

$$20 - 15 \div 5 + 4 \times 3 + 12$$

17. Which of the following is the value of the expression above?

    (A)  23

    (B)  25

    (C)  27

    (D)  41

    (E)  61

**GO ON TO THE NEXT PAGE.**

**USE THIS SPACE FOR FIGURING.**

18. What are the solutions to the equation $(x + 5)(x - 1) = 0$ ?

    (A)  $x = -1$ and $x = 5$
    (B)  $x = 1$ and $x = -5$
    (C)  $x = 1$ and $x = 5$
    (D)  $x = 4$ and $x = -5$
    (E)  $x = 4$ and $x = 1$

---

19. In the addition of the three-digit numbers shown, each of the letters A, B, C, and D represents one of the digits 0 through 9. Which of the following could be the sum A + B + C + D ?

    (A)  10
    (B)  13
    (C)  14
    (D)  16
    (E)  19

$$\begin{array}{r} A\ B\ C \\ +\ D\ B\ C \\ \hline 8\ 5\ 0 \end{array}$$

---

20. An isosceles right triangle has a leg of length 2. What is the length of the hypotenuse of this triangle?

    (A)  2
    (B)  4
    (C)  $\sqrt{2}$
    (D)  $2\sqrt{2}$
    (E)  $4\sqrt{2}$

---

21. Mr. Williams, a parking lot owner, sold 20% of his lot to his neighbor. Later that year he sold 20% of the remainder of his lot to another neighbor. What percent of Mr. Williams' original parking lot does he still own?

    (A)  16%
    (B)  40%
    (C)  60%
    (D)  64%
    (E)  80%

**GO ON TO THE NEXT PAGE.**

**USE THIS SPACE FOR FIGURING.**

22. In the figure, $C$ is the center of the circle. If the area of triangle $ACB$ is 8, what is the area of the shaded region?

    (A) $8 - 4\pi$
    (B) $8 - 8\pi$
    (C) $4\pi - 8$
    (D) $8\pi - 8$
    (E) $16\pi - 8$

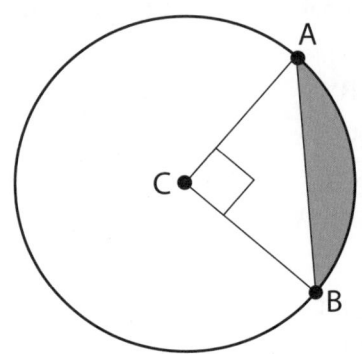

23. The heights of a maple tree and a cherry tree currently have a ratio of 5:2. If the maple tree grew 20 centimeters, and 20 centimeters was cut off the top of the cherry tree, the ratio of their heights would be 3:1. Currently, how much taller is the maple tree than the cherry tree, in centimeters?

    (A) 160
    (B) 240
    (C) 260
    (D) 280
    (E) 400

24. If $a > 0$, which of the following expressions is equivalent to $\sqrt[4]{a^9}$ ?

    (A) $a^{36}$
    (B) $a^5$
    (C) $a^3$
    (D) $(a^4)\sqrt[4]{a}$
    (E) $(a^2)\sqrt[4]{a}$

25. The cube shown is made up of 27 unpainted unit cubes. If the top and bottom faces of the cube are painted red, and the other faces are painted blue, how many unit cubes will be painted with only 1 color?

    (A) Ten
    (B) Nine
    (C) Eight
    (D) Seven
    (E) Six

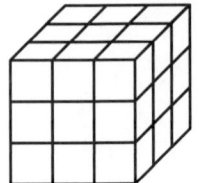

# STOP

**IF YOU FINISH BEFORE TIME IS CALLED, YOU MAY CHECK YOUR WORK ON THIS SECTION ONLY. DO NOT TURN TO ANY OTHER SECTION IN THE TEST.**

## SECTION 2
## 40 Questions

Read each passage carefully and then answer the questions about it. For each question, decide on the basis of the passage which one of the choices best answers the question.

---

Mr. Duffy lived in Chapelizod because he wished to live as far as possible from the city of which he was a citizen and because he found all other suburbs of Dublin mean, modern, and pretentious. He had been for many years cashier of a private bank in Baggot Street. Every morning he came in from Chapelizod by streetcar. At midday he went to Dan Burke's and took his lunch—a

*Line 5* bottle of lager beer and a small trayful of arrowroot biscuits. At four o'clock he was set free. He dined in an eating house on George's Street where he felt himself safe from the society of Dublin's gilded youth and where there was a certain plain honesty in the bill of fare. His evenings were spent either before his landlady's piano or roaming about the outskirts of the city. His liking for Mozart's music brought him sometimes to an opera or a concert. These were the only dissipations of his life.

---

1. The narrator's primary purpose in the passage is to
   (A) resolve a plot
   (B) create suspense
   (C) depict a location
   (D) impart a lesson
   (E) introduce a character

2. The passage suggests that Mr. Duffy preferred to live in Chapelizod because it was
   (A) near his place of business
   (B) culturally sophisticated
   (C) architecturally impressive
   (D) fashionable yet affordable
   (E) quaint and unassuming

3. The passage suggests that Mr. Duffy's attitude toward "Dublin's gilded youth" (lines 6-7) was one of
   (A) curiosity
   (B) disdain
   (C) admiration
   (D) indifference
   (E) jealousy

4. As portrayed in the passage, Mr. Duffy would be best described as a
   (A) cockeyed optimist
   (B) jack of all trades
   (C) creature of habit
   (D) frustrated artist
   (E) reclusive miser

5. The narrator uses the word "only" (line 9) to emphasize Mr. Duffy's
   (A) moderation
   (B) intelligence
   (C) generosity
   (D) impatience
   (E) loneliness

**GO ON TO THE NEXT PAGE.**

Being small, solitary, herbivorous, and cuddly has not been much help to the koala. In the early twentieth century, the two-foot tall Australian marsupial was hunted almost to extinction for its furry pelt. Only since the koala was declared a protected species in the late 1920s has it made something of a comeback. So perhaps the koala could be forgiven for thinking that life might be

*Line 5*   more bearable if it were closer to the size of a real bear.

In fact, it once was. Rooting around a southern Australian cave in 1985, spelunker Graham Pilkington uncovered a fossilized jaw fragment of a creature later identified as a giant koala, which probably inhabited the continent more than 1 million years ago. The jawbone and front molars are about twice the size of those of a present-day koala. This suggests that the creature was more than three

*10*   feet tall and weighed between 45 and 65 pounds. Not exactly a grizzly bear, but about two to three times as heavy as modern koalas.

Still, as the curator of fossils at the South Australian Museum explains, this larger size may have been a mixed blessing. Although the giant koala was perhaps better equipped to ward off foes, it probably subsisted on the same diet of eucalyptus leaves its descendants favor. Not all eucalyptus

*15*   branches could have supported that much weight, so dining out could have been an adventure for a giant koala. Worse still, late in the Pleistocene period, a series of droughts ravaged southeastern Australia, wiping out many species including the giant koala. Hardier and requiring less sustenance, only smaller members of the koala family survived.

6. The author suggests that if the koala were "closer to the size of a real bear" (line 5), it might

(A) not have been classified as a marsupial
(B) not have been hunted to near extinction
(C) not be perceived as warm and cuddly
(D) not have such a limited diet
(E) not be restricted to its current habitat

7. The last sentence of the first paragraph provides an example of which literary device?

(A) onomatopoeia
(B) alliteration
(C) hyperbole
(D) simile
(E) pun

8. The author's description of the size and behavior of the giant koala is based on

(A) historical documents
(B) conjecture from fossils
(C) direct observation
(D) traditional stories
(E) ancient cave paintings

9. In line 13, the author uses the word "Although" in order to

(A) contest a dubious claim
(B) point out a contradiction
(C) identify a false assumption
(D) acknowledge a possibility
(E) confirm a suspicion

10. The "adventure" mentioned in line 15 would most likely involve

(A) falling from a great height
(B) discovering a new diet
(C) encountering a predator
(D) migrating to a distant land
(E) exploring unknown terrain

**GO ON TO THE NEXT PAGE.**

Many people suppose the situation in an operating room to be like this: The atmosphere is tense; scarcely a word is spoken. The surgeon dominates the entire room with a powerful personality and expresses terse, authoritative commands. "Scalpel!" "Scissors!" "Sponge!" "Hemostat!" The rest of the team say nothing but carry out the orders like automatons.

*Line 5*        An operating room actually is not at all like this. It is the changing needs of the patient, as they develop in the course of the operation, that determine what everybody does. Say a small artery is cut and begins to bleed. The bleeding artery gives a simultaneous command to the three members of the team, all of whom have been watching the progress of the operation with equal attention. It says to the surgeon, "Get your hand out of the way until this is controlled." It says to the instrument

*10*        nurse, "Get a hemostat ready," and it says to the assistant, "Clamp that off." This is the highest and most efficient type of cooperation known. It is possible only where every member of the team knows enough about the total job and that of each other member to see the relationship of what he or she does to everything else that goes on.

11. The author uses the expression "like this" (line 1) in order to

   (A) demonstrate proper procedures
   (B) compare two opposing methods
   (C) relate an instructive anecdote
   (D) present a contrived scenario
   (E) exemplify a common problem

12. To describe how members of the surgical team "carry out the orders" (line 4), the author employs a simile drawn from the realm of

   (A) medical research
   (B) military operations
   (C) robotic technology
   (D) law enforcement
   (E) animal psychology

13. In the second paragraph, the author uses quotation marks to represent instructions given by the

   (A) surgeon
   (B) instrument nurse
   (C) assistant
   (D) bleeding artery
   (E) surgical handbook

14. In line 11, the author uses the word "only" to

   (A) specify an indispensable requirement
   (B) minimize the seriousness of a situation
   (C) emphasize the rarity of an occurrence
   (D) acknowledge an exception to a rule
   (E) define an area of specialization

15. A primary purpose of the passage is to

   (A) advocate reform of an outdated method
   (B) settle a longstanding controversy
   (C) expose flaws in a standard practice
   (D) highlight a technical advancement
   (E) correct a popular misconception

**GO ON TO THE NEXT PAGE.**

> Friends and fellow-citizens: I stand before you tonight under indictment for the alleged crime of having voted at the last Presidential election, without having a lawful right to vote. It shall be my work this evening to prove to you that in thus voting, I not only committed no crime, but, instead, simply exercised my citizen's rights, guaranteed to me and all United States citizens by the
>
> *Line 5* National Constitution.
>
> The preamble of the Federal Constitution says "We, the people of the United States, in order to form a more perfect union . . . and secure the blessings of liberty to ourselves and our posterity, do ordain and establish this Constitution for the United States of America." It was we, the people; not we, the White male citizens; nor yet we, the male citizens; but we, the whole people,
>
> *10* who formed the Union. And we formed it, not to give the blessings of liberty, but to secure them; not to the half of ourselves but to the whole people—women as well as men. And it is a downright mockery to talk to women of their enjoyment of the blessings of liberty, while they are denied the use of the only means of securing them—the ballot.
>
> The only question left to be settled now is: Are women persons? And I hardly believe any of
>
> *15* our opponents will have the hardihood to say they are not. Being persons, then, women are citizens; and no State has a right to make any law, or to enforce any old law, that shall abridge their privileges or immunities.

16. In her defense, the speaker argues that she
    - (A) did not vote and therefore committed no crime
    - (B) committed a crime by voting but did so for a just cause
    - (C) voted but committed no crime in so doing
    - (D) did not realize that it was a crime for her to vote
    - (E) has already been sufficiently punished for her crime

17. The speaker's defense focuses primarily on the
    - (A) establishment of an alibi
    - (B) the testimony of eye-witnesses
    - (C) analysis of physical evidence
    - (D) misconduct of prosecutors
    - (E) interpretation of a legal document

18. In line 10, the speaker uses the words "not" and "but" in order to distinguish between
    - (A) granting rights and safeguarding them
    - (B) having rights and exercising them
    - (C) enjoying rights and abusing them
    - (D) waiving rights and abolishing them
    - (E) demanding rights and earning them

19. In describing how some people "talk to women" (line 12), the speaker adopts a tone of
    - (A) regret
    - (B) disbelief
    - (C) indignation
    - (D) compromise
    - (E) sympathy

20. As it is used in line 15, the word "then" most nearly means
    - (A) next
    - (B) therefore
    - (C) previously
    - (D) at that time
    - (E) in addition

**GO ON TO THE NEXT PAGE.**

Approximately 28 percent of all energy used in the United States is devoted to transportation, and of that fraction, 40 percent is supplied in the form of gasoline to fuel the nation's nearly 255 million registered passenger vehicles. Americans use more energy to fuel their cars than they do for any other single purpose. The fuel used by American automobiles would just about

*Line 5*    fill all the energy needs of Japan, a nation of over 127 million and the world's largest consumer of energy after the United States and China. In an urgent effort to reduce consumption of an increasingly costly fuel whose chief reserves lie overseas, the government has rightly identified the American automobile and its utilization as prime targets for change.

21. The author makes reference to Japan in order to

   (A) call attention to the problem of population growth

   (B) put American fuel consumption into perspective

   (C) identify a principal competitor to the U.S. automobile industry

   (D) emphasize how far from the U.S. overseas fuel reserves lie

   (E) provide an example of fuel-efficient automobile design

22. As it is used in line 5, the word "fill" most nearly means

   (A) perform

   (B) occupy

   (C) pervade

   (D) satisfy

   (E) load

23. The author of the passage regards the government's "urgent effort" (line 6) with

   (A) astonishment

   (B) scepticism

   (C) approval

   (D) caution

   (E) pride

24. The author's description of the "fuel" (line 7) indicates that it is

   (A) becoming more expensive

   (B) harmful to the environment

   (C) difficult to transport

   (D) rapidly running out

   (E) of superior quality

25. In line 7, the word "whose" refers to

   (A) Japan

   (B) the United States

   (C) China

   (D) consumption

   (E) fuel

**GO ON TO THE NEXT PAGE.**

Thus having spoke, the illustrious chief of Troy
Stretched his fond arms to clasp the lovely boy.
The babe clung crying to his nurse's breast,
Scared at the dazzling helm and nodding crest.
*Line 5*   With secret pleasure each fond parent smiled,
And Hector hasted to relieve his child,
The glittering terrors from his brows unbound,
And placed the beaming helmet on the ground;
Then kissed the child, and, lifting high in air,
*10*   Thus to the gods preferred a father's prayer:
"O thou, whose glory fills the ethereal throne,
And all ye deathless powers, protect my son!
Grant him, like me, to purchase just renown,
To guard the Trojans, to defend the crown,
*15*   Against his country's foes the war to wage,
And rise the Hector of the future age,
So when, triumphant from successful toils,
Of heroes slain he bears the reeking spoils,
Whole hosts may hail him with deserved acclaim,
And say, 'This chief transcends his father's fame!'"

26. In line 2, the poet uses the word "Stretched" to depict

(A) a warrior holding out his shield
(B) an archer taking aim at the enemy
(C) a father reaching for his infant son
(D) a priest extending his hands in prayer
(E) two brothers embracing after a battle

27. In line 7, the expression "glittering terrors" refers to

(A) the nurse's flashing eyes
(B) stars twinkling ominously
(C) the child's recurrent nightmare
(D) Hector's gleaming headgear
(E) sudden thunder and lightning

28. In line 12, the expression "deathless powers" refers to

(A) immortal deities
(B) invincible armies
(C) defensive strategies
(D) inexhaustible energy
(E) magical properties

29. As it is used in line 18, the word "bears" most nearly means

(A) comports
(B) produces
(C) supports
(D) endures
(E) carries

30. In lines 11-20, Hector is depicted as wishing that

(A) he will survive to see his son grow up
(B) he will be surpassed in glory by his son
(C) his son will be crowned king of Troy
(D) his son will avenge his death in battle
(E) the gods will grant his son immortality

**GO ON TO THE NEXT PAGE.**

I am not sure that I can draw an exact line between wit and humor, but I am positive that humor is the more comfortable and livable quality. Humorous persons, if their gift is genuine, are always agreeable companions and they sit through the evening best. They have pleasant mouths turned up at the corners. To those corners the great Master of marionettes has fixed the strings and

*Line 5*   holds them with nimble fingers that twitch them at the slightest jest. But the mouth of a merely witty person is hard and sour until the moment of its discharge. Nor is the flash from a witty person always comforting, whereas a humorous person radiates a general pleasure and is like another candle in the room.

31. As it is used in line 1, the word "line" most nearly means

(A) connection
(B) distinction
(C) ancestry
(D) occupation
(E) sequence

32. In line 2, the author uses the word "if" in order to

(A) make a prediction
(B) express scepticism
(C) contradict an assertion
(D) qualify a generalization
(E) acknowledge an error

33. The author likens the "mouths" (line 3) of humorous persons to those of

(A) puppets
(B) clowns
(C) hyenas
(D) robots
(E) angels

34. The passage suggests that in comparison with a humorous person, a witty person

(A) is more intelligent
(B) laughs much louder
(C) smiles less readily
(D) is more entertaining
(E) speaks less clearly

35. To describe a "humorous person" (line 7), the author uses which of the following literary devices?

(A) Hyperbole
(B) Personification
(C) Alliteration
(D) Onomatopoeia
(E) Simile

**GO ON TO THE NEXT PAGE.**

Improvements in technology, in the tools and crafts men employ in making a living, have too often been ignored by the historical annalist. Farmers, carpenters, and miners live on a different level from philosophers, poets, and historians; the invention of the wheelbarrow, the windmill, and the horse collar were innovations of little interest to scholars on their high, intellectual plateau. This

*Line 5* gulf between theory and practice, between those who labor and those who think, has perverted the writing of history, giving it a one-sided, intellectualized interpretation. The humanists, for instance, when they peered backward from the fifteenth century, concluded that the thousand years following the collapse of Roman rule had been a dark age. It seemed so to them because arts and letters and other manifestations of the high intellectual tradition had declined when the Roman Empire in the

10 West disintegrated and had not revived until their own day.

Had the humanists paid more attention to technological developments, they might have modified their conception of the "dark ages," for the practical inventive genius of the European peoples continued to function although the Roman Empire dissolved. Medieval craftsmen devised and introduced labor-saving devices which even the Greeks and Romans had failed to invent when

15 their civilization was flourishing so brilliantly in the thousand years between 600 BCE and 400 CE. In some respects medieval society was neither static nor stagnant despite the contempt the humanists conceived for it.

36. The author criticizes "the historical annalist" (line 2) for

(A) failing to distinguish between theory and practice
(B) neglecting an important area of human achievement
(C) focusing too narrowly on war and political upheaval
(D) exaggerating the accomplishments of the Roman Empire
(E) misrepresenting the ideas of philosophers and poets

37. To describe the difference "between those who labor and those who think" (line 5), the author employs metaphors drawn from the realm of

(A) geography
(B) warfare
(C) agriculture
(D) medicine
(E) politics

38. According to the passage, which of the following occurred during the fifteenth century?

(A) The collapse of Roman rule
(B) The invention of the windmill
(C) The beginning of the dark ages
(D) A revival of arts and letters
(E) A technological revolution

39. As it is used in line 12, the word "for" most nearly means

(A) toward
(B) in favor of
(C) in place of
(D) despite
(E) because

40. The passage suggests that the humanists viewed "medieval society" (line 16) with

(A) disdain
(B) reverence
(C) ambivalence
(D) curiosity
(E) alarm

# STOP
**IF YOU FINISH BEFORE TIME IS CALLED, YOU MAY CHECK YOUR WORK ON THIS SECTION ONLY.
DO NOT TURN TO ANY OTHER SECTION IN THE TEST.**

## SECTION 3
## 60 Questions

This section consists of two different types of questions: synonyms and analogies. There are directions and a sample question for each type.

### Synonyms

Each of the following questions consists of one word followed by five words or phrases. You are to select the one word or phrase whose meaning is closest to the word in capital letters.

Sample Question:

> CHILLY:
> (A) lazy
> (B) nice
> (C) dry
> (D) cold
> (E) sunny
>
> Ⓐ Ⓑ Ⓒ ● Ⓔ

---

1. TERRACE:
   (A) hill
   (B) patio
   (C) roof
   (D) border
   (E) garden

2. DUBIOUS:
   (A) useful
   (B) devious
   (C) honest
   (D) doubtful
   (E) synchronous

3. REVENUE:
   (A) speed
   (B) income
   (C) entourage
   (D) arrival
   (E) location

4. CONSOLE:
   (A) hope
   (B) reward
   (C) comfort
   (D) advise
   (E) relax

5. SYNOPSIS:
   (A) request
   (B) theory
   (C) opinion
   (D) examination
   (E) summary

6. CORROBORATE:
   (A) assist
   (B) reveal
   (C) convict
   (D) confirm
   (E) approve

7. HUBBUB:
   (A) uproar
   (B) mistake
   (C) crossroad
   (D) nonsense
   (E) gadget

8. INSTIGATE:
   (A) stir up
   (B) cry out
   (C) go along
   (D) try again
   (E) do without

**GO ON TO THE NEXT PAGE.**

9. SUBLIME:
   (A) inferior
   (B) obscure
   (C) majestic
   (D) devious
   (E) elated

10. ENCUMBER:
    (A) repel
    (B) burden
    (C) agitate
    (D) disprove
    (E) disappoint

11. FLAMBOYANT:
    (A) showy
    (B) certain
    (C) aggressive
    (D) independent
    (E) accommodating

12. TENTATIVE:
    (A) stressful
    (B) enticing
    (C) thoughtless
    (D) interested
    (E) provisional

13. LABYRINTH:
    (A) castle
    (B) troll
    (C) shield
    (D) maze
    (E) spell

14. CALLOW:
    (A) immature
    (B) unfeeling
    (C) gloomy
    (D) envious
    (E) timid

15. QUALM:
    (A) lull
    (B) asset
    (C) problem
    (D) misgiving
    (E) obligation

16. IMPARTIAL:
    (A) complete
    (B) instructive
    (C) neutral
    (D) unaware
    (E) secure

17. ACUMEN:
    (A) humor
    (B) malice
    (C) insight
    (D) blame
    (E) vigor

18. PREDICAMENT:
    (A) introduction
    (B) quandary
    (C) question
    (D) reason
    (E) prophecy

19. VAUNT:
    (A) tempt
    (B) threaten
    (C) promise
    (D) boast
    (E) complain

20. COVERT:
    (A) small
    (B) false
    (C) weak
    (D) rapid
    (E) secret

**GO ON TO THE NEXT PAGE.**

21. IDIOSYNCRASY:
    (A) peculiarity
    (B) coincidence
    (C) malfunction
    (D) precision
    (E) ignorance

22. TRANSGRESSION:
    (A) journey
    (B) evolution
    (C) accident
    (D) exchange
    (E) violation

23. MAVEN:
    (A) tycoon
    (B) coward
    (C) expert
    (D) nanny
    (E) misfit

24. HAUGHTY:
    (A) arrogant
    (B) difficult
    (C) uncertain
    (D) awkward
    (E) frantic

25. BESTRIDE:
    (A) afflict
    (B) straddle
    (C) shriek
    (D) travel
    (E) inform

26. EQUILIBRIUM:
    (A) freedom
    (B) agreement
    (C) speed
    (D) balance
    (E) reaction

27. RELUCTANT:
    (A) disinclined
    (B) incompetent
    (C) unaware
    (D) resentful
    (E) disgusting

28. EDIFICE:
    (A) lesson
    (B) building
    (C) strategy
    (D) opening
    (E) pamphlet

29. RUMINATE:
    (A) ponder
    (B) delay
    (C) slander
    (D) boast
    (E) avoid

30. EPOCH:
    (A) dynasty
    (B) story
    (C) era
    (D) poem
    (E) species

**GO ON TO THE NEXT PAGE.**

## Analogies

The following questions ask you to find relationships between words. For each question, select the answer choice that best completes the meaning of the sentence.

Sample Question:

> Kitten is to cat as
> (A) fawn is to colt
> (B) puppy is to dog
> (C) cow is to bull
> (D) wolf is to bear
> (E) hen is to rooster    (A) ● (C) (D) (E)

Choice (B) is the best answer because a kitten is a young cat just as a puppy is a young dog. Of all the answer choices, (B) states a relationship that is most like the relationship between <u>kitten</u> and <u>cat</u>.

---

31. Barber is to scissors as

    (A) farmer is to crop
    (B) tailor is to garment
    (C) baker is to oven
    (D) sculptor is to chisel
    (E) carpenter is to wood

32. Theft is to crime as

    (A) victory is to trophy
    (B) mortgage is to loan
    (C) music is to instrument
    (D) guilt is to penalty
    (E) shrug is to uncertainty

33. Swagger is to walk as

    (A) command is to obey
    (B) attack is to fight
    (C) boast is to talk
    (D) scribble is to write
    (E) caress is to touch

34. General is to soldier as

    (A) warfare is to battle
    (B) incumbent is to voter
    (C) sovereign is to subject
    (D) command is to obedience
    (E) company is to employee

35. Shell is to egg as

    (A) seed is to apple
    (B) glove is to mitten
    (C) arm is to leg
    (D) planet is to Sun
    (E) skull is to brain

36. Novel is to fictional as

    (A) essay is to philosophical
    (B) treatise is to theological
    (C) pamphlet is to political
    (D) tragedy is to historical
    (E) memoir is to autobiographical

37. Wayfarer is to travel as

    (A) idol is to admire
    (B) tenant is to rent
    (C) creditor is to pay
    (D) orphan is to adopt
    (E) guest is to invite

38. Bridge is to ship as

    (A) cockpit is to airplane
    (B) horse is to wagon
    (C) caboose is to train
    (D) trunk is to automobile
    (E) yoke is to plow

**GO ON TO THE NEXT PAGE.**

39. Criticize is to castigate as
    (A) laugh is to amuse
    (B) err is to forgive
    (C) annoy is to bristle
    (D) reject is to spurn
    (E) damage is to repair

40. Peddler is to merchant as
    (A) patron is to artist
    (B) juggler is to circus
    (C) courier is to message
    (D) plaintiff is to attorney
    (E) troubadour is to singer

41. Visual is to sight as
    (A) audible is to ear
    (B) nasal is to smell
    (C) tactile is to touch
    (D) bitter is to taste
    (E) mental is to idea

42. Shovel is to dig as
    (A) stake is to drive
    (B) drill is to bore
    (C) plank is to saw
    (D) plow is to harvest
    (E) wedge is to insert

43. Capture is to custody as
    (A) correct is to error
    (B) pardon is to innocence
    (C) verify is to suspicion
    (D) imperil is to jeopardy
    (E) postpone is to patience

44. Barbell is to lift as
    (A) ball is to fly
    (B) javelin is to throw
    (C) track is to run
    (D) goal is to score
    (E) hurdle is to jump

45. Measure is to size as
    (A) prove is to hypothesis
    (B) appraise is to value
    (C) construct is to blueprint
    (D) accelerate is to speed
    (E) solve is to problem

46. Wedding is to marriage as
    (A) graduation is to diploma
    (B) banquet is to food
    (C) coronation is to reign
    (D) baptism is to water
    (E) party is to birthday

47. Implement is to plan as
    (A) realize is to dream
    (B) discuss is to agenda
    (C) retire is to career
    (D) aspire is to ambition
    (E) predict is to outcome

48. Secure is to danger as
    (A) affluent is to wealth
    (B) weary is to drudgery
    (C) immune is to obligation
    (D) profound is to insight
    (E) hostile is to hatred

49. Alibi is to exonerate as
    (A) testimonial is to endorse
    (B) obstruction is to unblock
    (C) punishment is to condemn
    (D) disaster is to recover
    (E) anger is to appease

50. Idle is to work as
    (A) steadfast is to resist
    (B) deceased is to live
    (C) docile is to teach
    (D) noxious is to harm
    (E) voracious is to eat

**GO ON TO THE NEXT PAGE.**

51. Debacle is to failure as
   (A) tempest is to storm
   (B) echo is to sound
   (C) peeve is to anger
   (D) slander is to truth
   (E) donation is to gift

52. Saga is to story as
   (A) myth is to reality
   (B) stanza is to verse
   (C) scandal is to gossip
   (D) odyssey is to journey
   (E) goal is to endeavor

53. Faithful is to loyalty as
   (A) guilty is to crime
   (B) heroic is to danger
   (C) sorry is to remorse
   (D) blithe is to anxiety
   (E) punctual is to time

54. Bother is to annoyance as
   (A) flatter is to insincerity
   (B) reprimand is to misconduct
   (C) vanish is to disappearance
   (D) implore is to sympathy
   (E) perplex is to puzzlement

55. Altitude is to high as
   (A) velocity is to far
   (B) angle is to acute
   (C) amplifier is to loud
   (D) breadth is to wide
   (E) speed is to distant

56. Inept is to skill as
   (A) dauntless is to fear
   (B) affluent is to wealth
   (C) remote is to distance
   (D) rueful is to remorse
   (E) toxic is to antidote

57. Cogent is to convince as
   (A) ambitious is to advance
   (B) subversive is to undermine
   (C) incessant is to stop
   (D) potable is to drink
   (E) obscure is to discern

58. Nuance is to distinction as
   (A) color is to vision
   (B) gesture is to action
   (C) hint is to suggestion
   (D) tangent is to digression
   (E) accuracy is to calculation

59. Taciturn is to speak as
   (A) fragile is to break
   (B) belligerent is to fight
   (C) facetious is to laugh
   (D) elusive is to capture
   (E) skeptical is to believe

60. Furtive is to stealth as
   (A) nocturnal is to darkness
   (B) circumspect is to caution
   (C) apathetic is to emotion
   (D) impeccable is to criticism
   (E) obsolete is to neglect

# STOP
**IF YOU FINISH BEFORE TIME IS CALLED, YOU MAY CHECK YOUR WORK ON THIS SECTION ONLY.
DO NOT TURN TO ANY OTHER SECTION IN THE TEST.**

## SECTION 4
## 25 Questions

Following each problem in this section, there are five suggested answers. Work each problem in your head or in the blank space provided at the right of the page. Then look at the five suggested answers and decide which one is best.

<u>Note:</u> Figures that accompany problems in this section are drawn as accurately as possible EXCEPT when it is stated in a specific problem that its figure is not drawn to scale.

Sample Problem:

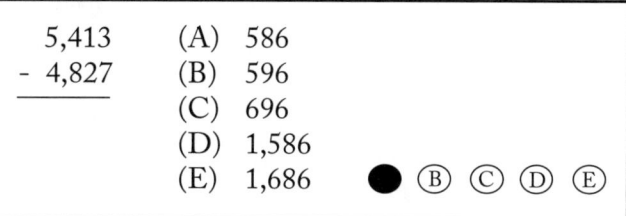

**USE THIS SPACE FOR FIGURING.**

1. If the area of a rectangle is 144 square centimeters, and its length is 16 centimeters, what is the width of the rectangle?

   (A)   7 centimeters
   (B)   8 centimeters
   (C)   9 centimeters
   (D) 10 centimeters
   (E) 12 centimeters

2. If $50 \times a = 50$, what is the value of $50 - a$?

   (A)   0

   (B)   $\frac{1}{50}$

   (C)   1
   (D) 49
   (E) 51

3. Gerald earns a base hourly rate of $8 per hour at his job. However, if he works more than 10 hours in a week, he earns $9 per hour for each hour he works after the first 10 hours. How much money does Gerald earn if he works 16 hours in one week?

   (A) $128
   (B) $134
   (C) $135
   (D) $138
   (E) $144

**GO ON TO THE NEXT PAGE.**

**USE THIS SPACE FOR FIGURING.**

4. If $\frac{1}{5} + x > 1$, which of the following could be a value of $x$ ?

(A) $\frac{1}{5}$

(B) $\frac{2}{5}$

(C) $\frac{1}{2}$

(D) $\frac{2}{3}$

(E) $\frac{9}{10}$

5. The diameter of a circle is 24 inches. What is the circumference, in inches, of the circle?

(A)   $6\pi$
(B)   $12\pi$
(C)   $24\pi$
(D)   $72\pi$
(E)   $144\pi$

6. A sequence is generated by repeating the pattern of the five symbols shown above in that order. Which of the following shows the 12th, 13th, 14th, 15th, and 16th symbols in the sequence?

(A) ●●●▲▲
(B) ●●▲▲●
(C) ●▲▲●●
(D) ▲▲●●●
(E) ▲●●●▲

7. What is the measure of $\angle ADC$ in the figure ?

(A) 145°
(B) 120°
(C) 95°
(D) 85°
(E) 60°

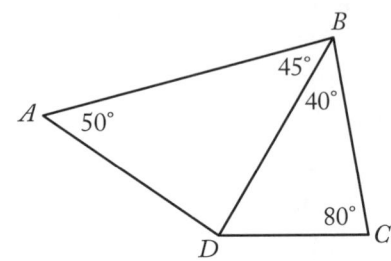

**GO ON TO THE NEXT PAGE.**

8.  Based on the bar graph, approximately what fractional part of the biologists were employed in education in year X ?

    (A) $\frac{1}{4}$

    (B) $\frac{7}{20}$

    (C) $\frac{1}{2}$

    (D) $\frac{3}{5}$

    (E) $\frac{7}{10}$

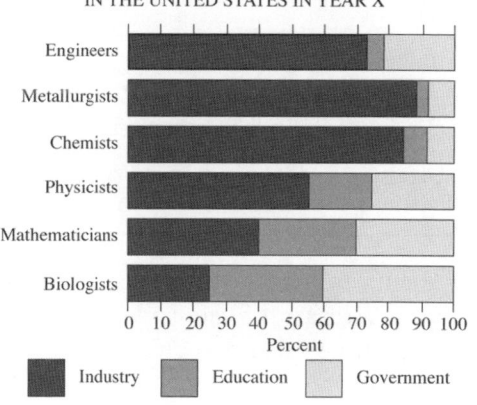

HOW SCIENTISTS AND ENGINEERS WERE EMPLOYED
IN THE UNITED STATES IN YEAR X

9.  The mass required to set off a mouse trap is 157 grams. Of the following, what is the largest mass of cheese, in grams, that can be put on the trap so that a 4-ounce mouse would <u>not</u> set off the trap? (1 ounce = 28 grams)

    (A)  28
    (B)  44
    (C)  45
    (D)  56
    (E)  112

10. If 60 percent of $t$ is 8, what is 30 percent of $2t$ ?

    (A)   2
    (B)   4
    (C)   8
    (D)  16
    (E)  24

11. Let  be defined by $a \blacklozenge b = \frac{2a}{b} + \frac{b}{a}$ where $a$ and $b$ are nonzero numbers. What is the value of $8 \blacklozenge 4$ ?

    (A) 2

    (B) $\frac{9}{4}$

    (C) $\frac{5}{2}$

    (D) 3

    (E) $\frac{9}{2}$

**GO ON TO THE NEXT PAGE.**

**USE THIS SPACE FOR FIGURING.**

12. In the figure, five lines intersect as shown. What is the measure of $\angle QTR$ ?

    (A)  30°
    (B)  40°
    (C)  50°
    (D)  60°
    (E)  70°

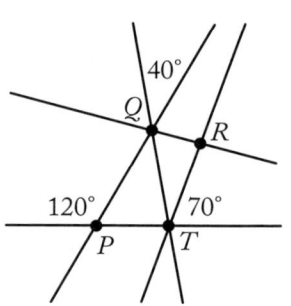

13. The mean height of four girls is 4.9 feet. The heights of two of these girls are 4.5 feet and 4.3 feet. What is the mean height, in feet, of the other two girls?

    (A)  5.1
    (B)  5.2
    (C)  5.3
    (D)  5.4
    (E)  5.5

14. The function $g$ is defined by $g(x) = (-x)^3 + 1$. What is the value of $g(-1)$ ?

    (A)  –2
    (B)  –1
    (C)   0
    (D)   2
    (E)   4

15. If $n$ is an odd integer, which of the following expressions is also an odd integer?

    (A)  $2n$
    (B)  $4n$
    (C)  $n + 1$
    (D)  $n + 2$
    (E)  $n + 3$

16. On Tuesday, there were 400 customers at a movie theater, and each customer paid $8 for a ticket. On Wednesday, the owner of the movie theater reduced the regular ticket price from $8 to $6 for tickets that were purchased before 6 p.m. If the daily ticket sales for the two days were the same, and 100 people paid $8 for a ticket on Wednesday, how many people paid $6 for a ticket on Wednesday?

    (A)  360
    (B)  400
    (C)  420
    (D)  480
    (E)  500

**GO ON TO THE NEXT PAGE.**

**114**

**USE THIS SPACE FOR FIGURING.**

17. Which of the following is equivalent to $4x^2 + 4xy + y^2$?

   (A) $4(x^2 + y^2)$
   (B) $4(x + y)^2$
   (C) $2(x + y)^2$
   (D) $(4x + y)^2$
   (E) $(2x + y)^2$

---

18. The numbers of miles that each of nine employees travels to work are 12, 22, 15, 36, 10, 32, 26, 9, and 32. What is the median number of miles traveled to work?

   (A) 22
   (B) 23
   (C) 24
   (D) 32
   (E) 36

---

19. Which of the following is an equation of line $k$ shown in the $xy$-coordinate plane?

   (A) $y = -\frac{1}{3}x + 3$

   (B) $y = -\frac{1}{3}x$

   (C) $y = \frac{1}{3}x + 3$

   (D) $y = \frac{1}{3}x$

   (E) $y = 3x + 3$

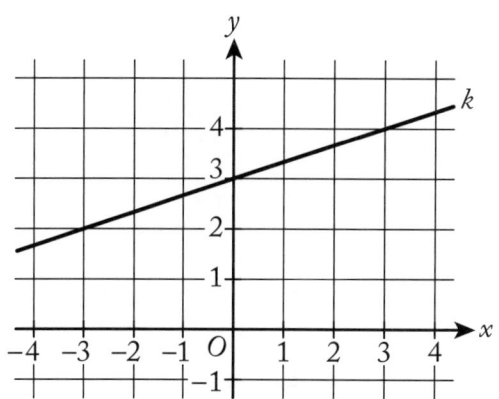

---

20. Grandma's Soup Company packages tomato soup in cylindrical cans that have a base diameter of 8 centimeters and a height of 10 centimeters. Each can contains four servings. The company also wants to package the soup in new cans that contain one serving. If the height of the new cans will be 10 centimeters, what should be the base diameter of these new cans, in centimeters?

   (A) 1
   (B) 2
   (C) 4
   (D) $\sqrt{2}$
   (E) $2\sqrt{2}$

**GO ON TO THE NEXT PAGE.**

21. Simplify: $(5x^3 + 7x - 3) - (x^3 - 2x^2 + 7x - 8)$

    (A) $4x^3 - 2x^2 + 14x - 11$

    (B) $4x^3 - 2x^2 - 11$

    (C) $4x^3 + 2x^2 - 14x + 5$

    (D) $4x^3 + 2x^2 - 11$

    (E) $4x^3 + 2x^2 + 5$

---

22. The triangle shown in the $xy$-coordinate plane is rotated 90 degrees clockwise about the point $(1, 1)$. Which of the following shows the resulting triangle?

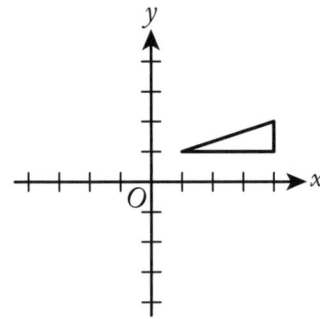

(A)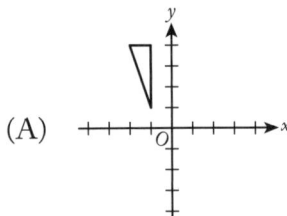

(B)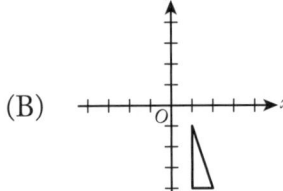

(C)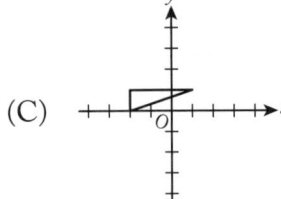

(D)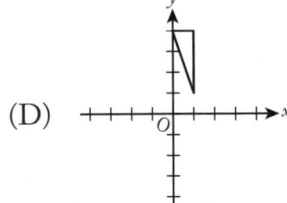

(E)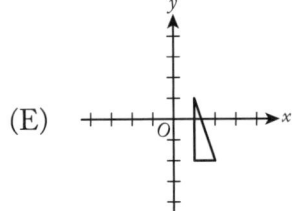

GO ON TO THE NEXT PAGE.

23. Ava, Cara, Emma, Lily, and Mia are to be seated together in a row. If Emma and Lily must sit next to each other, how many different ways can the five girls be seated?

    (A)  24
    (B)  48
    (C)  60
    (D)  120
    (E)  240

---

24. If $m$ is a positive integer, what is the least value of $m$ for which 225 is a factor of $120m$ ?

    (A)  3
    (B)  5
    (C)  15
    (D)  25
    (E)  30

---

25. In the $xy$-coordinate plane, the points $(4, 2)$ and $(-1, k)$ are on a line that is perpendicular to the line $y = 2x + 1$. What is the value of $k$ ?

    (A)  $-\frac{7}{2}$

    (B)  $-\frac{1}{2}$

    (C)  $\frac{7}{2}$

    (D)  $\frac{9}{2}$

    (E)  12

# STOP

**IF YOU FINISH BEFORE TIME IS CALLED, YOU MAY CHECK YOUR WORK ON THIS SECTION ONLY.
DO NOT TURN TO ANY OTHER SECTION IN THE TEST.**

THIS PAGE INTENTIONALLY LEFT BLANK.

# Practice Test II: Upper Level Answer Sheet

**Be sure each mark completely fills the circle.**
Start with number 1 for each new section of the test.

## Section 1

| | | | | |
|---|---|---|---|---|
| 1 Ⓐ Ⓑ Ⓒ Ⓓ Ⓔ | 6 Ⓐ Ⓑ Ⓒ Ⓓ Ⓔ | 11 Ⓐ Ⓑ Ⓒ Ⓓ Ⓔ | 16 Ⓐ Ⓑ Ⓒ Ⓓ Ⓔ | 21 Ⓐ Ⓑ Ⓒ Ⓓ Ⓔ |
| 2 Ⓐ Ⓑ Ⓒ Ⓓ Ⓔ | 7 Ⓐ Ⓑ Ⓒ Ⓓ Ⓔ | 12 Ⓐ Ⓑ Ⓒ Ⓓ Ⓔ | 17 Ⓐ Ⓑ Ⓒ Ⓓ Ⓔ | 22 Ⓐ Ⓑ Ⓒ Ⓓ Ⓔ |
| 3 Ⓐ Ⓑ Ⓒ Ⓓ Ⓔ | 8 Ⓐ Ⓑ Ⓒ Ⓓ Ⓔ | 13 Ⓐ Ⓑ Ⓒ Ⓓ Ⓔ | 18 Ⓐ Ⓑ Ⓒ Ⓓ Ⓔ | 23 Ⓐ Ⓑ Ⓒ Ⓓ Ⓔ |
| 4 Ⓐ Ⓑ Ⓒ Ⓓ Ⓔ | 9 Ⓐ Ⓑ Ⓒ Ⓓ Ⓔ | 14 Ⓐ Ⓑ Ⓒ Ⓓ Ⓔ | 19 Ⓐ Ⓑ Ⓒ Ⓓ Ⓔ | 24 Ⓐ Ⓑ Ⓒ Ⓓ Ⓔ |
| 5 Ⓐ Ⓑ Ⓒ Ⓓ Ⓔ | 10 Ⓐ Ⓑ Ⓒ Ⓓ Ⓔ | 15 Ⓐ Ⓑ Ⓒ Ⓓ Ⓔ | 20 Ⓐ Ⓑ Ⓒ Ⓓ Ⓔ | 25 Ⓐ Ⓑ Ⓒ Ⓓ Ⓔ |

## Section 2

| | | | | |
|---|---|---|---|---|
| 1 Ⓐ Ⓑ Ⓒ Ⓓ Ⓔ | 9 Ⓐ Ⓑ Ⓒ Ⓓ Ⓔ | 17 Ⓐ Ⓑ Ⓒ Ⓓ Ⓔ | 25 Ⓐ Ⓑ Ⓒ Ⓓ Ⓔ | 33 Ⓐ Ⓑ Ⓒ Ⓓ Ⓔ |
| 2 Ⓐ Ⓑ Ⓒ Ⓓ Ⓔ | 10 Ⓐ Ⓑ Ⓒ Ⓓ Ⓔ | 18 Ⓐ Ⓑ Ⓒ Ⓓ Ⓔ | 26 Ⓐ Ⓑ Ⓒ Ⓓ Ⓔ | 34 Ⓐ Ⓑ Ⓒ Ⓓ Ⓔ |
| 3 Ⓐ Ⓑ Ⓒ Ⓓ Ⓔ | 11 Ⓐ Ⓑ Ⓒ Ⓓ Ⓔ | 19 Ⓐ Ⓑ Ⓒ Ⓓ Ⓔ | 27 Ⓐ Ⓑ Ⓒ Ⓓ Ⓔ | 35 Ⓐ Ⓑ Ⓒ Ⓓ Ⓔ |
| 4 Ⓐ Ⓑ Ⓒ Ⓓ Ⓔ | 12 Ⓐ Ⓑ Ⓒ Ⓓ Ⓔ | 20 Ⓐ Ⓑ Ⓒ Ⓓ Ⓔ | 28 Ⓐ Ⓑ Ⓒ Ⓓ Ⓔ | 36 Ⓐ Ⓑ Ⓒ Ⓓ Ⓔ |
| 5 Ⓐ Ⓑ Ⓒ Ⓓ Ⓔ | 13 Ⓐ Ⓑ Ⓒ Ⓓ Ⓔ | 21 Ⓐ Ⓑ Ⓒ Ⓓ Ⓔ | 29 Ⓐ Ⓑ Ⓒ Ⓓ Ⓔ | 37 Ⓐ Ⓑ Ⓒ Ⓓ Ⓔ |
| 6 Ⓐ Ⓑ Ⓒ Ⓓ Ⓔ | 14 Ⓐ Ⓑ Ⓒ Ⓓ Ⓔ | 22 Ⓐ Ⓑ Ⓒ Ⓓ Ⓔ | 30 Ⓐ Ⓑ Ⓒ Ⓓ Ⓔ | 38 Ⓐ Ⓑ Ⓒ Ⓓ Ⓔ |
| 7 Ⓐ Ⓑ Ⓒ Ⓓ Ⓔ | 15 Ⓐ Ⓑ Ⓒ Ⓓ Ⓔ | 23 Ⓐ Ⓑ Ⓒ Ⓓ Ⓔ | 31 Ⓐ Ⓑ Ⓒ Ⓓ Ⓔ | 39 Ⓐ Ⓑ Ⓒ Ⓓ Ⓔ |
| 8 Ⓐ Ⓑ Ⓒ Ⓓ Ⓔ | 16 Ⓐ Ⓑ Ⓒ Ⓓ Ⓔ | 24 Ⓐ Ⓑ Ⓒ Ⓓ Ⓔ | 32 Ⓐ Ⓑ Ⓒ Ⓓ Ⓔ | 40 Ⓐ Ⓑ Ⓒ Ⓓ Ⓔ |

## Section 3

| | | | | |
|---|---|---|---|---|
| 1 Ⓐ Ⓑ Ⓒ Ⓓ Ⓔ | 13 Ⓐ Ⓑ Ⓒ Ⓓ Ⓔ | 25 Ⓐ Ⓑ Ⓒ Ⓓ Ⓔ | 37 Ⓐ Ⓑ Ⓒ Ⓓ Ⓔ | 49 Ⓐ Ⓑ Ⓒ Ⓓ Ⓔ |
| 2 Ⓐ Ⓑ Ⓒ Ⓓ Ⓔ | 14 Ⓐ Ⓑ Ⓒ Ⓓ Ⓔ | 26 Ⓐ Ⓑ Ⓒ Ⓓ Ⓔ | 38 Ⓐ Ⓑ Ⓒ Ⓓ Ⓔ | 50 Ⓐ Ⓑ Ⓒ Ⓓ Ⓔ |
| 3 Ⓐ Ⓑ Ⓒ Ⓓ Ⓔ | 15 Ⓐ Ⓑ Ⓒ Ⓓ Ⓔ | 27 Ⓐ Ⓑ Ⓒ Ⓓ Ⓔ | 39 Ⓐ Ⓑ Ⓒ Ⓓ Ⓔ | 51 Ⓐ Ⓑ Ⓒ Ⓓ Ⓔ |
| 4 Ⓐ Ⓑ Ⓒ Ⓓ Ⓔ | 16 Ⓐ Ⓑ Ⓒ Ⓓ Ⓔ | 28 Ⓐ Ⓑ Ⓒ Ⓓ Ⓔ | 40 Ⓐ Ⓑ Ⓒ Ⓓ Ⓔ | 52 Ⓐ Ⓑ Ⓒ Ⓓ Ⓔ |
| 5 Ⓐ Ⓑ Ⓒ Ⓓ Ⓔ | 17 Ⓐ Ⓑ Ⓒ Ⓓ Ⓔ | 29 Ⓐ Ⓑ Ⓒ Ⓓ Ⓔ | 41 Ⓐ Ⓑ Ⓒ Ⓓ Ⓔ | 53 Ⓐ Ⓑ Ⓒ Ⓓ Ⓔ |
| 6 Ⓐ Ⓑ Ⓒ Ⓓ Ⓔ | 18 Ⓐ Ⓑ Ⓒ Ⓓ Ⓔ | 30 Ⓐ Ⓑ Ⓒ Ⓓ Ⓔ | 42 Ⓐ Ⓑ Ⓒ Ⓓ Ⓔ | 54 Ⓐ Ⓑ Ⓒ Ⓓ Ⓔ |
| 7 Ⓐ Ⓑ Ⓒ Ⓓ Ⓔ | 19 Ⓐ Ⓑ Ⓒ Ⓓ Ⓔ | 31 Ⓐ Ⓑ Ⓒ Ⓓ Ⓔ | 43 Ⓐ Ⓑ Ⓒ Ⓓ Ⓔ | 55 Ⓐ Ⓑ Ⓒ Ⓓ Ⓔ |
| 8 Ⓐ Ⓑ Ⓒ Ⓓ Ⓔ | 20 Ⓐ Ⓑ Ⓒ Ⓓ Ⓔ | 32 Ⓐ Ⓑ Ⓒ Ⓓ Ⓔ | 44 Ⓐ Ⓑ Ⓒ Ⓓ Ⓔ | 56 Ⓐ Ⓑ Ⓒ Ⓓ Ⓔ |
| 9 Ⓐ Ⓑ Ⓒ Ⓓ Ⓔ | 21 Ⓐ Ⓑ Ⓒ Ⓓ Ⓔ | 33 Ⓐ Ⓑ Ⓒ Ⓓ Ⓔ | 45 Ⓐ Ⓑ Ⓒ Ⓓ Ⓔ | 57 Ⓐ Ⓑ Ⓒ Ⓓ Ⓔ |
| 10 Ⓐ Ⓑ Ⓒ Ⓓ Ⓔ | 22 Ⓐ Ⓑ Ⓒ Ⓓ Ⓔ | 34 Ⓐ Ⓑ Ⓒ Ⓓ Ⓔ | 46 Ⓐ Ⓑ Ⓒ Ⓓ Ⓔ | 58 Ⓐ Ⓑ Ⓒ Ⓓ Ⓔ |
| 11 Ⓐ Ⓑ Ⓒ Ⓓ Ⓔ | 23 Ⓐ Ⓑ Ⓒ Ⓓ Ⓔ | 35 Ⓐ Ⓑ Ⓒ Ⓓ Ⓔ | 47 Ⓐ Ⓑ Ⓒ Ⓓ Ⓔ | 59 Ⓐ Ⓑ Ⓒ Ⓓ Ⓔ |
| 12 Ⓐ Ⓑ Ⓒ Ⓓ Ⓔ | 24 Ⓐ Ⓑ Ⓒ Ⓓ Ⓔ | 36 Ⓐ Ⓑ Ⓒ Ⓓ Ⓔ | 48 Ⓐ Ⓑ Ⓒ Ⓓ Ⓔ | 60 Ⓐ Ⓑ Ⓒ Ⓓ Ⓔ |

## Section 4

| | | | | |
|---|---|---|---|---|
| 1 Ⓐ Ⓑ Ⓒ Ⓓ Ⓔ | 6 Ⓐ Ⓑ Ⓒ Ⓓ Ⓔ | 11 Ⓐ Ⓑ Ⓒ Ⓓ Ⓔ | 16 Ⓐ Ⓑ Ⓒ Ⓓ Ⓔ | 21 Ⓐ Ⓑ Ⓒ Ⓓ Ⓔ |
| 2 Ⓐ Ⓑ Ⓒ Ⓓ Ⓔ | 7 Ⓐ Ⓑ Ⓒ Ⓓ Ⓔ | 12 Ⓐ Ⓑ Ⓒ Ⓓ Ⓔ | 17 Ⓐ Ⓑ Ⓒ Ⓓ Ⓔ | 22 Ⓐ Ⓑ Ⓒ Ⓓ Ⓔ |
| 3 Ⓐ Ⓑ Ⓒ Ⓓ Ⓔ | 8 Ⓐ Ⓑ Ⓒ Ⓓ Ⓔ | 13 Ⓐ Ⓑ Ⓒ Ⓓ Ⓔ | 18 Ⓐ Ⓑ Ⓒ Ⓓ Ⓔ | 23 Ⓐ Ⓑ Ⓒ Ⓓ Ⓔ |
| 4 Ⓐ Ⓑ Ⓒ Ⓓ Ⓔ | 9 Ⓐ Ⓑ Ⓒ Ⓓ Ⓔ | 14 Ⓐ Ⓑ Ⓒ Ⓓ Ⓔ | 19 Ⓐ Ⓑ Ⓒ Ⓓ Ⓔ | 24 Ⓐ Ⓑ Ⓒ Ⓓ Ⓔ |
| 5 Ⓐ Ⓑ Ⓒ Ⓓ Ⓔ | 10 Ⓐ Ⓑ Ⓒ Ⓓ Ⓔ | 15 Ⓐ Ⓑ Ⓒ Ⓓ Ⓔ | 20 Ⓐ Ⓑ Ⓒ Ⓓ Ⓔ | 25 Ⓐ Ⓑ Ⓒ Ⓓ Ⓔ |

## Section 5

| | | | |
|---|---|---|---|
| 1 Ⓐ Ⓑ Ⓒ Ⓓ Ⓔ | 5 Ⓐ Ⓑ Ⓒ Ⓓ Ⓔ | 9 Ⓐ Ⓑ Ⓒ Ⓓ Ⓔ | 13 Ⓐ Ⓑ Ⓒ Ⓓ Ⓔ |
| 2 Ⓐ Ⓑ Ⓒ Ⓓ Ⓔ | 6 Ⓐ Ⓑ Ⓒ Ⓓ Ⓔ | 10 Ⓐ Ⓑ Ⓒ Ⓓ Ⓔ | 14 Ⓐ Ⓑ Ⓒ Ⓓ Ⓔ |
| 3 Ⓐ Ⓑ Ⓒ Ⓓ Ⓔ | 7 Ⓐ Ⓑ Ⓒ Ⓓ Ⓔ | 11 Ⓐ Ⓑ Ⓒ Ⓓ Ⓔ | 15 Ⓐ Ⓑ Ⓒ Ⓓ Ⓔ |
| 4 Ⓐ Ⓑ Ⓒ Ⓓ Ⓔ | 8 Ⓐ Ⓑ Ⓒ Ⓓ Ⓔ | 12 Ⓐ Ⓑ Ⓒ Ⓓ Ⓔ | 16 Ⓐ Ⓑ Ⓒ Ⓓ Ⓔ |

**Experimental Section – See page 9 for details.**

THIS PAGE INTENTIONALLY LEFT BLANK.

**Writing Sample**

Schools would like to get to know you better through an essay you write. If you choose to write a personal essay, base your essay on the topic presented in A. If you choose to write a general essay, base your essay on the topic presented in B. Please fill in the circle next to your choice.

Ⓐ What one event do you look forward to the most all year and why?

Ⓑ What is something that you think needs to be invented and why?

**Use this page and the next page to complete your writing sample.**

*Continue on next page*

**SECTION 1**
**25 Questions**

Following each problem in this section, there are five suggested answers. Work each problem in your head or in the blank space provided at the right of the page. Then look at the five suggested answers and decide which one is best.

<u>Note:</u> Figures that accompany problems in this section are drawn as accurately as possible EXCEPT when it is stated in a specific problem that its figure is not drawn to scale.

Sample Problem:

| | |
|---|---|
| 5,413 | (A) 586 |
| - 4,827 | (B) 596 |
| | (C) 696 |
| | (D) 1,586 |
| | (E) 1,686 ● Ⓑ Ⓒ Ⓓ Ⓔ |

---

**USE THIS SPACE FOR FIGURING.**

1. Which point on the graph shown has an *x*-coordinate of 6 ?

   (A) *A*
   (B) *B*
   (C) *C*
   (D) *D*
   (E) *E*

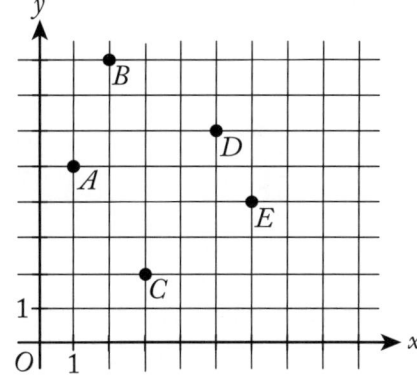

---

2. Six equally-sized pieces are cut from a piece of rope that has a length of 88 inches. Each of the six pieces has a length of 14 inches. What is the length, in inches, of the leftover piece?

   (A) 2
   (B) 4
   (C) 8
   (D) 14
   (E) 38

**GO ON TO THE NEXT PAGE.**

**USE THIS SPACE FOR FIGURING.**

3. If $10x - 5 = 5x + 15$, what is the value of $x$ ?

    (A) $\frac{2}{3}$

    (B) $\frac{3}{2}$

    (C) 2

    (D) 4

    (E) 5

---

4. Calculate: $\left(-\frac{5}{4}\right)^3$

    (A) $-\frac{125}{64}$

    (B) $-\frac{15}{64}$

    (C) $\frac{125}{64}$

    (D) $-\frac{15}{12}$

    (E) $\frac{15}{12}$

---

5. What is the measure of each exterior angle of an equilateral triangle?

    (A) 60°

    (B) 120°

    (C) 150°

    (D) 180°

    (E) 240°

---

> The sum of 3 times a number and 4 times another number is greater than or equal to 27.

6. The statement in the box above can be represented by which of the following inequalities?

    (A) $3a \times 4b \geq 27$

    (B) $3a \times 4b \leq 27$

    (C) $3a + 4b \geq 27$

    (D) $3a + 4b \leq 27$

    (E) $3a \div 4b \geq 27$

**GO ON TO THE NEXT PAGE.**

**USE THIS SPACE FOR FIGURING.**

7. There are 30 girls and 20 boys in a class. In the class, $\frac{2}{3}$ of the girls are wearing blue shirts and 75% of the boys are wearing green shirts. There are how many more girls wearing blue shirts than there are boys wearing green shirts?

   (A)   5
   (B)   10
   (C)   15
   (D)   20
   (E)   35

---

8. In the Venn diagram shown, set $A$ consists of all the multiples of 3, and set $B$ consists of all the multiples of 4. Which of the following values could be included in the shaded region?

   (A)   6
   (B)   8
   (C)   12
   (D)   16
   (E)   30

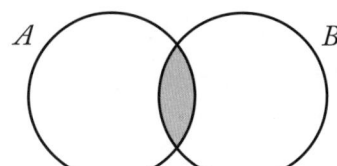

---

9. Let ▲ be defined as $x$ ▲ $y = (x - y)^y$ for all integer values of $x$ and $y$. What is the value of $0$ ▲ $4$ ?

   (A)   –256
   (B)   –16
   (C)     1
   (D)    16
   (E)   256

---

10. Enrico is buying bottles of water for an upcoming business meeting. He has \$20 to spend, and each bottle of water costs \$1.50. The function $f$ gives the relationship between the amount of money, $f(x)$, in dollars, Enrico has remaining after buying $x$ bottles of water. Which of the following defines $f$ ?

   (A)  $f(x) = 1.5 - 20x$
   (B)  $f(x) = 1.5x - 20$
   (C)  $f(x) = 18.5x$
   (D)  $f(x) = 20 - 1.5x$
   (E)  $f(x) = 20x - 1.5$

**GO ON TO THE NEXT PAGE.**

**USE THIS SPACE FOR FIGURING.**

11. The perimeter of an octagon is 20 units. If the length of each side of the figure is increased by 2 units, what is the perimeter of the new figure?

(A) 22 units
(B) 28 units
(C) 30 units
(D) 36 units
(E) 40 units

12. If the average (arithmetic mean) of the numbers $x$ and $y$ is 100, which of the following must be true ?

(A) $x - 100 = 100 - y$
(B) $x = 100 + y$
(C) $x + y = 100$
(D) $x - y = 50$
(E) $x = 100$ and $y = 100$

13. A dairy farm has a tank that contains 500 gallons of milk. Of the following, what is the best approximation for the number of 26-fluid-ounce containers that can be filled from the tank? (1 gallon = 128 fluid ounces)

(A) 6,400
(B) 2,400
(C) 1,500
(D) 1,000
(E) 100

14. What is the area of the figure shown?

(A) 35
(B) 60
(C) 85
(D) 110
(E) 120

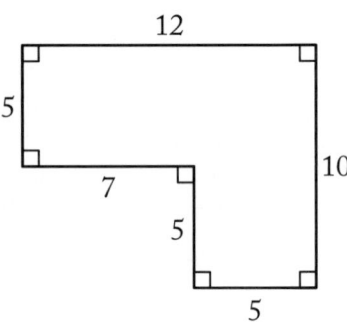

**GO ON TO THE NEXT PAGE.**

$$(2x + 3)(3x - 5)$$

15. Which of the following is equivalent to the expression above?

(A) $6x^2 - 15$
(B) $6x^2 - 19x + 15$
(C) $6x^2 - 19x - 15$
(D) $6x^2 - x + 15$
(E) $6x^2 - x - 15$

16. Johnny's house is 16 miles due north from the deli and Hannah's house is 12 miles due east from the same deli. In total miles, what is the distance from Johnny's house to Hannah's house?

(A)  4
(B)  5
(C) 20
(D) 28
(E) 32

17. If $x^2 + 5x = 6$, what are all possible values of $x$?

(A) $x = -6$ and $1$
(B) $x = -3$ and $-2$
(C) $x = -3$ and $2$
(D) $x = 2$ and $3$
(E) $x = 6$ and $1$

$$\frac{112}{a^2}, \frac{56}{a}, 28, 14a, \ldots$$

18. In the sequence above, the first term is $\frac{112}{a^2}$, where $a \neq 0$. Each term after the first is formed by multiplying the preceding term by the same expression. What is the next term in the sequence?

(A) 0

(B) 7

(C) $\dfrac{7}{a^2}$

(D) $7a^2$

(E) $14a^2$

**GO ON TO THE NEXT PAGE.**

**USE THIS SPACE FOR FIGURING.**

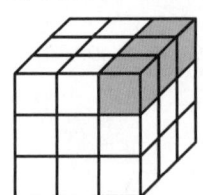

19. The large cube shown consists of 27 unit cubes of equal size, of which 3 cubes are shaded. If the shaded cubes are removed from the large cube, how will the surface area of the resulting figure compare with the surface area of the large cube?

    (A) The surface area will be the same as the original area.
    (B) The surface area will be 1 square unit less than the original area.
    (C) The surface area will be 2 square units less than the original area.
    (D) The surface area will be 6 square units less than the original area.
    (E) The surface area will be 8 square units less than the original area.

20. A lookout tower has 360 steps from the bottom to the top. Owen and Jillian are having a race. Owen is at the bottom of the tower and races to the top at a rate of 40 steps per minute. Jillian is at the top of the tower and races to the bottom at a rate of 80 steps per minute. If they start at the same time, after how many minutes will they be on the same step?

    (A) 2
    (B) 3
    (C) 4.5
    (D) 9
    (E) 13.5

21. In the $xy$-coordinate plane, the line passing through the points $(3, -4)$ and $(c, 2)$ has a slope of $-3$ What is the value of $c$ ?

    (A) -6
    (B) -5
    (C) 0
    (D) 1
    (E) 5

22. In the figure, segments $\overline{AF}$, $\overline{BG}$, $\overline{CE}$, and $\overline{DF}$ intersect as shown. If $\overline{BG} \parallel \overline{CE}$, what is the value of $x$ ?

    (A) 40
    (B) 60
    (C) 80
    (D) 140
    (E) 280

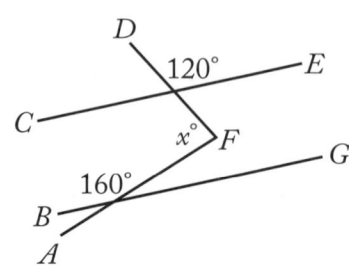

**GO ON TO THE NEXT PAGE.**

**USE THIS SPACE FOR FIGURING.**

23. Simplify: $\left(x^{\frac{1}{2}}\right)^3 (x^3)^{-\frac{1}{2}}$ for $x > 0$.

   (A)  0

   (B)  1

   (C)  $x$

   (D)  $x^{-\frac{9}{4}}$

   (E)  $x^{-3}$

---

24. What is the total surface area, in square centimeters, of the right circular cylinder shown?

   (A)  $100\pi$
   (B)  $125\pi$
   (C)  $150\pi$
   (D)  $200\pi$
   (E)  $300\pi$

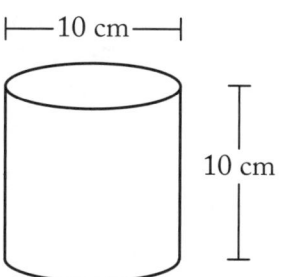

---

25. Which of the following is equivalent to $\frac{2}{x} + \frac{3}{x-1}$ for $x > 1$ ?

   (A)  $\dfrac{5}{x^2 - x}$

   (B)  $\dfrac{5x - 2}{x^2 - 1}$

   (C)  $\dfrac{5x - 3}{x^2 - 1}$

   (D)  $\dfrac{5x - 2}{x^2 - x}$

   (E)  $\dfrac{5x - 3}{x^2 - x}$

# STOP
**IF YOU FINISH BEFORE TIME IS CALLED, YOU MAY CHECK YOUR WORK ON THIS SECTION ONLY.**
**DO NOT TURN TO ANY OTHER SECTION IN THE TEST.**

**SECTION 2**
**40 Questions**

Read each passage carefully and then answer the questions about it. For each question, decide on the basis of the passage which one of the choices best answers the question.

---

Chopin's own playing was the counterpart of his personality. Every characteristic that could be distinguished in the man was apparent in the pianist—the same precision; the horror of excess and all that is careless and uncontrolled; the same good manners and high tone of character, combined with poetic warmth and a romantic fervor of expression. No one had ever heard such
*Line 5*     polished playing, although others could make a more overwhelming impression by their rush and violence. It is a mistake, encouraged by sentimental legend, to believe that Chopin's playing was limited by a delicacy which was equivalent to weakness. Even in the last stages of tuberculosis, he could rally and play with an energy that surprised the audience, who saw in front of them "a slight, frail-looking person." At his final public appearance in November 1848, less than a year before the
*10*     end, he managed to play "with his usual brilliance."

---

1. According to the passage Chopin's playing and personality were characterized by

   (A) wild flights of fancy
   (B) uncertainty and hesitation
   (C) dramatic changes of mood
   (D) discipline and moderation
   (E) indifference to popular opinion

2. According to the passage, Chopin "surprised the audience" (line 8) with his

   (A) frail appearance
   (B) gruff manner
   (C) loss of control
   (D) unusual repertoire
   (E) energetic playing

3. The "end" mentioned in line 10 most likely refers to

   (A) Chopin's retirement from public life
   (B) the decline of Chopin's genius
   (C) a cure for Chopin's illness
   (D) Chopin's death in 1849
   (E) the finale of a concert piece

4. This passage deals primarily with Chopin's

   (A) musical compositions
   (B) musical performance
   (C) debilitating illness
   (D) aristocratic personality
   (E) romantic fervor

5. When discussing Chopin, the author uses a tone best described as

   (A) admiring
   (B) brusque
   (C) ironic
   (D) cautious
   (E) naïve

**GO ON TO THE NEXT PAGE.**

> Among partnerships in the sea, one of the most fascinating is that of the brightly colored clown fish and the poisonous sea anemone. The clown fish is only three inches long but its brilliant orange color and slow speed make it a perfect target for enemies. It has no natural camouflage, but it is not defenseless. The clown fish is immune to the sea anemone's poison and can hide among the
> *Line 5* anemone's tentacles in safety. In return, the clown fish brings food to the anemone, which cannot move about in the sea but is anchored in the ocean floor.

6. The passage suggests that, on its own, the clown fish is at a disadvantage because it cannot

   (A) blend into its surroundings
   (B) poison its enemies
   (C) detect natural predators
   (D) find food for itself
   (E) swim as fast as the sea anemone

7. According to the passage, the clown fish serves the sea anemone by

   (A) helping it to move
   (B) attracting its prey
   (C) distracting its predators
   (D) providing nourishment
   (E) providing protection

8. According to the passage, all of the following are true of the clown fish EXCEPT that it is

   (A) small in size
   (B) a slow swimmer
   (C) very poisonous
   (D) brightly colored
   (E) pursued by other creatures

9. As it is used in line 5, the word "return" most nearly means

   (A) retaliation
   (B) recurrence
   (C) reciprocation
   (D) homecoming
   (E) profit

10. What is the main idea of the passage?

    (A) The clown fish is easy prey for other sea creatures.
    (B) The clown fish is immune to the sea anemone's poison.
    (C) The sea anemone cannot swim.
    (D) The sea anemone gives protection to the clown fish.
    (E) The clown fish and the sea anemone help each other.

**GO ON TO THE NEXT PAGE.**

> Washington is full of green politicians mindlessly supporting whatever causes other people demand they support. But the so-called seasoned politicians are no better. Though they portray themselves as independent thinkers, they generally take uncontroversial stances that capture the public's interest and pay off in the currency of fame.
>
> *Line 5*   But there is another, all too rare kind of politician: the authentic professional who steeps himself or herself in the art of public service with dazzling skill and persuasiveness. What marks these politicians, besides integrity, is their drive to achieve impressive results rather than fame, despite all the temptations of publicity and self-indulgence. Most began their careers in local government, and for many, helping the little guy remains their top priority, despite the temptation
>
> *10*   to overlook the powerless. Above all, they seek to pose the unanswered questions—to make an honorable mark on an often false town.

11. The author uses the word "green" (line 1) to suggest that certain politicians

    (A) support environmental causes
    (B) have little political experience
    (C) are interested only in making money
    (D) are envious of their colleagues
    (E) have an unhealthy appearance

12. The author suggests that many "seasoned politicians" (line 2) are

    (A) corrupt
    (B) unpopular
    (C) unresponsive
    (D) hypocritical
    (E) lazy

13. To describe how politicians achieve "fame" (line 4), the author uses a metaphor drawn from the realm of

    (A) sports
    (B) medicine
    (C) commerce
    (D) warfare
    (E) entertainment

14. The author's tone in the first paragraph is best described as

    (A) scathing
    (B) lighthearted
    (C) neutral
    (D) scholarly
    (E) boastful

15. As it is used in line 6, the word "marks" most nearly means

    (A) defaces
    (B) grades
    (C) notates
    (D) observes
    (E) distinguishes

**GO ON TO THE NEXT PAGE.**

We had a dreary morning's work before us, for there was no sign of any wind, and the boats had to be got out and manned, and the ship warped three or four miles round the corner of the island and up the narrow passage to the haven behind Skeleton Island. I volunteered for one of the boats, where I had, of course, no business. The heat was sweltering, and the men grumbled fiercely

*Line 5*   over their work. Anderson was in command of my boat, and instead of keeping the crew in order, he grumbled as loud as the worst.

"Well," he said with an oath, "it's not forever."

I thought this was a very bad sign, for up to that day the men had gone briskly and willingly about their business; but the very sight of the island had relaxed the cords of discipline.

*10*   We brought up just where the anchor was in the chart, about a third of a mile from each shore, the mainland on one side and Skeleton Island on the other. The bottom was clean sand. The plunge of our anchor sent up clouds of birds wheeling and crying over the woods, but in less than a minute they were down again and all was once more silent.

If the conduct of the men had been alarming in the boat, it became truly threatening when

*15*   they had come aboard. They lay about the deck growling together in talk. The slightest order was received with a black look and grudgingly and carelessly obeyed. Even the honest hands must have caught the infection, for there was not one man aboard to mend another. Mutiny it was plain, hung over us like a thunder-cloud.

16. With the phrase "of course" (line 4) the narrator acknowledges that he

(A) regretted having volunteered
(B) was eager to explore the island
(C) was unsuited to his chosen task
(D) wanted to be in command of a boat
(E) expected no profit from the venture

17. As depicted in the passage, the mood of the crew is

(A) sullen
(B) relaxed
(C) worried
(D) perplexed
(E) cooperative

18. The narrator observes that for the ship's crew the "sight of the island" (line 9) was

(A) inspiring
(B) terrifying
(C) mystifying
(D) satisfying
(E) demoralizing

19. In the last paragraph, the narrator uses a medical metaphor in order to emphasize

(A) the prevalence of an attitude
(B) the need to take precautions
(C) the effectiveness of a strategy
(D) the importance of following orders
(E) the seaworthiness of the ship

20. To describe the potential "Mutiny" (line 17), the narrator uses which of the following literary devices?

(A) Hyperbole
(B) Onomatopoeia
(C) Rhetorical question
(D) Simile
(E) Personification

**GO ON TO THE NEXT PAGE.**

Dinitrogen tetroxide is a chemical compound made up of nitrogen and oxygen. It is abbreviated $N_2O_4$ and is often simply called nitrogen tetroxide or NTO. Propelling rockets is one of the best examples of the use to which nitrogen tetroxide can be put. It is often combined with a hydrazine-based rocket fuel. Because it burns on contact without needing a separate source to ignite

*Line 5*    it, it is one of the most important rocket propellants ever developed.

By the late 1950s, NTO was the storable oxidizer of choice for U.S. and Soviet rockets. It was used on the space shuttle, and continues to be used on most geo-stationary satellites and many deep-space probes. However, its use is not without risk. NTO poisoning nearly killed three astronauts when dangerous fumes were vented inside their cabin by mistake.

21. As it is used in line 2, the word "called" most nearly means

(A) summoned
(B) designated
(C) telephoned
(D) challenged
(E) judged

22. It can be inferred from the passage that nitrogen tetroxide

(A) is extremely expensive
(B) was discovered by Soviet scientists
(C) is used only for propelling rockets
(D) has been vital to the space program
(E) must not be combined with any other substance

23. Which of the following titles best describes the content of the passage?

(A) Fire Prevention in Space
(B) A Chemical Experiment
(C) Why Nitrogen Tetroxide Is No Longer Used
(D) Nitrogen Tetroxide and the Soviets
(E) An Introduction to Nitrogen Tetroxide

24. The author uses the phrase "on contact" (line 4) to indicate that nitrogen tetroxide is

(A) not to be touched
(B) highly flammable
(C) not easily transported
(D) also used as a weapon
(E) too dangerous to use in industry

25. With the word "However" (line 8), the author adopts a tone best described as

(A) outraged
(B) intimate
(C) cautionary
(D) humorous
(E) enthusiastic

**GO ON TO THE NEXT PAGE.**

> There was a sound of revelry by night,
>     And Belgium's Capital had gathered then
>     Her Beauty and her Chivalry, and bright
>     The lamps shone o'er fair women and brave men;
> *Line 5*    A thousand hearts beat happily; and when
>     Music arose with its voluptuous swell,
>     Soft eyes looked love to eyes which spake again,
>     And all went merry as a marriage bell;
>     But hush! hark! a deep sound strikes like a rising knell!
>
> 10   Did ye not hear it?—No; 'twas but the wind,
>     Or the car rattling o'er the stony street;
>     On with the dance! let joy be unconfined;
>     No sleep till morn, when Youth and Pleasure meet
>     To chase the glowing Hours with flying feet—
> 15   But hark!—that heavy sound breaks in once more,
>     As if the clouds its echo would repeat;
>     And nearer, clearer, deadlier than before!
>
> Arm! Arm! it is—it is—the cannon's opening roar!

26. In lines 1-4, the poet depicts

    (A) a solemn ceremony
    (B) a boisterous celebration
    (C) a diplomatic conference
    (D) a looming disaster
    (E) a fierce battle

27. The poet's description of the "swell" (line 6) suggests that the music was very

    (A) fast
    (B) loud
    (C) somber
    (D) sensual
    (E) dignified

28. In line 9, the poet introduces a tone of

    (A) alarm
    (B) whimsy
    (C) despair
    (D) nostalgia
    (E) jubilation

29. The statement "twas but the wind" (line 10) is most likely meant to be

    (A) ironic
    (B) humorous
    (C) reassuring
    (D) misleading
    (E) mysterious

30. The "heavy sound" (line 15) signifies

    (A) vigorous dancing
    (B) a musical crescendo
    (C) a sudden thunderstorm
    (D) uproarious laughter
    (E) the outbreak of war

**GO ON TO THE NEXT PAGE.**

About 70 percent of the tea America drinks each year comes from countries in tropical or subtropical climates, where it is warm and where a great deal of rain falls. Paradoxically, although the tea plant grows most luxuriantly in the heat, teas grown in cooler altitudes of 3,000 to 7,000 feet are of the finest quality produced. The slower growth at higher altitudes adds to the flavor of tea, but the yield is smaller, making this high-grown tea rarer and more expensive.

*Line 5*

A jungle plant, tea grows best in jungle soils but also grows in soil ranging from the lightest sands to the stiffest clays. However, while it demands a great deal of rain, it refuses to grow in swampy land. Otherwise, tea is a hardy plant that will take much punishment from both climate and soil.

*10*

Tea is usually grown from seeds obtained by allowing some of the plants to grow unchecked until they become trees 15 or 20 feet high. Then, seeds are taken from the small, white, sweet-smelling flowers that cover these trees.

At planting time the seeds, much like hazel nuts in size and appearance, are laid out 6 inches apart. When the plants are 6 to 18 months old, they are removed to the tea garden. Early in its growth, the young plant is cut back, or pruned, to encourage the main stem to grow more side branches. Each plant is kept cut to about 3 or 4 feet in height and width so that the harvesters can reach all of its leaves. After the tea plant has been transplanted and pruned, 3 to 5 years pass before it is ready to yield choice leaves.

*15*

31. It can be inferred from the passage that the part of the tea plant used to prepare tea for consumers is the

   (A) flower
   (B) seed
   (C) branch
   (D) leaf
   (E) nut

32. According to the passage, tea plants need to be pruned early in their growth so that

   (A) more side branches will grow
   (B) they can be transplanted easily
   (C) more seeds can develop
   (D) the tree will grow faster
   (E) high-quality tea can be produced

33. According to the passage, the primary reason high-grown tea is more expensive than others is that it

   (A) requires more irrigation
   (B) is more costly to transport
   (C) requires more workers to harvest
   (D) tastes better
   (E) is less plentiful

34. Which of the following questions is NOT answered in the passage?

   (A) In what climate does tea grow best?
   (B) What countries produce tea?
   (C) How long after transplanting is tea ready for picking?
   (D) What is the relationship between altitude and yield of tea?
   (E) What kind of soil is good for growing tea?

35. The passage makes all of the following statements about the tea plant EXCEPT

   (A) It grows best in jungle climates.
   (B) It needs considerable rain.
   (C) It grows in various soils.
   (D) It produces small white flowers.
   (E) Its leaves are produced within 6 to 18 months.

**GO ON TO THE NEXT PAGE.**

English sympathy at the outset of the American Civil War leaned toward the South. The Tory aristocracy, which understood and appreciated the kindred Southern planter class, looked forward with satisfaction to the possible downfall of democracy anywhere. Many English liberals also favored the South, for their favorite doctrine then was free trade, and the South seemed to be

*Line 5* deeply committed to a free trade policy. English manufacturers hoped that a direct exchange of Southern cotton for English wares would be facilitated by the success of the Southern army.

The North, however, was not without its friends in England. Some reformers, although distressed at the newly adopted tariff policy of the United States, saw clearly that a Northern victory must result in the abolition of slavery. With the issue thus reduced to a struggle between

10 free labor and slave labor, their sympathies could lie only with the North. With the issuing of the Emancipation Proclamation, the number of Northern sympathizers was greatly increased. The mill workers of Manchester, in spite of the suffering that the failure of the American cotton supply had caused them, urged a complete "erasure of that foul blot upon civilization." To some extent, perhaps, British sympathy for the North was purchased by the greater need for Northern wheat

15 than for Southern cotton. In addition, there can be no doubt that the profits of neutrality were widely regarded as preferable to a hazardous war over the issue of Southern independence.

36. According to the passage, the Tory aristocracy was

(A) sympathetic toward the North's tariff policy
(B) sympathetic toward those who advocated the abolition of slavery
(C) in favor of protecting the rights of working people
(D) opposed to a war that would result in Southern independence
(E) opposed to any form of rule by the people

37. The author discusses British attitudes about the Civil War primarily in terms of

(A) immoral basis
(B) economic effects
(C) military strategy
(D) cultural impact
(E) historical antecedents

38. It can be inferred from the passage that the North's policy on trade was

(A) designed to protect cotton planters
(B) sympathetic toward the Tory views
(C) based on the needs of English manufacturers
(D) contrary to the South's policy
(E) difficult to define

39. In lines 13-16, the author implies that British sympathy for the North was motivated primarily by

(A) isolationism
(B) well-established loyalties
(C) self-interest
(D) gratitude
(E) ill-defined priorities

40. According to the passage, the Tory aristocracy regarded Southern planters as

(A) foolhardy
(B) unpredictable
(C) destructive
(D) similar to English liberals
(E) similar to themselves

## STOP
**IF YOU FINISH BEFORE TIME IS CALLED, YOU MAY CHECK YOUR WORK ON THIS SECTION ONLY.
DO NOT TURN TO ANY OTHER SECTION IN THE TEST.**

## SECTION 3
## 60 Questions

This section consists of two different types of questions: synonyms and analogies. There are directions and a sample question for each type.

**Synonyms**

Each of the following questions consists of one word followed by five words or phrases. You are to select the one word or phrase whose meaning is closest to the word in capital letters.

Sample Question:

CHILLY:

(A) lazy
(B) nice
(C) dry
(D) cold
(E) sunny

Ⓐ Ⓑ Ⓒ ● Ⓔ

---

1. ESTEEM:

   (A) wealth
   (B) power
   (C) desire
   (D) beauty
   (E) respect

2. AMIABLE:

   (A) friendly
   (B) obvious
   (C) competent
   (D) modest
   (E) careful

3. UNSAVORY:

   (A) dangerous
   (B) ignorant
   (C) obscure
   (D) distasteful
   (E) useless

4. SEER:

   (A) guardian
   (B) prophet
   (C) spy
   (D) poet
   (E) fairy

5. EXEMPLIFY:

   (A) protect
   (B) illustrate
   (C) question
   (D) increase
   (E) correct

6. DETACH:

   (A) uncover
   (B) prevent
   (C) separate
   (D) extend
   (E) gather

7. SUPERFLUOUS:

   (A) unnecessary
   (B) fantastic
   (C) shallow
   (D) fleeting
   (E) incomparable

8. SCALAWAG:

   (A) sailor
   (B) joker
   (C) peddler
   (D) novice
   (E) rogue

**GO ON TO THE NEXT PAGE.**

9. ACCOLADE:

(A) procession

(B) payment

(C) praise

(D) campaign

(E) deception

10. BEWILDER:

(A) banish

(B) confuse

(C) celebrate

(D) abandon

(E) arouse

11. CONGENITAL:

(A) inborn

(B) courteous

(C) permanent

(D) identical

(E) widespread

12. EXQUISITE:

(A) foreign

(B) elegant

(C) curious

(D) costly

(E) obsolete

13. BASTION:

(A) market

(B) symbol

(C) weapon

(D) stronghold

(E) descendant

14. AUDACITY:

(A) clamor

(B) boldness

(C) freedom

(D) potential

(E) reluctance

15. DETEST:

(A) hate

(B) doubt

(C) fail

(D) relax

(E) tell

16. RATIONALE:

(A) allotment

(B) proposal

(C) solution

(D) answer

(E) justification

17. PROCLAMATION:

(A) forewarning

(B) liberation

(C) assistance

(D) announcement

(E) citizenship

18. AMEND:

(A) punish

(B) encourage

(C) improve

(D) supplement

(E) apologize

19. ENDEAVOR:

(A) recommend

(B) attempt

(C) challenge

(D) explore

(E) terminate

20. APPARITION:

(A) ghost

(B) remedy

(C) equality

(D) compensation

(E) performance

**GO ON TO THE NEXT PAGE.**

21. THRONG:
    (A) edge
    (B) crowd
    (C) noise
    (D) ache
    (E) shock

22. FEIGN:
    (A) pretend
    (B) weaken
    (C) disappear
    (D) request
    (E) conceal

23. REBUKE:
    (A) mutter
    (B) deny
    (C) slander
    (D) disturb
    (E) chide

24. AMBIANCE:
    (A) flavor
    (B) luster
    (C) atmosphere
    (D) uncertainty
    (E) trance

25. QUASH:
    (A) moisten
    (B) scream
    (C) tremble
    (D) suppress
    (E) disturb

26. AUSPICIOUS:
    (A) favorable
    (B) untrustworthy
    (C) impressive
    (D) skeptical
    (E) protective

27. DWINDLE:
    (A) delay
    (B) rotate
    (C) chatter
    (D) shrink
    (E) steal

28. CLEFT:
    (A) ledge
    (B) split
    (C) blade
    (D) mound
    (E) noise

29. CONVALESCE:
    (A) disappear
    (B) combine
    (C) recuperate
    (D) fortify
    (E) overpower

30. TUMULT:
    (A) uproar
    (B) downfall
    (C) mound
    (D) feast
    (E) error

**GO ON TO THE NEXT PAGE.**

## Analogies

The following questions ask you to find relationships between words. For each question, select the answer choice that best completes the meaning of the sentence.

Sample Question:

> Kitten is to cat as
> (A) fawn is to colt
> (B) puppy is to dog
> (C) cow is to bull
> (D) wolf is to bear
> (E) hen is to rooster

Choice (B) is the best answer because a kitten is a young cat just as a puppy is a young dog. Of all the answer choices, (B) states a relationship that is most like the relationship between <u>kitten</u> and <u>cat</u>.

---

31. Fib is to deception as

    (A) theft is to property
    (B) setback is to progress
    (C) glitch is to malfunction
    (D) symptom is to disease
    (E) error is to accident

32. Watch is to see as

    (A) give is to take
    (B) listen is to hear
    (C) raise is to rise
    (D) speak is to talk
    (E) toss is to throw

33. Facilitate is to easy as

    (A) augment is to large
    (B) believe is to plausible
    (C) resurrect is to dead
    (D) lament is to sad
    (E) refine is to crude

34. Femur is to bone as

    (A) blood is to vessel
    (B) strength is to muscle
    (C) joint is to limb
    (D) tendon is to leg
    (E) kidney is to organ

35. Detrimental is to harm as

    (A) contentious is to controversy
    (B) guilty is to culprit
    (C) omniscient is to knowledge
    (D) ruthless is to mercy
    (E) neutral is to partisan

36. Imprison is to custody as

    (A) quarantine is to disease
    (B) hoard is to surplus
    (C) disgrace is to dignity
    (D) endanger is to jeopardy
    (E) arrive is to destination

37. Census is to population as

    (A) election is to government
    (B) budget is to expenditure
    (C) experiment is to theory
    (D) inventory is to stock
    (E) tax is to revenue

38. Textile is to weave as

    (A) jewelry is to sparkle
    (B) sculpture is to shape
    (C) furniture is to arrange
    (D) vehicle is to transport
    (E) music is to listen

**GO ON TO THE NEXT PAGE.**

39. Inquisitive is to ask as
    (A) defiant is to resist
    (B) incessant is to stop
    (C) eligible is to choose
    (D) needy is to give
    (E) aloof is to reach

40. Minuscule is to small as
    (A) extreme is to moderate
    (B) vertical is to tall
    (C) mythic is to epic
    (D) recent is to nearby
    (E) precipitous is to steep

41. Legend is to story as
    (A) fashion is to trend
    (B) drama is to plot
    (C) rumor is to gossip
    (D) custom is to practice
    (E) icon is to hero

42. Prowess is to skillful as
    (A) discretion is to prudent
    (B) novice is to inexperienced
    (C) euphoria is to pleasant
    (D) restraint is to extravagant
    (E) charity is to grateful

43. Ripple is to wave as
    (A) shore is to sea
    (B) crater is to volcano
    (C) eddy is to whirlpool
    (D) star is to galaxy
    (E) cloud is to sky

44. Boast is to pride as
    (A) thank is to generosity
    (B) console is to grief
    (C) request is to permission
    (D) grumble is to dissatisfaction
    (E) applaud is to performance

45. Tapestry is to thread as
    (A) mural is to wall
    (B) mosaic is to tile
    (C) painting is to portrait
    (D) shroud is to burial
    (E) statue is to pedestal

46. Summarize is to synopsis as
    (A) appraise is to assessment
    (B) diagnose is to illness
    (C) refute is to falsehood
    (D) abridge is to dictionary
    (E) recite is to memory

47. Consensus is to agree as
    (A) paralysis is to move
    (B) asylum is to protect
    (C) placebo is to medicate
    (D) exodus is to depart
    (E) mandate is to obey

48. Trajectory is to air as
    (A) map is to location
    (B) route is to land
    (C) boat is to river
    (D) orbit is to planet
    (E) distance is to area

49. Cottage is to house as
    (A) anchor is to boat
    (B) hamlet is to village
    (C) summit is to mountain
    (D) whisper is to secret
    (E) stanza is to poem

50. Lull is to sleep as
    (A) begin is to finish
    (B) ponder is to decide
    (C) kindle is to burn
    (D) travel is to arrive
    (E) attack is to defend

**GO ON TO THE NEXT PAGE.**

51. Hermit is to reclusive as
    (A) charlatan is to gullible
    (B) vagabond is to stable
    (C) witness is to truthful
    (D) descendant is to proud
    (E) turncoat is to disloyal

52. Asset is to valuable as
    (A) nuance is to obvious
    (B) poverty is to affluent
    (C) anomaly is to irregular
    (D) pardon is to innocent
    (E) acclaim is to critical

53. Pure is to adulterate as
    (A) impromptu is to plan
    (B) vigilant is to watch
    (C) compliant is to protest
    (D) rotten is to decay
    (E) flexible is to bend

54. Disguise is to identity as
    (A) pretext is to purpose
    (B) confession is to guilt
    (C) remedy is to illness
    (D) cache is to storage
    (E) alibi is to location

55. Raze is to demolition as
    (A) restrict is to freedom
    (B) hoard is to accumulation
    (C) shirk is to obligation
    (D) thwart is to progress
    (E) descend is to altitude

56. Callous is to sensitive as
    (A) afraid is to dangerous
    (B) random is to fortunate
    (C) contagious is to immune
    (D) bogus is to genuine
    (E) frigid is to cold

57. Oblivious is to awareness as
    (A) devout is to religion
    (B) destructive is to ruin
    (C) dominant is to control
    (D) impeccable is to flaw
    (E) obsolete is to disuse

58. Suggestible is to influence as
    (A) greedy is to acquire
    (B) skittish is to frighten
    (C) evasive is to confront
    (D) quarrelsome is to argue
    (E) illiterate is to read

59. Endorse is to approval as
    (A) invest is to risk
    (B) praise is to merit
    (C) suffer is to hardship
    (D) embark is to journey
    (E) counsel is to advice

60. Celestial is to heaven as
    (A) profound is to thought
    (B) annual is to date
    (C) maritime is to sea
    (D) chronic is to disease
    (E) intrepid is to fear

## STOP
**IF YOU FINISH BEFORE TIME IS CALLED, YOU MAY CHECK YOUR WORK ON THIS SECTION ONLY. DO NOT TURN TO ANY OTHER SECTION IN THE TEST.**

**SECTION 4**
**25 Questions**

Following each problem in this section, there are five suggested answers. Work each problem in your head or in the blank space provided at the right of the page. Then look at the five suggested answers and decide which one is best.

Note: Figures that accompany problems in this section are drawn as accurately as possible EXCEPT when it is stated in a specific problem that its figure is not drawn to scale.

Sample Problem:

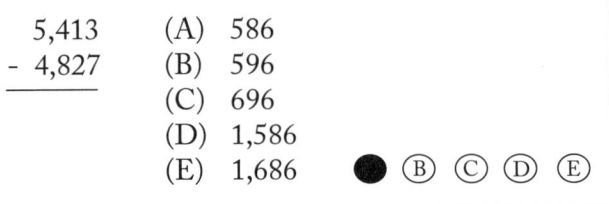

| 5,413 | (A) 586 |
| - 4,827 | (B) 596 |
| | (C) 696 |
| | (D) 1,586 |
| | (E) 1,686 |

● Ⓑ Ⓒ Ⓓ Ⓔ

1. Of the following, which is closest to $1.998 \times 2,001$ ?

    (A) 2,000
    (B) 3,000
    (C) 4,000
    (D) 5,000
    (E) 6,000

**USE THIS SPACE FOR FIGURING.**

2. What is the value of $2x - y^2$ when $x = 5$ and $y = 3$ ?

    (A) 1
    (B) 4
    (C) 16
    (D) 19
    (E) 49

3. According to the line graph, which day had the greatest increase in the number of cars produced when compared with the number of cars produced on the previous day?

    (A) Monday
    (B) Tuesday
    (C) Wednesday
    (D) Thursday
    (E) Friday

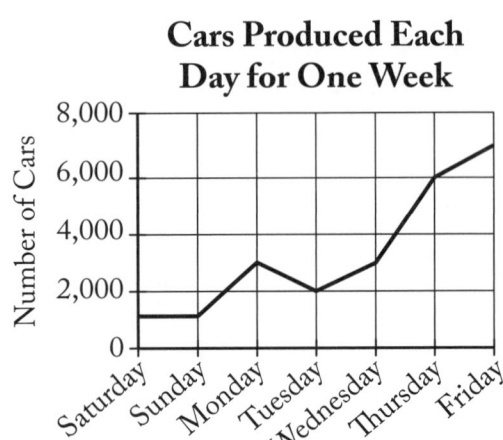

**Cars Produced Each Day for One Week**

**GO ON TO THE NEXT PAGE.**

**USE THIS SPACE FOR FIGURING.**

927.<u>6</u>4

4. What is the value of the underlined digit in the number above?

(A) 6 hundredths
(B) 6 tenths
(C) 6 oneths
(D) 6 tens
(E) 6 ones

---

5. Which of the following is the graph of $y = \frac{x}{2}$ ?

(A)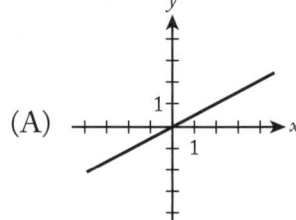

(B)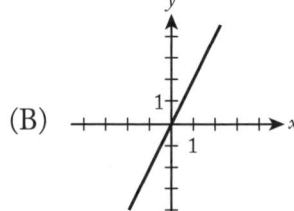

(C)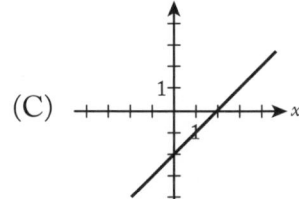

(D)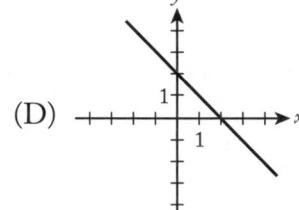

(E)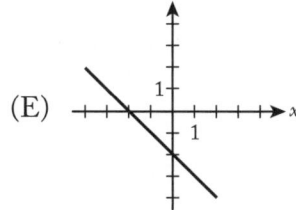

**GO ON TO THE NEXT PAGE.**

**USE THIS SPACE FOR FIGURING.**

$$2, 2, 3, 4, 5, 6, 7, 8$$

6. A number is to be selected at random from the list above. What is the probability that the number selected will be an even number?

(A) 0

(B) $\frac{3}{8}$

(C) $\frac{1}{2}$

(D) $\frac{5}{8}$

(E) 1

7. Solve the inequality: $4x - 5 \geq 2x - 3$

(A) $x \geq -4$

(B) $x \geq -1$

(C) $x \geq 1$

(D) $x \geq 2$

(E) $x \geq 4$

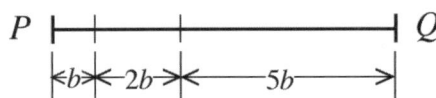

8. In the figure, if $b$ is a whole number, which of the following could be the length of segment $\overline{PQ}$ ?

(A) 7

(B) 10

(C) 14

(D) 15

(E) 16

**GO ON TO THE NEXT PAGE.**

**USE THIS SPACE FOR FIGURING.**

9.  To make 4 gallons of a certain shade of purple paint, Denise mixes 2.5 gallons of red paint with 1.5 gallons of blue paint. What is the ratio of the number of gallons of red paint to the number of gallons of blue paint in Denise's mixture?

    (A)  3:5
    (B)  3:8
    (C)  5:3
    (D)  5:8
    (E)  8:3

10. In the $xy$-coordinate plane shown, $\triangle ABC$ is to be translated 3 units left and 2 units down to form $\triangle A'B'C'$. What are the coordinates of the point $B'$?

    (A)  $(5, 3)$
    (B)  $(4, 4)$
    (C)  $(3, 2)$
    (D)  $(-1, 1)$
    (E)  $(-3, -2)$

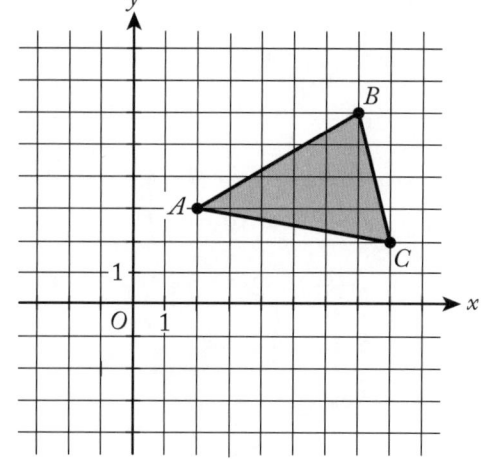

11. If $x + 2y = 8$, and $x - y = 5$, what is the value of $x$?

    (A)  1
    (B)  2
    (C)  3
    (D)  6
    (E)  18

12. If the volume of a cube is 512 cubic inches, what is the edge length of the cube, in inches?

    (A)  6
    (B)  8
    (C)  12
    (D)  32
    (E)  64

**GO ON TO THE NEXT PAGE.**

**USE THIS SPACE FOR FIGURING.**

13. There are 3 trucks of equal weight in a parking lot. One third of the weight of each truck is 2.4 tons. The total weight of the 3 trucks can be determined by multiplying 2.4 by which of the following numbers?

   (A) $\frac{1}{3}$

   (B) $\frac{2}{3}$

   (C) $\frac{4}{3}$

   (D) 3

   (E) 9

---

14. Factor: $5x^2y^2 + 10x^2y + 5xy^2$

   (A) $xy(5xy + 2x + y)$
   (B) $5xy(xy + 2 + y)$
   (C) $5xy(xy + 2x + y)$
   (D) $5x^2y(y + 2 + xy)$
   (E) $5x^2y^2(1 + 2y + x)$

---

15. Which of the following could be the length of the sides of a triangle?
   (A) $3, 3, 6$
   (B) $1, 2, 3$
   (C) $3, 5, 9$
   (D) $3, 5, 8$
   (E) $8, 8, 15$

**GO ON TO THE NEXT PAGE.**

**USE THIS SPACE FOR FIGURING.**

16. Omar begins training for a 5 km race by running 0.75 km the first day, 0.85 km the second day, and 0.95 km the third day. If he keeps increasing his distance each day according to the pace of his first three days, what is the first day in his training program that Omar will run greater than 5 km?

(A) The 42nd day
(B) The 43rd day
(C) The 44th day
(D) The 50th day
(E) The 500th day

$$10, 10, 15, 20, 20, 25, 40$$

17. Which of the following pairs of numbers when included in the list above will make the median of the list greater than the mode of the list?

(A) $5, 25$
(B) $10, 30$
(C) $20, 20$
(D) $20, 30$
(E) $25, 25$

18. If $a + b$ is divisible by 11, which of the following is also divisible by 11 ?

(A) $(a + b) + 11$

(B) $a + (11 \times b)$

(C) $(11 \times a) + b$

(D) $(2 \times a) \times (2 \times b)$

(E) $\dfrac{a - b}{11}$

19. In the rectangle shown, what is the area of the shaded region?

(A) 4.5
(B) 7.5
(C) 9
(D) 12
(E) 15

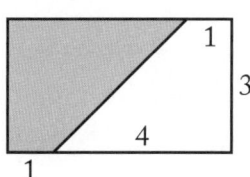

**GO ON TO THE NEXT PAGE.**

**USE THIS SPACE FOR FIGURING.**

20. What is the value of $20 - 6 \times 3 + 7$ ?

 (A) −40
 (B) −5
 (C) 9
 (D) 49
 (E) 140

---

21. A bag contains 7 marbles: 4 red, 2 yellow, and 1 green. Three marbles are to be selected from the bag, one at a time, without replacement. If the order of selection does not matter, how many color combinations of the three marbles are possible?

 (A) Six
 (B) Seven
 (C) Eight
 (D) Nine
 (E) Ten

---

22. Let the functions $f$ and $g$ be defined as $f(x) = 9 - x$ and $g(x) = 3x^2$. If $g(-2) = k$, what is the value of $f(k)$ ?

 (A) −3
 (B) 12
 (C) 21
 (D) 147
 (E) 363

---

23. Which of the following is equivalent to $\sqrt{45} - \sqrt{5}$ ?

 (A) $2\sqrt{5}$

 (B) $\sqrt{10}$

 (C) $2\sqrt{10}$

 (D) 2

 (E) 3

**GO ON TO THE NEXT PAGE.**

24. Each of the houses shown is painted one of the five colors: red, yellow, blue, green, or white. There is exactly one house between the red house and the blue house. There are exactly two houses between the green house and the white house. House *A* cannot be which of the following colors?

    (A) Red
    (B) Yellow
    (C) Blue
    (D) Green
    (E) White

**USE THIS SPACE FOR FIGURING.**

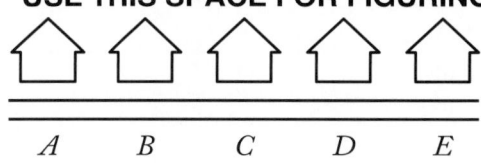

25. Point *B* is the center of the circle shown, and the length of arc $\overparen{AC}$ is $8\pi$. What is the radius of the circle?

    (A) 4
    (B) 8
    (C) 9
    (D) 18
    (E) 36

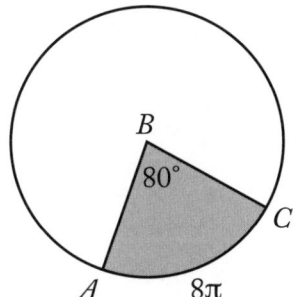

# STOP

**IF YOU FINISH BEFORE TIME IS CALLED, YOU MAY CHECK YOUR WORK ON THIS SECTION ONLY.
DO NOT TURN TO ANY OTHER SECTION IN THE TEST.**

THIS PAGE INTENTIONALLY LEFT BLANK.

# Practice Test III: Upper Level Answer Sheet

**Be sure each mark completely fills the circle.**
Start with number 1 for each new section of the test.

## Section 1

1 Ⓐ Ⓑ Ⓒ Ⓓ Ⓔ  6 Ⓐ Ⓑ Ⓒ Ⓓ Ⓔ  11 Ⓐ Ⓑ Ⓒ Ⓓ Ⓔ  16 Ⓐ Ⓑ Ⓒ Ⓓ Ⓔ  21 Ⓐ Ⓑ Ⓒ Ⓓ Ⓔ
2 Ⓐ Ⓑ Ⓒ Ⓓ Ⓔ  7 Ⓐ Ⓑ Ⓒ Ⓓ Ⓔ  12 Ⓐ Ⓑ Ⓒ Ⓓ Ⓔ  17 Ⓐ Ⓑ Ⓒ Ⓓ Ⓔ  22 Ⓐ Ⓑ Ⓒ Ⓓ Ⓔ
3 Ⓐ Ⓑ Ⓒ Ⓓ Ⓔ  8 Ⓐ Ⓑ Ⓒ Ⓓ Ⓔ  13 Ⓐ Ⓑ Ⓒ Ⓓ Ⓔ  18 Ⓐ Ⓑ Ⓒ Ⓓ Ⓔ  23 Ⓐ Ⓑ Ⓒ Ⓓ Ⓔ
4 Ⓐ Ⓑ Ⓒ Ⓓ Ⓔ  9 Ⓐ Ⓑ Ⓒ Ⓓ Ⓔ  14 Ⓐ Ⓑ Ⓒ Ⓓ Ⓔ  19 Ⓐ Ⓑ Ⓒ Ⓓ Ⓔ  24 Ⓐ Ⓑ Ⓒ Ⓓ Ⓔ
5 Ⓐ Ⓑ Ⓒ Ⓓ Ⓔ  10 Ⓐ Ⓑ Ⓒ Ⓓ Ⓔ  15 Ⓐ Ⓑ Ⓒ Ⓓ Ⓔ  20 Ⓐ Ⓑ Ⓒ Ⓓ Ⓔ  25 Ⓐ Ⓑ Ⓒ Ⓓ Ⓔ

## Section 2

1 Ⓐ Ⓑ Ⓒ Ⓓ Ⓔ  9 Ⓐ Ⓑ Ⓒ Ⓓ Ⓔ  17 Ⓐ Ⓑ Ⓒ Ⓓ Ⓔ  25 Ⓐ Ⓑ Ⓒ Ⓓ Ⓔ  33 Ⓐ Ⓑ Ⓒ Ⓓ Ⓔ
2 Ⓐ Ⓑ Ⓒ Ⓓ Ⓔ  10 Ⓐ Ⓑ Ⓒ Ⓓ Ⓔ  18 Ⓐ Ⓑ Ⓒ Ⓓ Ⓔ  26 Ⓐ Ⓑ Ⓒ Ⓓ Ⓔ  34 Ⓐ Ⓑ Ⓒ Ⓓ Ⓔ
3 Ⓐ Ⓑ Ⓒ Ⓓ Ⓔ  11 Ⓐ Ⓑ Ⓒ Ⓓ Ⓔ  19 Ⓐ Ⓑ Ⓒ Ⓓ Ⓔ  27 Ⓐ Ⓑ Ⓒ Ⓓ Ⓔ  35 Ⓐ Ⓑ Ⓒ Ⓓ Ⓔ
4 Ⓐ Ⓑ Ⓒ Ⓓ Ⓔ  12 Ⓐ Ⓑ Ⓒ Ⓓ Ⓔ  20 Ⓐ Ⓑ Ⓒ Ⓓ Ⓔ  28 Ⓐ Ⓑ Ⓒ Ⓓ Ⓔ  36 Ⓐ Ⓑ Ⓒ Ⓓ Ⓔ
5 Ⓐ Ⓑ Ⓒ Ⓓ Ⓔ  13 Ⓐ Ⓑ Ⓒ Ⓓ Ⓔ  21 Ⓐ Ⓑ Ⓒ Ⓓ Ⓔ  29 Ⓐ Ⓑ Ⓒ Ⓓ Ⓔ  37 Ⓐ Ⓑ Ⓒ Ⓓ Ⓔ
6 Ⓐ Ⓑ Ⓒ Ⓓ Ⓔ  14 Ⓐ Ⓑ Ⓒ Ⓓ Ⓔ  22 Ⓐ Ⓑ Ⓒ Ⓓ Ⓔ  30 Ⓐ Ⓑ Ⓒ Ⓓ Ⓔ  38 Ⓐ Ⓑ Ⓒ Ⓓ Ⓔ
7 Ⓐ Ⓑ Ⓒ Ⓓ Ⓔ  15 Ⓐ Ⓑ Ⓒ Ⓓ Ⓔ  23 Ⓐ Ⓑ Ⓒ Ⓓ Ⓔ  31 Ⓐ Ⓑ Ⓒ Ⓓ Ⓔ  39 Ⓐ Ⓑ Ⓒ Ⓓ Ⓔ
8 Ⓐ Ⓑ Ⓒ Ⓓ Ⓔ  16 Ⓐ Ⓑ Ⓒ Ⓓ Ⓔ  24 Ⓐ Ⓑ Ⓒ Ⓓ Ⓔ  32 Ⓐ Ⓑ Ⓒ Ⓓ Ⓔ  40 Ⓐ Ⓑ Ⓒ Ⓓ Ⓔ

## Section 3

1 Ⓐ Ⓑ Ⓒ Ⓓ Ⓔ  13 Ⓐ Ⓑ Ⓒ Ⓓ Ⓔ  25 Ⓐ Ⓑ Ⓒ Ⓓ Ⓔ  37 Ⓐ Ⓑ Ⓒ Ⓓ Ⓔ  49 Ⓐ Ⓑ Ⓒ Ⓓ Ⓔ
2 Ⓐ Ⓑ Ⓒ Ⓓ Ⓔ  14 Ⓐ Ⓑ Ⓒ Ⓓ Ⓔ  26 Ⓐ Ⓑ Ⓒ Ⓓ Ⓔ  38 Ⓐ Ⓑ Ⓒ Ⓓ Ⓔ  50 Ⓐ Ⓑ Ⓒ Ⓓ Ⓔ
3 Ⓐ Ⓑ Ⓒ Ⓓ Ⓔ  15 Ⓐ Ⓑ Ⓒ Ⓓ Ⓔ  27 Ⓐ Ⓑ Ⓒ Ⓓ Ⓔ  39 Ⓐ Ⓑ Ⓒ Ⓓ Ⓔ  51 Ⓐ Ⓑ Ⓒ Ⓓ Ⓔ
4 Ⓐ Ⓑ Ⓒ Ⓓ Ⓔ  16 Ⓐ Ⓑ Ⓒ Ⓓ Ⓔ  28 Ⓐ Ⓑ Ⓒ Ⓓ Ⓔ  40 Ⓐ Ⓑ Ⓒ Ⓓ Ⓔ  52 Ⓐ Ⓑ Ⓒ Ⓓ Ⓔ
5 Ⓐ Ⓑ Ⓒ Ⓓ Ⓔ  17 Ⓐ Ⓑ Ⓒ Ⓓ Ⓔ  29 Ⓐ Ⓑ Ⓒ Ⓓ Ⓔ  41 Ⓐ Ⓑ Ⓒ Ⓓ Ⓔ  53 Ⓐ Ⓑ Ⓒ Ⓓ Ⓔ
6 Ⓐ Ⓑ Ⓒ Ⓓ Ⓔ  18 Ⓐ Ⓑ Ⓒ Ⓓ Ⓔ  30 Ⓐ Ⓑ Ⓒ Ⓓ Ⓔ  42 Ⓐ Ⓑ Ⓒ Ⓓ Ⓔ  54 Ⓐ Ⓑ Ⓒ Ⓓ Ⓔ
7 Ⓐ Ⓑ Ⓒ Ⓓ Ⓔ  19 Ⓐ Ⓑ Ⓒ Ⓓ Ⓔ  31 Ⓐ Ⓑ Ⓒ Ⓓ Ⓔ  43 Ⓐ Ⓑ Ⓒ Ⓓ Ⓔ  55 Ⓐ Ⓑ Ⓒ Ⓓ Ⓔ
8 Ⓐ Ⓑ Ⓒ Ⓓ Ⓔ  20 Ⓐ Ⓑ Ⓒ Ⓓ Ⓔ  32 Ⓐ Ⓑ Ⓒ Ⓓ Ⓔ  44 Ⓐ Ⓑ Ⓒ Ⓓ Ⓔ  56 Ⓐ Ⓑ Ⓒ Ⓓ Ⓔ
9 Ⓐ Ⓑ Ⓒ Ⓓ Ⓔ  21 Ⓐ Ⓑ Ⓒ Ⓓ Ⓔ  33 Ⓐ Ⓑ Ⓒ Ⓓ Ⓔ  45 Ⓐ Ⓑ Ⓒ Ⓓ Ⓔ  57 Ⓐ Ⓑ Ⓒ Ⓓ Ⓔ
10 Ⓐ Ⓑ Ⓒ Ⓓ Ⓔ  22 Ⓐ Ⓑ Ⓒ Ⓓ Ⓔ  34 Ⓐ Ⓑ Ⓒ Ⓓ Ⓔ  46 Ⓐ Ⓑ Ⓒ Ⓓ Ⓔ  58 Ⓐ Ⓑ Ⓒ Ⓓ Ⓔ
11 Ⓐ Ⓑ Ⓒ Ⓓ Ⓔ  23 Ⓐ Ⓑ Ⓒ Ⓓ Ⓔ  35 Ⓐ Ⓑ Ⓒ Ⓓ Ⓔ  47 Ⓐ Ⓑ Ⓒ Ⓓ Ⓔ  59 Ⓐ Ⓑ Ⓒ Ⓓ Ⓔ
12 Ⓐ Ⓑ Ⓒ Ⓓ Ⓔ  24 Ⓐ Ⓑ Ⓒ Ⓓ Ⓔ  36 Ⓐ Ⓑ Ⓒ Ⓓ Ⓔ  48 Ⓐ Ⓑ Ⓒ Ⓓ Ⓔ  60 Ⓐ Ⓑ Ⓒ Ⓓ Ⓔ

## Section 4

1 Ⓐ Ⓑ Ⓒ Ⓓ Ⓔ  6 Ⓐ Ⓑ Ⓒ Ⓓ Ⓔ  11 Ⓐ Ⓑ Ⓒ Ⓓ Ⓔ  16 Ⓐ Ⓑ Ⓒ Ⓓ Ⓔ  21 Ⓐ Ⓑ Ⓒ Ⓓ Ⓔ
2 Ⓐ Ⓑ Ⓒ Ⓓ Ⓔ  7 Ⓐ Ⓑ Ⓒ Ⓓ Ⓔ  12 Ⓐ Ⓑ Ⓒ Ⓓ Ⓔ  17 Ⓐ Ⓑ Ⓒ Ⓓ Ⓔ  22 Ⓐ Ⓑ Ⓒ Ⓓ Ⓔ
3 Ⓐ Ⓑ Ⓒ Ⓓ Ⓔ  8 Ⓐ Ⓑ Ⓒ Ⓓ Ⓔ  13 Ⓐ Ⓑ Ⓒ Ⓓ Ⓔ  18 Ⓐ Ⓑ Ⓒ Ⓓ Ⓔ  23 Ⓐ Ⓑ Ⓒ Ⓓ Ⓔ
4 Ⓐ Ⓑ Ⓒ Ⓓ Ⓔ  9 Ⓐ Ⓑ Ⓒ Ⓓ Ⓔ  14 Ⓐ Ⓑ Ⓒ Ⓓ Ⓔ  19 Ⓐ Ⓑ Ⓒ Ⓓ Ⓔ  24 Ⓐ Ⓑ Ⓒ Ⓓ Ⓔ
5 Ⓐ Ⓑ Ⓒ Ⓓ Ⓔ  10 Ⓐ Ⓑ Ⓒ Ⓓ Ⓔ  15 Ⓐ Ⓑ Ⓒ Ⓓ Ⓔ  20 Ⓐ Ⓑ Ⓒ Ⓓ Ⓔ  25 Ⓐ Ⓑ Ⓒ Ⓓ Ⓔ

## Section 5

1 Ⓐ Ⓑ Ⓒ Ⓓ Ⓔ  5 Ⓐ Ⓑ Ⓒ Ⓓ Ⓔ  9 Ⓐ Ⓑ Ⓒ Ⓓ Ⓔ  13 Ⓐ Ⓑ Ⓒ Ⓓ Ⓔ
2 Ⓐ Ⓑ Ⓒ Ⓓ Ⓔ  6 Ⓐ Ⓑ Ⓒ Ⓓ Ⓔ  10 Ⓐ Ⓑ Ⓒ Ⓓ Ⓔ  14 Ⓐ Ⓑ Ⓒ Ⓓ Ⓔ
3 Ⓐ Ⓑ Ⓒ Ⓓ Ⓔ  7 Ⓐ Ⓑ Ⓒ Ⓓ Ⓔ  11 Ⓐ Ⓑ Ⓒ Ⓓ Ⓔ  15 Ⓐ Ⓑ Ⓒ Ⓓ Ⓔ
4 Ⓐ Ⓑ Ⓒ Ⓓ Ⓔ  8 Ⓐ Ⓑ Ⓒ Ⓓ Ⓔ  12 Ⓐ Ⓑ Ⓒ Ⓓ Ⓔ  16 Ⓐ Ⓑ Ⓒ Ⓓ Ⓔ

**Experimental Section – See page 9 for details.**

THIS PAGE INTENTIONALLY LEFT BLANK.

## Writing Sample

Schools would like to get to know you better through an essay you write. If you choose to write a personal essay, base your essay on the topic presented in A. If you choose to write a general essay, base your essay on the topic presented in B. Please fill in the circle next to your choice.

Ⓐ With what literary character do you most identify and why?

Ⓑ When making important decisions, should you rely only on factual information, or is it sometimes better to follow your gut instinct? Support your answer with reasons and examples.

**Use this page and the next page to complete your writing sample.**

*Continue on next page*

## SECTION 1
## 25 Questions

Following each problem in this section, there are five suggested answers. Work each problem in your head or in the blank space provided at the right of the page. Then look at the five suggested answers and decide which one is best.

<u>Note</u>: Figures that accompany problems in this section are drawn as accurately as possible EXCEPT when it is stated in a specific problem that its figure is not drawn to scale.

Sample Problem:

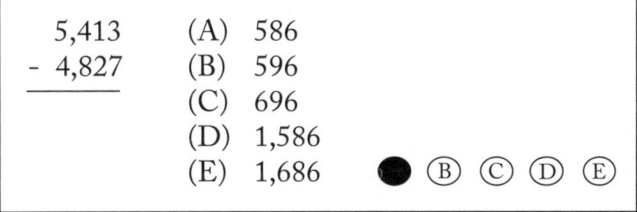

$$\begin{array}{r} 5{,}413 \\ -\ 4{,}827 \\ \hline \end{array}$$

(A)  586
(B)  596
(C)  696
(D)  1,586
(E)  1,686

**USE THIS SPACE FOR FIGURING.**

1.  Each of the following has the same value EXCEPT

(A)  $3 \times \frac{2}{3}$

(B)  $6 \times \frac{2}{6}$

(C)  $9 \times \frac{2}{9}$

(D)  $12 \times \frac{1}{6}$

(E)  $14 \times \frac{1}{6}$

2.  Which of the following is a possible value of $x$ for which
$2x(x - 4) = 0$ ?

(A)  −4
(B)  −2
(C)  2
(D)  4
(E)  8

**GO ON TO THE NEXT PAGE.**

**USE THIS SPACE FOR FIGURING.**

3. Cho has 14 books, and Amy has *b* more books than Cho. In terms of *b*, how many books does Amy have?

(A) $\dfrac{b}{14}$

(B) $\dfrac{14}{b}$

(C) $b - 14$

(D) $14 - b$

(E) $14 + b$

---

4. In the square shown, *M* is the midpoint of side $\overline{CD}$. If the shaded region has an area of 1 square centimeter, what is the area of the square, in square centimeters?

(A) 10
(B) 8
(C) 7
(D) 6
(E) 5

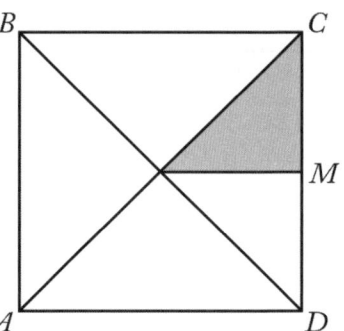

---

5. In the figure, lines *l* and *m* intersect, as shown. What is the value of *x* ?

(A) 40
(B) 50
(C) 80
(D) 100
(E) 160

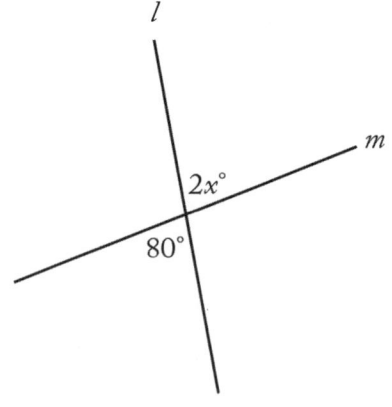

---

50, 10, 40, 20, 70, 60, 20

6. What is the median of the list of numbers above?

(A) 20
(B) 30
(C) 40
(D) 50
(E) 60

**GO ON TO THE NEXT PAGE.**

**USE THIS SPACE FOR FIGURING.**

$$(3x^2 - 2x + 1) - (2x^2 + x)$$

7. Which of the following is equivalent to the expression above?

(A) $5x^2 - 2x + 1$
(B) $5x^2 - x + 1$
(C) $x^2 - 3x + 1$
(D) $x^2 - 2x + 1$
(E) $x^2 - x + 1$

---

8. Factor: $x^2 - x - 2$

(A) $2x(x - 1)$
(B) $(x - 1)(x - 2)$
(C) $(x - 1)(x + 2)$
(D) $(x + 1)(x - 2)$
(E) $(x + 1)(x + 2)$

---

$$-2, 0, 2, 0, -2, 0, 2, 0, \ldots$$

9. In the sequence above, $-2$ is the first term.
If the pattern $-2, 0, 2, 0$ repeats itself indefinitely, which of the following terms has a value of $-2$?

(A) 32nd
(B) 33rd
(C) 34th
(D) 35th
(E) 36th

---

10. If $4(x - 1) = 2(8 + x)$, what is the value of $x$?

(A) 2
(B) 3
(C) 5
(D) 9
(E) 10

**GO ON TO THE NEXT PAGE.**

**USE THIS SPACE FOR FIGURING.**

11. There are 10 people waiting in line for a carriage ride to the park. No more than four people can go in each carriage. If no two carriages have the same number of people, what is the least number of carriages required to accommodate the 10 people?

(A) Two
(B) Four
(C) Five
(D) Eight
(E) Ten

12. It takes $\frac{2}{3}$ of a minute for a machine to make one bolt. What is the greatest number of bolts the machine can make in an hour?

(A) 20
(B) 40
(C) 80
(D) 90
(E) 120

13. The graph of the inequality $y < x$ is shown in the $xy$-coordinate plane. If point $A$ is contained within the shaded region, which of the following could be the coordinates of $A$?

(A) $(-2, 0)$
(B) $(0, 1)$
(C) $(1, 1)$
(D) $(1, 2)$
(E) $(2, 1)$

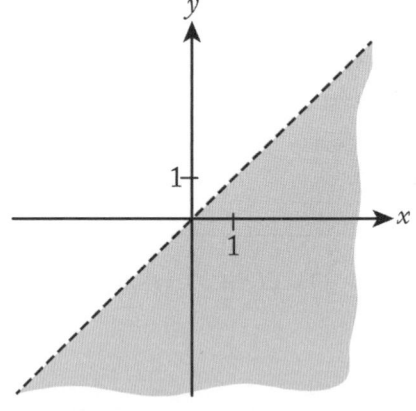

14. What is the perimeter, in centimeters, of the figure shown?

(A) 23
(B) 31
(C) 38
(D) 40
(E) 41

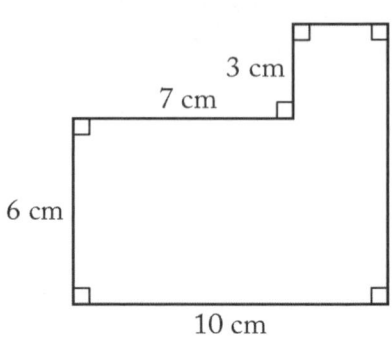

**GO ON TO THE NEXT PAGE.**

**USE THIS SPACE FOR FIGURING.**

15. In the $xy$-coordinate plane, the coordinates of $\triangle ABC$ are $A(2, 3)$, $B(8, 3)$, and $C(2, -5)$. What is the length of side $\overline{BC}$?

    (A)  7
    (B)  8.5
    (C)  9
    (D) 10
    (E) 14

---

16. Which of the following must be true if two numbers, $x$ and $y$, have a mean of 40 and $y$ is less than $x$?

    (A)  $x = 40 + y$
    (B)  $x + y = 40$
    (C)  $x - y = 20$
    (D)  $x = 40$ and $y = 40$
    (E)  $x - 40 = 40 - y$

---

17. In a survey taken of 60 households, 40 households reported having a dog and 30 households reported having a cat. If half of all households having a cat also have a dog, how many households reported having neither a dog nor a cat?

    (A)  5
    (B) 10
    (C) 15
    (D) 20
    (E) 25

---

18. Taxi fare is \$1.50 for the first mile and \$0.40 for each additional $\frac{1}{2}$ mile. How many miles can a passenger ride for \$6.30?

    (A) 7
    (B) 7.5
    (C) 8
    (D) 8.5
    (E) 9

**GO ON TO THE NEXT PAGE.**

**EMA**
**SSAT**

19. If $a = 2b$ and $3b = 5c$, what is the value of $\frac{c}{a}$ ?

(A) $\frac{3}{10}$

(B) $\frac{3}{5}$

(C) $\frac{5}{6}$

(D) $\frac{10}{3}$

(E) It cannot be determined from the information given.

---

20. In a particular deck of cards, each card has A, B, or C on the front and either a circle or a square on the back. Michael claims that every card with a C on the front has a circle on the back. Which of the following cards from the deck of cards would <u>disprove</u> Michael's claim?

(A) A on the front, circle on the back
(B) A on the front, square on the back
(C) B on the front, circle on the back
(D) B on the front, square on the back
(E) C on the front, square on the back

---

21. If a number is increased by 50% of its value and the result is then decreased by 50% of this new value, what will be the percent change from the original number to the final result?

(A) 25% decrease
(B) 50% decrease
(C) 0% change
(D) 25% increase
(E) 50% increase

---

22. If $a + b$ represents a positive number that is divisible by 7, which of the following must also be divisible by 7 ?

(A) $a - \frac{b}{7}$

(B) $(a \times b) + 7$

(C) $a + (7 \times b)$

(D) $(7 \times a) + b$

(E) $(2 \times a) + (2 \times b)$

**GO ON TO THE NEXT PAGE.**

**USE THIS SPACE FOR FIGURING.**

23. At an online retailer, each bag of potting soil costs $32.30 and each flower pot costs $7.64. If Tucker uses a $100 gift card to buy 2 bags of potting soil and 1 flower pot, and no taxes or shipping charges are applied, how much money will be left on the gift card?

    (A) $27.76
    (B) $38.86
    (C) $47.58
    (D) $52.42
    (E) $72.24

24. In the circle shown, segment $\overline{AD}$ is the diameter of the circle, and $AB = BC = CD = 4$. What is the circumference of the circle?

    (A)  $7\pi$
    (B)  $12\pi$
    (C)  $14\pi$
    (D)  $24\pi$
    (E)  $36\pi$

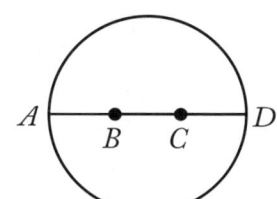

25. What is the value of $8 - 16 \div 8 - 4$ ?

    (A)  −5
    (B)  −2
    (C)   2
    (D)   4
    (E)  10

# STOP

**IF YOU FINISH BEFORE TIME IS CALLED, YOU MAY CHECK YOUR WORK ON THIS SECTION ONLY.**
**DO NOT TURN TO ANY OTHER SECTION IN THE TEST.**

 EMA
SSAT

SECTION 2
40 Questions

Enrollment
Management
Association

Read each passage carefully and then answer the questions about it. For each question, decide on the basis of the passage which one of the choices best answers the question.

---

Being small, solitary, herbivorous, and cuddly has not been much help to the koala. Long before it could blame its troubles on an airline advertising campaign, the two-foot tall Australian marsupial was hunted almost to extinction for its furry pelt. Only since the koala was declared a protected species in the late 1920s has it made something of a comeback. So perhaps
*Line 5* the koala could be forgiven for thinking that life might be more bearable if it were closer to the size of a real bear.

In fact, it once was. Rooting around a southern Australian cave in 1985, spelunker Graham Pilkington uncovered a fossilized jaw fragment of a creature later identified as a giant koala, which probably inhabited the continent more than a million years ago. The jawbone and front molars are
10 about twice the size of those of a present-day koala. This suggests that the creature was more than three feet tall and weighed between 45 and 65 pounds. Not exactly a grizzly bear, but about two to three times as heavy as modern koalas.

Still, as the curator of fossils at the South Australian Museum explains, this larger size may have been a mixed blessing. Although the giant koala was perhaps better equipped to ward
15 off foes, it probably subsisted on the same diet of eucalyptus leaves its descendants favor. Not all eucalyptus branches could have supported that much weight, so dining out could have been an adventure for a giant koala. Worse still, late in the Pleistocene period, a series of droughts ravaged southeastern Australia, wiping out many species including the giant koala. Hardier and requiring less sustenance, only smaller members of the koala family survived.

---

1. According to the passage, which of the following is true of the giant koalas?

   (A) They were not able to climb eucalyptus trees.
   (B) They were less than two feet tall.
   (C) They were frequently attacked by other animals.
   (D) They became extinct during the Pleistocene period.
   (E) They became a protected species in the 1920s.

2. It can be inferred from the passage that grizzly bears are

   (A) larger than giant koalas
   (B) extremely ferocious
   (C) an endangered species
   (D) herbivorous creatures
   (E) usually found in caves

3. The author's use of which of the following words is an example of a pun?

   (A) "solitary" (line 1)
   (B) "hunted" (line 3)
   (C) "pelt" (line 3)
   (D) "bearable" (line 5)
   (E) "favor" (line 15)

4. "Rooting around" (line 7) could be replaced by which of the following without changing the author's meaning?

   (A) Camping near
   (B) Hurrying through
   (C) Striding toward
   (D) Falling across
   (E) Poking about

5. The passage contains information to answer which of the following questions?

   (A) How many front molars did the giant koala have?
   (B) How long ago did the giant koalas probably live in Australia?
   (C) How did the giant koala defend itself against its enemies?
   (D) What were the pelts of koalas used for?
   (E) What troubles can the present-day koala blame on an airline advertising campaign?

**GO ON TO THE NEXT PAGE.**

Radiation from the Sun continuously breaks two-atom oxygen molecules into single atoms. Some of these link up with ordinary oxygen molecules and form ozone. Some rejoin other free singles and revert to stable molecules. This Sun-energy process, if left undisturbed, maintains a fairly constant supply of ozone above the Earth's surface. The ozone layer begins about eight miles
*Line 5* up and is distributed thinly to about thirty miles up. This lofty umbrella of ozone shields the Earth from much of the Sun's deadly ultraviolet rays. Without the ozone cover, life on Earth would be literally sunburned to death.

Some scientists believe that relatively small amounts of synthetic chemicals, such as spray-can fluorocarbon or jet exhaust, reach the upper limits of the atmosphere and break down the
10 three-atom ozone molecules. It is also believed that just one atom of spray-can or jet pollutant can affect vast numbers of ozone molecules. Weather research satellites have observed the ozone shield in great detail, but their data have neither put to rest the "doomsday theories" nor incited a global campaign to stop destroying the Earth's protective covering.

6. According to the passage, ozone is a
   (A) kind of radiation
   (B) deadly ultraviolet ray
   (C) combination of oxygen atoms
   (D) synthetic chemical
   (E) free-floating atom

7. Concern about ozone has recently increased because it is thought that
   (A) ultraviolet rays are destroying the ozone
   (B) radiation is breaking up the ozone molecules
   (C) synthetic chemicals are damaging the ozone shield
   (D) pollutants are causing the ozone layer to drop closer to Earth
   (E) jets are endangering their passengers by entering the ozone shield

8. From the passage, it can be concluded that life on Earth would be threatened if
   (A) ozone ever combined with ordinary molecules
   (B) scientists stopped producing synthetic chemicals
   (C) atmospheric forces drastically changed the weather
   (D) ultraviolet radiation reaching Earth's surface rose significantly
   (E) Earth's ozone layer expanded to a multiple of its present size

9. Which of the following would be the best title for the passage?
   (A) The Many Uses of Weather Satellites
   (B) Dangers Caused by Radiation
   (C) The Discovery of Ultraviolet Rays
   (D) Scientists Study the Sun-Energy Process
   (E) Some Facts and Theories About the Ozone Layer

**GO ON TO THE NEXT PAGE.**

Since communities were first established, women have been involved in statecraft. In ancient Egypt, however, the few who exerted more than nominal power possessed extraordinary qualities. One of the first women of distinction was Hatshepsut, the only woman pharaoh in history, who ruled Egypt between 1503 and 1482 B.C. Whereas previous Egyptian consorts had used indirect
*Line 5* influence in government, Hatshepsut ruled openly after her husband, the pharaoh, died. She was sufficiently influential to exercise supreme power when she became regent to her husband's six-year-old son.

Hatshepsut surrounded herself with people of outstanding administrative and intellectual abilities. When she renounced the regency and declared herself pharaoh, she successfully chal-
*10* lenged the 2,000-year-old tradition of masculine rule in an extremely conservative civilization.

She also avoided what had been the pharaoh's major occupation, waging war. Her 20-year reign was devoted to peace and prosperity. She encouraged agriculture and trade and established sea routes to replace long, arduous, overland journeys. The arts, especially architecture, flourished under her patronage, as her funerary temple at Deir al-Bahri and the two obelisks at Karnak dem-
*15* onstrate.

When she died, her constructive influence ended and her husband's son became pharaoh. He smashed her statues and erased her name from monuments, thus belittling Queen Hatshepsut's accomplishments. To this day, Hatshepsut is less renowned even though she was a far more capable ruler than the famous Queen Cleopatra.

10. The author suggests that in ancient Egypt before Hatshepsut's time, women had

(A) not been involved in trade
(B) frequently held minor posts in Egyptian government
(C) not been allowed to take part in public functions
(D) shown little interest in government
(E) wielded little direct political power

11. It can be inferred from the passage that before Hatshepsut's reign, Egypt was

(A) not concerned with education
(B) often engaged in military conflict
(C) hampered by inept rulers
(D) often conquered by rival nations
(E) not a world power

12. The author's attitude toward Hatshepsut can best be described as

(A) tactfully critical
(B) tentatively favorable
(C) openly admiring
(D) mildly condescending
(E) smugly disdainful

13. The passage provides information that helps answer which of the following questions?

I. What role had women played in Egyptian politics before Hatshepsut's time?

II. What effect did Hatshepsut's rule have on Egypt?

III. What products were transported over the trade routes established by Hatshepsut?

(A) I only
(B) II only
(C) III only
(D) I and II only
(E) II and III only

14. Which of the following titles best fits the content of the passage?

(A) A Most Unusual Pharaoh
(B) The First Pharaohs of Egypt
(C) Statecraft in the Pre-Christian Era
(D) Pharaohs: Rulers of Limited Influence
(E) Rulers of Egypt: 1500 B.C.E. to the Present

**GO ON TO THE NEXT PAGE.**

Dance Theater of Harlem is one of the great successes of our time. The survival of the company and the way it has found a secure place in an increasingly crowded dance world are considerable accomplishments. Of greater significance, though, are the consistently high levels of the company's dancing and the unfailing enthusiasm of each performer. Of all the ballet companies

Line 5     that regularly appear in New York, it shows the least danger of succumbing to routine.

Arthur Mitchell's Dance Theater of Harlem is animated by a sense of purpose that is largely moral in nature. In the midst of the despair that followed the assassination of Dr. Martin Luther King, Jr., in 1968, Mitchell was determined to give Black people a place in ballet. He sought to help other Black dancers so that they would not have to face the difficulties he

10     faced.

Nobody was better qualified than Mitchell to understand what Black dancers could do in ballet if given the incentive and the opportunity, and time has proved his faith well-founded. But Mitchell is too shrewd an artistic administrator and too serious an artist not to know that the only standard he and his company can in the long run be guided by is artistic. As he said in an

15     interview, ". . . maybe, eventually, we'll get to the day when Dance Theater of Harlem is no longer thought of as a good Black company, but a good ballet company."

That day, so far as I'm concerned, has already arrived.

15. The author's primary purpose is to
(A) encourage the establishment of more African American ballet companies
(B) clarify the motives underlying the formation of ballet companies
(C) contrast the artistic qualities of various ballet companies
(D) discuss the success of one ballet company
(E) describe how a ballet company is formed

16. Which of the following could be used in place of "a secure" (line 2) without changing the author's meaning?
(A) a shielded
(B) a private
(C) an overconfident
(D) an orderly
(E) an assured

17. The author implies which of the following about ballet companies?
(A) Many contemporary ballet companies have incorporated modern dance into their repertoires.
(B) Not all ballet companies survive against their competitors.
(C) The best dancers often leave the ballet companies that gave them their start.
(D) Most ballet companies regularly appear in New York City.
(E) Most ballet companies maintain high levels of performance.

18. The author's attitude toward Dance Theater of Harlem can best be described as one of
(A) enthusiastic approval
(B) cautious optimism
(C) perplexed bewilderment
(D) theoretical justification
(E) impulsive criticism

**GO ON TO THE NEXT PAGE.**

19. In lines 14-16 the author indicates that Mitchell's view of the artistic standards by which the Dance Theater of Harlem will be judged is

(A) regrettable
(B) simplistic
(C) noncommittal
(D) unselfish
(E) realistic

20. The passage provides information to answer all of the following questions EXCEPT

(A) Does Dance Theater of Harlem perform frequently in New York City?
(B) How do the dancers in the company view Dance Theater of Harlem?
(C) Has Dance Theater of Harlem begun to be fully accepted by ballet audiences?
(D) Has Dance Theater of Harlem justified the faith of its founder?
(E) Why did Mitchell establish Dance Theater of Harlem?

**GO ON TO THE NEXT PAGE.**

The barrier islands are slender, shifting piles of sand hugging the Atlantic and Gulf coasts of the United States from Maine to Texas. Actually, not all are islands, many are peninsulas or sand spits with tenuous connections to the mainland. The barriers include some of the country's bleakest yet most beautiful beaches, as well as many that are depressing waterfront strips of high-rise apart-
*Line 5* ments and fast-food places.

But now many barrier beaches are washing away, largely because too many people are living on them. Communities that once faced broad seashores now huddle behind stone walls, just yards from the ocean. Construction of seawalls helps save houses but ultimately destroys beaches by ignoring an unalterable fact—it is natural for barrier beaches to move. High seas and powerful
10 storms normally fling sand from the front of the island toward the sound behind, slowly pushing the barrier back over on itself. The barriers have been shifting this way ever since they were formed. Any structure built to hold the beaches in place interferes with powerful ocean forces and ends up increasing erosion it was meant to prevent.

The dilemma of the barrier beaches is that whether people leave them alone or try to mold
15 them to suit human needs, someone loses. One way out of the dilemma is to move the cottages and resorts off the beach. Abandoning the beaches seems an admission of defeat, but no human is a match for the ocean. Many miles of beaches have already been irreversibly destroyed. We now are confronted with two mutually exclusive choices—buildings or beaches.

21. The author's primary purpose is to

(A) recount the history of the barrier beaches

(B) compare the erosion on the Atlantic coast with the erosion on the Gulf coast

(C) highlight the threat to barrier beaches

(D) give examples of the power of the ocean

(E) explain why people build resorts on the barrier beaches

22. According to the passage, the barrier beaches are in danger of washing away primarily because they are

(A) overdeveloped

(B) shifting

(C) slender

(D) delicate

(E) unreinforced

23. The passage provides information to answer which of the following questions?

I. When were barrier beaches first formed?

II. How do seawalls affect barrier beaches?

III. Which barrier beaches have been destroyed so far?

(A) I only

(B) II only

(C) III only

(D) I and II only

(E) I, II, and III

24. The passage was most likely taken from a

(A) vacation brochure

(B) guidebook about the Gulf coast

(C) glossary of geologic terms

(D) popular science magazine

(E) textbook on marine biology

**GO ON TO THE NEXT PAGE.**

25. According to the passage, the tendency of barrier beaches to move and change is

    (A) inexplicable
    (B) diminishing
    (C) normal
    (D) unpredictable
    (E) limited

26. By saying that we have "two mutually exclusive choices" (line 18), the author means that we

    (A) can rebuild some of the barrier beaches or we can destroy them all
    (B) can have either beaches or buildings on the barrier islands, but not both
    (C) must mold the beaches to suit our needs or stop trying to develop them at all
    (D) must design beachfront homes more carefully or risk their destruction
    (E) must build more seawalls to protect the beaches or resign ourselves to losing all barrier beaches

**GO ON TO THE NEXT PAGE.**

Human longing for social participation leads to a fear of being alone, and the desire for occasional solitude tends to be overcome by this fear. Thus the need for privacy may eventually be completely submerged in the overpowering need to be *with*. When such an annihilation of privacy is achieved, a person is, indeed, in danger of self-annihilation, of becoming a living automaton

*Line 5* at the mercy of anyone who knows how to make him or her tick. In such a society one becomes grateful to "Big Brother" for assuming the task of directing the life one is no longer capable of directing oneself. In this way does the annihilation of privacy lead to the annihilation of the person, and of society; for the healthy society depends up on the ability of individuals to think and reflect upon what true society is—and without the privacy to think and reflect, people and society are lost.

27. The author's primary purpose in the passage is to present his views about

(A) the value of social participation to the individual

(B) the importance of social responsibility in a democracy

(C) the dangers of a lack of individual privacy

(D) several characteristics of a healthy society

(E) techniques for ensuring privacy

28. According to the author, why is the privacy of individuals so important to society?

(A) Society depends on social participation.

(B) Privacy fosters the development of democratic values.

(C) Without privacy the individual personality cannot respond to "Big Brother."

(D) Privacy enables individuals to reflect on the nature of society.

(E) Group effort is impossible without privacy.

29. The author suggests that all of the following could be in danger of destruction EXCEPT

(A) the individual personality

(B) human longing for social participation

(C) society as it now exists

(D) a person's ability to think independently

(E) the individual's desire for privacy

30. In the sentence beginning "When such an annihilation" (lines 3-4), a human being is compared to a

(A) time bomb

(B) guinea pig

(C) martyr

(D) statue

(E) robot

**GO ON TO THE NEXT PAGE.**

Social scientists agree that everyone in a generation is not identical. Nevertheless, many demographers assert that generalizations about the distinct characters of birth groups are helpful for social analysis. They aid in designing policy and education targeted toward the unique characteristics of specific cohorts. A case in point are those born between 1981 and 2000, dubbed "The Millennial
*Line 5* Generation" because they are the first adults of the 21st century. According to the Pew Research Center, a think tank, the current group of 13 to 29 year-olds is more ethnically and racially diverse than any other similarly-aged cohort in our history. Many believe this explains their tendency to see themselves as global citizens. Millennials have been described as "digital natives" because of their total comfort with technology. This is in stark contrast with previous generations, such as the Silent
10 Generation, born before 1946; the Baby Boomers, born during the spike in births between 1946-1964 that followed World War II; or even Generation X, born between 1965-1980. Millennials inhabit a world where personal devices have always existed and are all around us, as ubiquitous as the air we breathe. Because two-thirds of Millennials voted for Barack Obama for president in 2008, some suggest that Millennials are more politically progressive than previous generations. While some
15 authors call Millennials narcissistic, others believe rather that this generation is notably unselfish and eager to be of service to others. Many sociologists believe that understanding Millennials will make those who work with them more productive citizens.

31. In line 7, "cohort" refers to a

(A) research facility
(B) racial minority
(C) detachment of soldiers
(D) group of contemporaries
(E) team of social scientists

32. The passage indicates that the predecessors of the Baby Boomers

(A) were born after 1946
(B) belonged to Generation X
(C) were called the Boomers
(D) belonged to the Silent Generation
(E) were more progressive than Millennials

33. The passage suggests that Baby Boomers

(A) fought in the Second World War
(B) were born before 1946
(C) are younger than Generation X
(D) are more diverse than the Millennials
(E) are less progressive than the Millennials

34. Which of the following can be concluded based on the information in the passage?

(A) The Pew Research Center studies the voting habits of distinct generational cohorts.
(B) Generalizations about generational cohorts may enhance educational practices.
(C) Some members of Generation X are beginning to shun electronic devices.
(D) Generational cohorts are assigned nicknames that reflect their members' natures.
(E) It is a principle of social science that it is necessary to categorize generations.

**GO ON TO THE NEXT PAGE.**

Women played an important part in Iroquois society. The fields, the crops, the houses, belonged to them. Descent was traced through the women; a child belonged to its mother's clan. Men, when they married, went to live with their wives. If the marriage broke up, the man went home to mother, leaving his children behind him.

*Line 5* Each clan was divided into "lineages" whose members were all descended from a common ancestor. At the head of each lineage was an older woman, the matron. Certain lineages were called "noble" and from them the various chiefs or sachems were chosen. The term "sachem" is used here for those chiefs who sat in the tribal council and helped to rule the tribe.

When a sachem died, the matron of his lineage selected his successor from among the men of
10 his lineage, then announced her choice to the other women of her longhouse, the name of the communal dwelling, and then to the clan as a whole. Undoubtedly the choice was talked over carefully among the women before it was announced, because once made public, the choice was almost always ratified. When the period of mourning for the dead chief ended, the candidate was installed and presented with the official deer horns.

15 If the new sachem did badly, the matron warned him three times. If he still did not improve, she would "remove the horns" by asking the council to depose him. The council seldom failed to do so. In short, although the women did not rule or give orders, they did choose the rulers and, by their power of recall, had a good deal of influence over them.

35. Which of the following best expresses the main idea of the passage?

(A) The Iroquois were governed by a tribal council.
(B) Women exerted a great deal of influence among the Iroquois.
(C) Iroquois women were wealthier than Iroquois men.
(D) Iroquois women were responsible for deciding the period of mourning for a chief.
(E) Only Iroquois from "noble" lineages could help rule the tribe.

36. If an Iroquois marriage failed, what probably happened to the couple's fields?

(A) They remained in the wife's possession.
(B) They reverted to the husband's family.
(C) They were turned over to the entire tribe.
(D) They were confiscated by the sachems.
(E) They were held in trust for the children.

37. It can be inferred from the passage that a sachem was

(A) the oldest man in his lineage
(B) the husband of the matron of his lineage
(C) chosen by members of the tribal council
(D) named by the previous sachem as a successor
(E) subject to the approval of the women of his clan

38. According to the passage, a sachem who ruled badly and failed to heed advice was usually

(A) given a mild warning by the tribal council
(B) banished by his clan
(C) removed from office by the tribal council
(D) subjected to public ridicule
(E) ostracized by the other sachems on the tribal council

**GO ON TO THE NEXT PAGE.**

39. It can be inferred from the passage that deer horns

  (A) identified a chief's lineage
  (B) represented material wealth
  (C) were awarded for physical prowess
  (D) signified a state of mourning
  (E) were a chief's symbol of office

40. The tone of the passage is primarily

  (A) colloquial
  (B) explanatory
  (C) humorous
  (D) contemplative
  (E) combative

## STOP

**IF YOU FINISH BEFORE TIME IS CALLED, YOU MAY CHECK YOUR WORK ON THIS SECTION ONLY.
DO NOT TURN TO ANY OTHER SECTION IN THE TEST.**

## SECTION 3
## 60 Questions

This section consists of two different types of questions: synonyms and analogies. There are directions and a sample question for each type.

### Synonyms

Each of the following questions consists of one word followed by five words or phrases. You are to select the one word or phrase whose meaning is closest to the word in capital letters.

Sample Question:

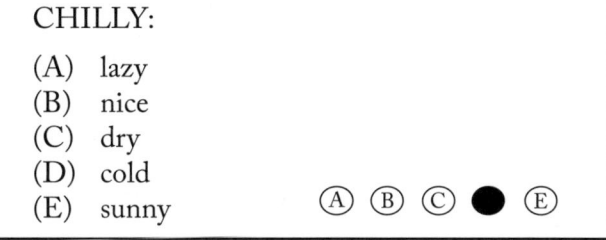

CHILLY:

(A) lazy
(B) nice
(C) dry
(D) cold
(E) sunny

---

1. SUITABLE:

   (A) successful
   (B) appropriate
   (C) exceptional
   (D) resilient
   (E) genuine

2. ROGUE:

   (A) vagrant
   (B) prisoner
   (C) impostor
   (D) scoundrel
   (E) lunatic

3. EXPEL:

   (A) destroy
   (B) pause
   (C) depart
   (D) invest
   (E) eject

4. AUTHENTIC:

   (A) formal
   (B) genuine
   (C) guaranteed
   (D) confident
   (E) original

5. PROSPER:

   (A) thrive
   (B) relax
   (C) explore
   (D) renew
   (E) suggest

6. CONFER:

   (A) verify
   (B) agree
   (C) bestow
   (D) delay
   (E) adhere

7. CLARIFICATION:

   (A) explanation
   (B) amendment
   (C) overcharge
   (D) reproduction
   (E) connection

8. PROVOKE:

   (A) steal
   (B) endorse
   (C) assault
   (D) incite
   (E) recall

**GO ON TO THE NEXT PAGE.**

9. LAVISH:

(A) greedy

(B) emphatic

(C) sentimental

(D) extravagant

(E) festive

10. ARMISTICE:

(A) truce

(B) barracks

(C) brigade

(D) strategy

(E) arsenal

11. DISMANTLE:

(A) run into

(B) argue with

(C) give away

(D) work on

(E) take apart

12. MAGISTRATE:

(A) judge

(B) wizard

(C) soldier

(D) monarch

(E) virtuoso

13. SAGE:

(A) free

(B) lenient

(C) arrogant

(D) placid

(E) wise

14. STRONGHOLD:

(A) prison

(B) vise

(C) fortress

(D) lock

(E) shackle

15. DESTITUTE:

(A) outmoded

(B) melancholy

(C) impoverished

(D) unavoidable

(E) unlawful

16. SOMBER:

(A) alarming

(B) gloomy

(C) feeble

(D) cruel

(E) resistant

17. PANORAMA:

(A) elaborate celebration

(B) universal experience

(C) comprehensive view

(D) extensive collection

(E) total expenditure

18. ETHICAL:

(A) viable

(B) glorious

(C) competent

(D) persuasive

(E) moral

19. MALADY:

(A) crime

(B) mishap

(C) hatred

(D) illness

(E) penalty

20. BOLSTER:

(A) wallop

(B) support

(C) attach

(D) harass

(E) prance

**GO ON TO THE NEXT PAGE.**

21. CONCUR:
    (A) award
    (B) agree
    (C) submit
    (D) discuss
    (E) proceed

22. RELINQUISH:
    (A) surrender
    (B) undermine
    (C) justify
    (D) neglect
    (E) presume

23. MOTIF:
    (A) method
    (B) reason
    (C) theme
    (D) gesture
    (E) gadget

24. CHARACTERIZE:
    (A) describe
    (B) review
    (C) select
    (D) guess
    (E) allege

25. INCORRIGIBLE:
    (A) unjustifiable
    (B) ridiculous
    (C) arrogant
    (D) unattainable
    (E) unmanageable

26. PETULANT:
    (A) indifferent
    (B) faithful
    (C) irritable
    (D) affectionate
    (E) reckless

27. BANAL:
    (A) commonplace
    (B) burdensome
    (C) profound
    (D) harmful
    (E) obscure

28. COMPRISE:
    (A) control
    (B) understand
    (C) invalidate
    (D) contain
    (E) seize

29. FIASCO:
    (A) wall painting
    (B) total failure
    (C) unruly mob
    (D) loud noise
    (E) large vessel

30. DEBILITATE:
    (A) cancel
    (B) weaken
    (C) annoy
    (D) forbid
    (E) dishonor

**GO ON TO THE NEXT PAGE.**

## Analogies

The following questions ask you to find relationships between words. For each question, select the answer choice that best completes the meaning of the sentence.

Sample Question:

> Kitten is to cat as
> (A) fawn is to colt
> (B) puppy is to dog
> (C) cow is to bull
> (D) wolf is to bear
> (E) hen is to rooster
>
> (A) ● (C) (D) (E)

Choice (B) is the best answer because a kitten is a young cat just as a puppy is a young dog. Of all the answer choices, (B) states a relationship that is most like the relationship between <u>kitten</u> and <u>cat</u>.

---

31. Umbrella is to soak as

    (A) lantern is to see
    (B) roof is to protect
    (C) glove is to handle
    (D) sunshine is to bleach
    (E) shield is to wound

32. Scale is to weight as

    (A) decibel is to volume
    (B) map is to destination
    (C) speedometer is to velocity
    (D) calendar is to appointment
    (E) microscope is to size

33. Famine is to food as

    (A) epidemic is to disease
    (B) earthquake is to shelter
    (C) drought is to rain
    (D) hurricane is to storm
    (E) catastrophe is to disaster

34. Wax is to wane as

    (A) advance is to retreat
    (B) plan is to execute
    (C) permit is to allow
    (D) force is to persuade
    (E) whisper is to speak

35. Sponsor is to funding as

    (A) guest is to hospitality
    (B) mediator is to conflict
    (C) dignitary is to rank
    (D) avenger is to injustice
    (E) muse is to inspiration

36. Crude is to refinement as

    (A) deep is to clarity
    (B) bland is to flavor
    (C) irksome is to peeve
    (D) devout is to religion
    (E) tragic is to drama

37. Swarm is to bees as

    (A) drove is to cattle
    (B) stable is to horses
    (C) pond is to frogs
    (D) sky is to birds
    (E) insect is to ants

38. Barrier is to obstruct as

    (A) fortress is to besiege
    (B) anchor is to disembark
    (C) camouflage is to conceal
    (D) boycott is to purchase
    (E) veto is to legislate

**GO ON TO THE NEXT PAGE.**

39. Flirt is to courtship as
    (A) concede is to argument
    (B) achieve is to purpose
    (C) compete is to victory
    (D) exchange is to merchandise
    (E) banter is to conversation

40. Yacht is to boat as
    (A) portrait is to sketch
    (B) constellation is to star
    (C) tragedy is to drama
    (D) banquet is to meal
    (E) palace is to royalty

41. Hover is to airborne as
    (A) protrude is to sharp
    (B) rotate is to clockwise
    (C) totter is to unstable
    (D) capsize is to sunken
    (E) recline is to prone

42. Hungry is to ravenous as
    (A) tiresome is to weary
    (B) fragile is to broken
    (C) friendly is to aloof
    (D) happy is to jubilant
    (E) generous is to needy

43. Flexibility is to bend as
    (A) darkness is to illuminate
    (B) stamina is to endure
    (C) conviction is to prosecute
    (D) uncertainty is to decide
    (E) latitude is to restrict

44. Grope is to search as
    (A) swagger is to walk
    (B) speak is to write
    (C) guess is to predict
    (D) demand is to ask
    (E) throw is to catch

45. Incumbent is to office as
    (A) champion is to title
    (B) tenant is to landlord
    (C) ancestor is to family
    (D) captive is to ransom
    (E) veteran is to army

46. Writing is to erase as
    (A) budget is to exceed
    (B) invitation is to refuse
    (C) building is to demolish
    (D) experiment is to fail
    (E) appliance is to unplug

47. Versatile is to adapt as
    (A) unaware is to notify
    (B) bankrupt is to repay
    (C) reticent is to speak
    (D) strenuous is to exert
    (E) buoyant is to float

48. Abbreviate is to short as
    (A) fortify is to strong
    (B) persist is to durable
    (C) deceive is to false
    (D) accuse is to guilty
    (E) civilize is to wild

49. Invaluable is to worthless as
    (A) immense is to enormous
    (B) belligerent is to peaceful
    (C) famous is to notorious
    (D) vertical is to diagonal
    (E) fearless is to frightening

50. Clientele is to customer as
    (A) management is to company
    (B) neighborhood is to city
    (C) faculty is to student
    (D) electorate is to voter
    (E) audience is to performer

**GO ON TO THE NEXT PAGE.**

51. Appease is to anger as

    (A) wander is to location

    (B) enlighten is to ignorance

    (C) forgive is to transgression

    (D) inquire is to curiosity

    (E) lament is to sorrow

52. Invade is to enter as

    (A) promote is to hire

    (B) construct is to destroy

    (C) contribute is to give

    (D) dislodge is to remove

    (E) require is to need

53. Outcast is to shun as

    (A) idol is to worship

    (B) decoy is to distract

    (C) impostor is to identify

    (D) prophet is to believe

    (E) censor is to prohibit

54. Divulge is to public as

    (A) adorn is to plain

    (B) avoid is to inevitable

    (C) comply is to obedient

    (D) trust is to suspicious

    (E) rectify is to right

55. Plausible is to believe as

    (A) arrogant is to presume

    (B) inquisitive is to question

    (C) cryptic is to understand

    (D) conspicuous is to notice

    (E) jocular is to amuse

56. Survivor is to succumb as

    (A) bachelor is to marry

    (B) benefactor is to donate

    (C) glutton is to devour

    (D) nominee is to support

    (E) defendant is to allege

57. Merciful is to clemency as

    (A) amorous is to jealousy

    (B) culpable is to condemnation

    (C) fastidious is to satisfaction

    (D) privileged is to resentment

    (E) contrite is to remorse

58. Pretense is to reason as

    (A) theory is to evidence

    (B) façade is to appearance

    (C) alibi is to innocence

    (D) error is to correction

    (E) discount is to purchase

59. Obsolete is to disuse as

    (A) timid is to confidence

    (B) vigilant is to danger

    (C) chaotic is to confusion

    (D) content is to ambition

    (E) naïve is to knowledge

60. Impromptu is to preparation as

    (A) logical is to reason

    (B) absurd is to laughter

    (C) reckless is to caution

    (D) courteous is to etiquette

    (E) confidential is to secrecy

# STOP

**IF YOU FINISH BEFORE TIME IS CALLED, YOU MAY CHECK YOUR WORK ON THIS SECTION ONLY.
DO NOT TURN TO ANY OTHER SECTION IN THE TEST.**

## SECTION 4
## 25 Questions

Following each problem in this section, there are five suggested answers. Work each problem in your head or in the blank space provided at the right of the page. Then look at the five suggested answers and decide which one is best.

<u>Note:</u> Figures that accompany problems in this section are drawn as accurately as possible EXCEPT when it is stated in a specific problem that its figure is not drawn to scale.

Sample Problem:

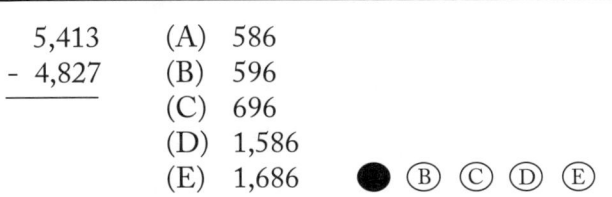

$$
\begin{array}{rl}
5{,}413 & \text{(A)} \quad 586 \\
-\,4{,}827 & \text{(B)} \quad 596 \\
& \text{(C)} \quad 696 \\
& \text{(D)} \quad 1{,}586 \\
& \text{(E)} \quad 1{,}686
\end{array}
$$

● Ⓑ Ⓒ Ⓓ Ⓔ

---

**USE THIS SPACE FOR FIGURING.**

1. In the figure shown, what is the *y*-coordinate of point *J* ?
   - (A) −4
   - (B) −3
   - (C) −2
   - (D) 2
   - (E) 3

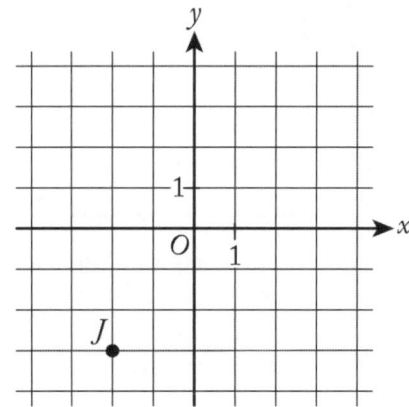

---

2. Of the following, which is closest to the result when 8,105 is divided by 309 ?
   - (A) 15
   - (B) 20
   - (C) 25
   - (D) 30
   - (E) 35

**GO ON TO THE NEXT PAGE.**

$$3x - 7 = 2x - 5$$

3. What value of $x$ is the solution to the equation above?

   (A)  $-12$

   (B)  $-\dfrac{12}{5}$

   (C)  $-2$

   (D)  $\dfrac{2}{5}$

   (E)  $2$

---

4. If the perimeter of a square is 64 inches, what is the length of a side of the square?

   (A)  4 inches
   (B)  6 inches
   (C)  8 inches
   (D)  16 inches
   (E)  32 inches

---

5. A bag contains equal-sized disks that are either red, green, yellow, or blue. There are 6 red disks, 3 green disks, 6 yellow disks, and 5 blue disks. If a disk is selected at random from the bag, what is the probability that the disk will be either red or yellow?

   (A)  $\dfrac{1}{12}$

   (B)  $\dfrac{2}{7}$

   (C)  $\dfrac{3}{5}$

   (D)  $\dfrac{3}{10}$

   (E)  $\dfrac{4}{7}$

**GO ON TO THE NEXT PAGE.**

**USE THIS SPACE FOR FIGURING.**

6. What is the tens digit in the largest 5-digit <u>odd</u> number that can be formed from the digits $4, 0, 5, 6, 2$, where each digit is used once?

   (A) 6
   (B) 5
   (C) 4
   (D) 2
   (E) 0

7. If 4 pears cost $2.80, then, at this rate, how much would 7 pears cost?

   (A) $3.10
   (B) $3.50
   (C) $4.20
   (D) $4.90
   (E) $5.80

8. How many quadrilaterals are there in the figure shown?

   (A) Four
   (B) Five
   (C) Six
   (D) Seven
   (E) Eight

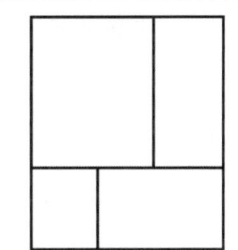

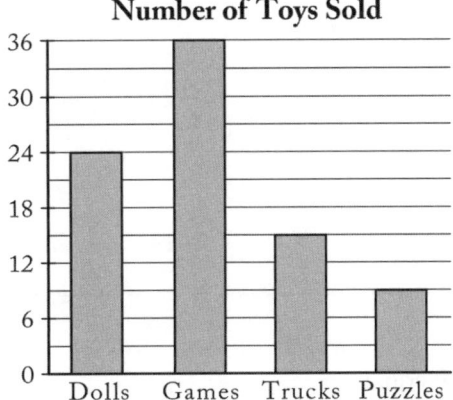

**Number of Toys Sold**

9. Based on the bar graph shown, which of the following statements is correct?

   (A) The number of games sold was more than twice the number of trucks sold.
   (B) The number of games sold was two more than the number of dolls sold.
   (C) The number of dolls sold was greater than the total number of trucks and puzzles sold.
   (D) The number of trucks sold was twice the number of puzzles sold.
   (E) The number of games sold was greater than the total number of dolls and trucks sold.

**GO ON TO THE NEXT PAGE.**

**USE THIS SPACE FOR FIGURING.**

10. If $f(x) = 2x + 5$, then $f(4) + f(7) =$

   (A)  25

   (B)  27

   (C)  32

   (D)  42

   (E)  77

---

$$(x^3)(x^3)x$$

11. Which of the following is equivalent to the expression above?

   (A)  $x^6$

   (B)  $x^7$

   (C)  $x^9$

   (D)  $2x^7$

   (E)  $3x^9$

---

12. In the figure shown, lines $l$ and $m$ are perpendicular. What is the value of $x$ ?

   (A)  40

   (B)  45

   (C)  50

   (D)  55

   (E)  60

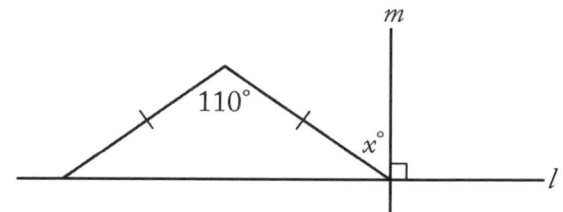

---

13. Which of the following is equivalent to $(x + 4)(x - 4)$ ?

   (A)  $x^2$

   (B)  $x^2 - 8$

   (C)  $x^2 - 16$

   (D)  $x^2 + 8x - 16$

   (E)  $x^2 - 8x - 16$

---

$$3x - 2y = -6$$

14. In the $xy$-coordinate plane, the graph of the equation above is a line that intersects the $x$-axis at point $A$. What are the coordinates of $A$ ?

   (A)  $(-2, 0)$

   (B)  $(2, 0)$

   (C)  $(0, -3)$

   (D)  $(0, 3)$

   (E)  $(3, -2)$

**GO ON TO THE NEXT PAGE.**

   

**USE THIS SPACE FOR FIGURING.**

15. The mean age of three male students is 21, and the mean age of two female students is 19. What is the mean age of all five students?

    (A) 20
    (B) 20.1
    (C) 20.2
    (D) 20.4
    (E) 20.5

16. In the $xy$-coordinate plane, if point $P(4, 3)$ is reflected across the $y$-axis and then translated down 5 units, what are the coordinates of the resulting point?

    (A) $(-9, -2)$
    (B) $(-9, 3)$
    (C) $(-4, -2)$
    (D) $(-1, -3)$
    (E) $(4, -8)$

17. Which of the following is equivalent to $\sqrt{8} + \sqrt{18}$ ?

    (A) 5
    (B) $5\sqrt{2}$
    (C) $6\sqrt{2}$
    (D) $\sqrt{26}$
    (E) $2\sqrt{2} + 2\sqrt{3}$

18. Wendy lives 6 miles from a swimming pool, and Grant lives 14 miles from the same pool. In miles, how far is Wendy's house from Grant's house?

    (A) 8
    (B) 15
    (C) 21
    (D) 28
    (E) It cannot be determined from the information given.

**GO ON TO THE NEXT PAGE.**

19. What is the least common multiple of 6, 10, and 28 ?

    (A)    140
    (B)    210
    (C)    420
    (D)    840
    (E)  1,680

20. Figure 1 shown consists of a single one-inch square.
    Figures 2 and 3 are created by adding one-inch squares
    around the perimeter of the previous figure in the
    sequence, as shown. If this pattern is continued, what
    will be the total number of one-inch squares in Figure 4 ?

    (A)  17
    (B)  19
    (C)  21
    (D)  23
    (E)  25

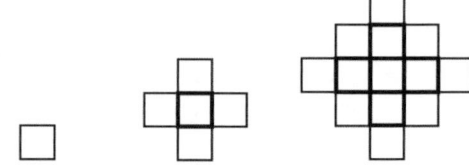

Figure 1    Figure 2    Figure 3

21. How many centimeters are there in 10 kilometers?

    (A)          100
    (B)        1,000
    (C)       10,000
    (D)      100,000
    (E)    1,000,000

22. Isabella has to take five courses next semester:
    Composition, US Geography, Statistics, Chemistry, and
    a seminar. She needs to register for each course. She
    must choose from 2 composition courses, 3 geography
    courses, 2 statistics courses, 5 chemistry courses, and
    7 seminar courses. If no courses meet at the same time,
    how many different combinations of courses are possible
    for Isabella to choose from?

    (A)      17
    (B)      19
    (C)     210
    (D)     420
    (E)   2,100

**GO ON TO THE NEXT PAGE.**

USE THIS SPACE FOR FIGURING.

23. What is the volume of the right triangular prism shown?

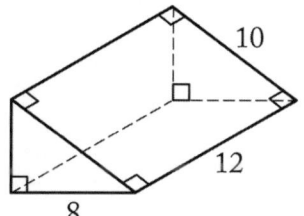

(A) 288

(B) 480

(C) 576

(D) 720

(E) 960

24. The product of $3n$ and 2 less than $n$ equals 9.

Which of the following could be $n$ ?

(A) −3

(B) −2

(C) 1

(D) 2

(E) 3

25. In the $xy$-coordinate plane, what is the slope of a line that is perpendicular to the line with equation $2x + 3y = 6$ ?

(A) $-\frac{3}{2}$

(B) $-\frac{2}{3}$

(C) $-\frac{1}{2}$

(D) $\frac{2}{3}$

(E) $\frac{3}{2}$

## STOP
**IF YOU FINISH BEFORE TIME IS CALLED, YOU MAY CHECK YOUR WORK ON THIS SECTION ONLY.**
**DO NOT TURN TO ANY OTHER SECTION IN THE TEST.**

THIS PAGE INTENTIONALLY LEFT BLANK.

# Practice Test IV: Upper Level Answer Sheet

**Be sure each mark completely fills the circle.**
Start with number 1 for each new section of the test.

## Section 1

| | | | | |
|---|---|---|---|---|
| 1 Ⓐ Ⓑ Ⓒ Ⓓ Ⓔ | 6 Ⓐ Ⓑ Ⓒ Ⓓ Ⓔ | 11 Ⓐ Ⓑ Ⓒ Ⓓ Ⓔ | 16 Ⓐ Ⓑ Ⓒ Ⓓ Ⓔ | 21 Ⓐ Ⓑ Ⓒ Ⓓ Ⓔ |
| 2 Ⓐ Ⓑ Ⓒ Ⓓ Ⓔ | 7 Ⓐ Ⓑ Ⓒ Ⓓ Ⓔ | 12 Ⓐ Ⓑ Ⓒ Ⓓ Ⓔ | 17 Ⓐ Ⓑ Ⓒ Ⓓ Ⓔ | 22 Ⓐ Ⓑ Ⓒ Ⓓ Ⓔ |
| 3 Ⓐ Ⓑ Ⓒ Ⓓ Ⓔ | 8 Ⓐ Ⓑ Ⓒ Ⓓ Ⓔ | 13 Ⓐ Ⓑ Ⓒ Ⓓ Ⓔ | 18 Ⓐ Ⓑ Ⓒ Ⓓ Ⓔ | 23 Ⓐ Ⓑ Ⓒ Ⓓ Ⓔ |
| 4 Ⓐ Ⓑ Ⓒ Ⓓ Ⓔ | 9 Ⓐ Ⓑ Ⓒ Ⓓ Ⓔ | 14 Ⓐ Ⓑ Ⓒ Ⓓ Ⓔ | 19 Ⓐ Ⓑ Ⓒ Ⓓ Ⓔ | 24 Ⓐ Ⓑ Ⓒ Ⓓ Ⓔ |
| 5 Ⓐ Ⓑ Ⓒ Ⓓ Ⓔ | 10 Ⓐ Ⓑ Ⓒ Ⓓ Ⓔ | 15 Ⓐ Ⓑ Ⓒ Ⓓ Ⓔ | 20 Ⓐ Ⓑ Ⓒ Ⓓ Ⓔ | 25 Ⓐ Ⓑ Ⓒ Ⓓ Ⓔ |

## Section 2

| | | | | |
|---|---|---|---|---|
| 1 Ⓐ Ⓑ Ⓒ Ⓓ Ⓔ | 9 Ⓐ Ⓑ Ⓒ Ⓓ Ⓔ | 17 Ⓐ Ⓑ Ⓒ Ⓓ Ⓔ | 25 Ⓐ Ⓑ Ⓒ Ⓓ Ⓔ | 33 Ⓐ Ⓑ Ⓒ Ⓓ Ⓔ |
| 2 Ⓐ Ⓑ Ⓒ Ⓓ Ⓔ | 10 Ⓐ Ⓑ Ⓒ Ⓓ Ⓔ | 18 Ⓐ Ⓑ Ⓒ Ⓓ Ⓔ | 26 Ⓐ Ⓑ Ⓒ Ⓓ Ⓔ | 34 Ⓐ Ⓑ Ⓒ Ⓓ Ⓔ |
| 3 Ⓐ Ⓑ Ⓒ Ⓓ Ⓔ | 11 Ⓐ Ⓑ Ⓒ Ⓓ Ⓔ | 19 Ⓐ Ⓑ Ⓒ Ⓓ Ⓔ | 27 Ⓐ Ⓑ Ⓒ Ⓓ Ⓔ | 35 Ⓐ Ⓑ Ⓒ Ⓓ Ⓔ |
| 4 Ⓐ Ⓑ Ⓒ Ⓓ Ⓔ | 12 Ⓐ Ⓑ Ⓒ Ⓓ Ⓔ | 20 Ⓐ Ⓑ Ⓒ Ⓓ Ⓔ | 28 Ⓐ Ⓑ Ⓒ Ⓓ Ⓔ | 36 Ⓐ Ⓑ Ⓒ Ⓓ Ⓔ |
| 5 Ⓐ Ⓑ Ⓒ Ⓓ Ⓔ | 13 Ⓐ Ⓑ Ⓒ Ⓓ Ⓔ | 21 Ⓐ Ⓑ Ⓒ Ⓓ Ⓔ | 29 Ⓐ Ⓑ Ⓒ Ⓓ Ⓔ | 37 Ⓐ Ⓑ Ⓒ Ⓓ Ⓔ |
| 6 Ⓐ Ⓑ Ⓒ Ⓓ Ⓔ | 14 Ⓐ Ⓑ Ⓒ Ⓓ Ⓔ | 22 Ⓐ Ⓑ Ⓒ Ⓓ Ⓔ | 30 Ⓐ Ⓑ Ⓒ Ⓓ Ⓔ | 38 Ⓐ Ⓑ Ⓒ Ⓓ Ⓔ |
| 7 Ⓐ Ⓑ Ⓒ Ⓓ Ⓔ | 15 Ⓐ Ⓑ Ⓒ Ⓓ Ⓔ | 23 Ⓐ Ⓑ Ⓒ Ⓓ Ⓔ | 31 Ⓐ Ⓑ Ⓒ Ⓓ Ⓔ | 39 Ⓐ Ⓑ Ⓒ Ⓓ Ⓔ |
| 8 Ⓐ Ⓑ Ⓒ Ⓓ Ⓔ | 16 Ⓐ Ⓑ Ⓒ Ⓓ Ⓔ | 24 Ⓐ Ⓑ Ⓒ Ⓓ Ⓔ | 32 Ⓐ Ⓑ Ⓒ Ⓓ Ⓔ | 40 Ⓐ Ⓑ Ⓒ Ⓓ Ⓔ |

## Section 3

| | | | | |
|---|---|---|---|---|
| 1 Ⓐ Ⓑ Ⓒ Ⓓ Ⓔ | 13 Ⓐ Ⓑ Ⓒ Ⓓ Ⓔ | 25 Ⓐ Ⓑ Ⓒ Ⓓ Ⓔ | 37 Ⓐ Ⓑ Ⓒ Ⓓ Ⓔ | 49 Ⓐ Ⓑ Ⓒ Ⓓ Ⓔ |
| 2 Ⓐ Ⓑ Ⓒ Ⓓ Ⓔ | 14 Ⓐ Ⓑ Ⓒ Ⓓ Ⓔ | 26 Ⓐ Ⓑ Ⓒ Ⓓ Ⓔ | 38 Ⓐ Ⓑ Ⓒ Ⓓ Ⓔ | 50 Ⓐ Ⓑ Ⓒ Ⓓ Ⓔ |
| 3 Ⓐ Ⓑ Ⓒ Ⓓ Ⓔ | 15 Ⓐ Ⓑ Ⓒ Ⓓ Ⓔ | 27 Ⓐ Ⓑ Ⓒ Ⓓ Ⓔ | 39 Ⓐ Ⓑ Ⓒ Ⓓ Ⓔ | 51 Ⓐ Ⓑ Ⓒ Ⓓ Ⓔ |
| 4 Ⓐ Ⓑ Ⓒ Ⓓ Ⓔ | 16 Ⓐ Ⓑ Ⓒ Ⓓ Ⓔ | 28 Ⓐ Ⓑ Ⓒ Ⓓ Ⓔ | 40 Ⓐ Ⓑ Ⓒ Ⓓ Ⓔ | 52 Ⓐ Ⓑ Ⓒ Ⓓ Ⓔ |
| 5 Ⓐ Ⓑ Ⓒ Ⓓ Ⓔ | 17 Ⓐ Ⓑ Ⓒ Ⓓ Ⓔ | 29 Ⓐ Ⓑ Ⓒ Ⓓ Ⓔ | 41 Ⓐ Ⓑ Ⓒ Ⓓ Ⓔ | 53 Ⓐ Ⓑ Ⓒ Ⓓ Ⓔ |
| 6 Ⓐ Ⓑ Ⓒ Ⓓ Ⓔ | 18 Ⓐ Ⓑ Ⓒ Ⓓ Ⓔ | 30 Ⓐ Ⓑ Ⓒ Ⓓ Ⓔ | 42 Ⓐ Ⓑ Ⓒ Ⓓ Ⓔ | 54 Ⓐ Ⓑ Ⓒ Ⓓ Ⓔ |
| 7 Ⓐ Ⓑ Ⓒ Ⓓ Ⓔ | 19 Ⓐ Ⓑ Ⓒ Ⓓ Ⓔ | 31 Ⓐ Ⓑ Ⓒ Ⓓ Ⓔ | 43 Ⓐ Ⓑ Ⓒ Ⓓ Ⓔ | 55 Ⓐ Ⓑ Ⓒ Ⓓ Ⓔ |
| 8 Ⓐ Ⓑ Ⓒ Ⓓ Ⓔ | 20 Ⓐ Ⓑ Ⓒ Ⓓ Ⓔ | 32 Ⓐ Ⓑ Ⓒ Ⓓ Ⓔ | 44 Ⓐ Ⓑ Ⓒ Ⓓ Ⓔ | 56 Ⓐ Ⓑ Ⓒ Ⓓ Ⓔ |
| 9 Ⓐ Ⓑ Ⓒ Ⓓ Ⓔ | 21 Ⓐ Ⓑ Ⓒ Ⓓ Ⓔ | 33 Ⓐ Ⓑ Ⓒ Ⓓ Ⓔ | 45 Ⓐ Ⓑ Ⓒ Ⓓ Ⓔ | 57 Ⓐ Ⓑ Ⓒ Ⓓ Ⓔ |
| 10 Ⓐ Ⓑ Ⓒ Ⓓ Ⓔ | 22 Ⓐ Ⓑ Ⓒ Ⓓ Ⓔ | 34 Ⓐ Ⓑ Ⓒ Ⓓ Ⓔ | 46 Ⓐ Ⓑ Ⓒ Ⓓ Ⓔ | 58 Ⓐ Ⓑ Ⓒ Ⓓ Ⓔ |
| 11 Ⓐ Ⓑ Ⓒ Ⓓ Ⓔ | 23 Ⓐ Ⓑ Ⓒ Ⓓ Ⓔ | 35 Ⓐ Ⓑ Ⓒ Ⓓ Ⓔ | 47 Ⓐ Ⓑ Ⓒ Ⓓ Ⓔ | 59 Ⓐ Ⓑ Ⓒ Ⓓ Ⓔ |
| 12 Ⓐ Ⓑ Ⓒ Ⓓ Ⓔ | 24 Ⓐ Ⓑ Ⓒ Ⓓ Ⓔ | 36 Ⓐ Ⓑ Ⓒ Ⓓ Ⓔ | 48 Ⓐ Ⓑ Ⓒ Ⓓ Ⓔ | 60 Ⓐ Ⓑ Ⓒ Ⓓ Ⓔ |

## Section 4

| | | | | |
|---|---|---|---|---|
| 1 Ⓐ Ⓑ Ⓒ Ⓓ Ⓔ | 6 Ⓐ Ⓑ Ⓒ Ⓓ Ⓔ | 11 Ⓐ Ⓑ Ⓒ Ⓓ Ⓔ | 16 Ⓐ Ⓑ Ⓒ Ⓓ Ⓔ | 21 Ⓐ Ⓑ Ⓒ Ⓓ Ⓔ |
| 2 Ⓐ Ⓑ Ⓒ Ⓓ Ⓔ | 7 Ⓐ Ⓑ Ⓒ Ⓓ Ⓔ | 12 Ⓐ Ⓑ Ⓒ Ⓓ Ⓔ | 17 Ⓐ Ⓑ Ⓒ Ⓓ Ⓔ | 22 Ⓐ Ⓑ Ⓒ Ⓓ Ⓔ |
| 3 Ⓐ Ⓑ Ⓒ Ⓓ Ⓔ | 8 Ⓐ Ⓑ Ⓒ Ⓓ Ⓔ | 13 Ⓐ Ⓑ Ⓒ Ⓓ Ⓔ | 18 Ⓐ Ⓑ Ⓒ Ⓓ Ⓔ | 23 Ⓐ Ⓑ Ⓒ Ⓓ Ⓔ |
| 4 Ⓐ Ⓑ Ⓒ Ⓓ Ⓔ | 9 Ⓐ Ⓑ Ⓒ Ⓓ Ⓔ | 14 Ⓐ Ⓑ Ⓒ Ⓓ Ⓔ | 19 Ⓐ Ⓑ Ⓒ Ⓓ Ⓔ | 24 Ⓐ Ⓑ Ⓒ Ⓓ Ⓔ |
| 5 Ⓐ Ⓑ Ⓒ Ⓓ Ⓔ | 10 Ⓐ Ⓑ Ⓒ Ⓓ Ⓔ | 15 Ⓐ Ⓑ Ⓒ Ⓓ Ⓔ | 20 Ⓐ Ⓑ Ⓒ Ⓓ Ⓔ | 25 Ⓐ Ⓑ Ⓒ Ⓓ Ⓔ |

## Section 5

| | | | |
|---|---|---|---|
| 1 Ⓐ Ⓑ Ⓒ Ⓓ Ⓔ | 5 Ⓐ Ⓑ Ⓒ Ⓓ Ⓔ | 9 Ⓐ Ⓑ Ⓒ Ⓓ Ⓔ | 13 Ⓐ Ⓑ Ⓒ Ⓓ Ⓔ |
| 2 Ⓐ Ⓑ Ⓒ Ⓓ Ⓔ | 6 Ⓐ Ⓑ Ⓒ Ⓓ Ⓔ | 10 Ⓐ Ⓑ Ⓒ Ⓓ Ⓔ | 14 Ⓐ Ⓑ Ⓒ Ⓓ Ⓔ |
| 3 Ⓐ Ⓑ Ⓒ Ⓓ Ⓔ | 7 Ⓐ Ⓑ Ⓒ Ⓓ Ⓔ | 11 Ⓐ Ⓑ Ⓒ Ⓓ Ⓔ | 15 Ⓐ Ⓑ Ⓒ Ⓓ Ⓔ |
| 4 Ⓐ Ⓑ Ⓒ Ⓓ Ⓔ | 8 Ⓐ Ⓑ Ⓒ Ⓓ Ⓔ | 12 Ⓐ Ⓑ Ⓒ Ⓓ Ⓔ | 16 Ⓐ Ⓑ Ⓒ Ⓓ Ⓔ |

**Experimental Section – See page 9 for details.**

THIS PAGE INTENTIONALLY LEFT BLANK.

## Writing Sample

Schools would like to get to know you better through an essay you write. If you choose to write a personal essay, base your essay on the topic presented in A. If you choose to write a general essay, base your essay on the topic presented in B. Please fill in the circle next to your choice.

Ⓐ What motivates you to learn in school and why?

Ⓑ Is it always best to "live and let live," allowing people to do what they want, or is it sometimes necessary to oppose the actions of others? Support your answer with reasons and examples.

**Use this page and the next page to complete your writing sample.**

*Continue on next page*

## SECTION 1
## 25 Questions

Following each problem in this section, there are five suggested answers. Work each problem in your head or in the blank space provided at the right of the page. Then look at the five suggested answers and decide which one is best.

<u>Note:</u> Figures that accompany problems in this section are drawn as accurately as possible EXCEPT when it is stated in a specific problem that its figure is not drawn to scale.

Sample Problem:

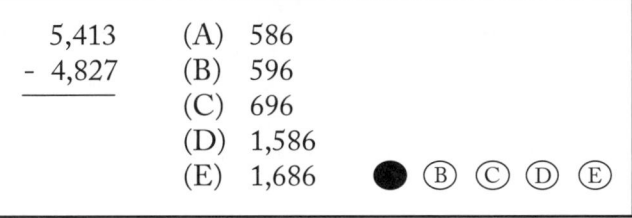

```
   5,413      (A)  586
 - 4,827      (B)  596
 _____      (C)  696
              (D)  1,586
              (E)  1,686      ● Ⓑ Ⓒ Ⓓ Ⓔ
```

---

1. Laura purchased a shirt for $30. She had a coupon that gave her a 20% discount. What was the final cost of the shirt?

   (A)  $6.00
   (B)  $10.00
   (C)  $15.00
   (D)  $24.00
   (E)  $29.40

**USE THIS SPACE FOR FIGURING.**

---

2. The point with coordinates $(4, 7)$ in the $xy$-coordinate plane is translated 3 units to the left and 2 units down. What will be the coordinates of the new point?

   (A)  $(1, 5)$
   (B)  $(1, 9)$
   (C)  $(2, 4)$
   (D)  $(4, 2)$
   (E)  $(5, 1)$

---

3. If A = {2, 6, 15, 30} and B = {5, 6, 15, 20}, what is the intersection of sets A and B?

   (A)  {6}
   (B)  {6, 15}
   (C)  {2, 30}
   (D)  {2, 5, 20, 30}
   (E)  {2, 5, 6, 15, 20, 30}

**GO ON TO THE NEXT PAGE.**

**USE THIS SPACE FOR FIGURING.**

4. The mean of two numbers is 23. Which of the following could be the two numbers?

(A) 3 and 20
(B) 3 and 26
(C) 10 and 13
(D) 10 and 56
(E) 20 and 26

---

5. A triangle has a base length of $x$. The height is 3 less than the length of the base. Which expression represents the area of the triangle?

(A) $x(x-3)$

(B) $x(3-x)$

(C) $2x(x-3)$

(D) $\frac{1}{2}x(3-x)$

(E) $\frac{1}{2}x(x-3)$

---

6. Calculate: $\dfrac{75 \times 0 \times 2 \times 3}{75}$

(A) 0
(B) 2
(C) 3
(D) 5
(E) 6

---

7. Which of the following is equivalent to $6x^2 + 8x$ ?

(A) $14x^3$
(B) $6x(x+2)$
(C) $2x(x+4)$
(D) $2x(3x+2)$
(E) $2x(3x+4)$

**GO ON TO THE NEXT PAGE.**

**USE THIS SPACE FOR FIGURING.**

8.  What can you conclude from the following
    two statements?

    • ∠A and ∠B are complementary
    • ∠B and ∠C are complementary

    (A)  ∠A and ∠B are congruent
    (B)  ∠B and ∠C are congruent
    (C)  ∠B and ∠C are supplementary
    (D)  ∠A and ∠C are congruent
    (E)  ∠A and ∠C are supplementary

---

9.  The square of 5 is divided by the cube root of 27.
    What is the remainder?

    (A)  0
    (B)  1
    (C)  2
    (D)  3
    (E)  4

---

10. Solve: $\frac{1}{3}(w - 6) \geq -3$

    (A)  $w \geq -3$

    (B)  $w \geq 1$

    (C)  $w \geq 3$

    (D)  $w \geq 5$

    (E)  $w \geq 15$

---

11. On the number line in the figure, if $P$ points to a number
    $\frac{1}{4}$ of the distance from 0.02 to 0.03, what is this number?

    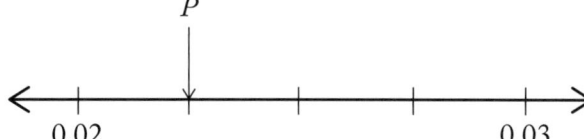

    (A)  0.0021
    (B)  0.0024
    (C)  0.0225
    (D)  0.025
    (E)  0.25

**GO ON TO THE NEXT PAGE.**

**USE THIS SPACE FOR FIGURING.**

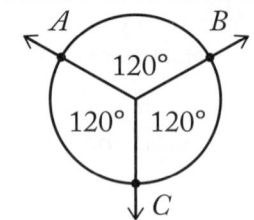

12. The figure represents the map of a circular walk 1,860 meters in length around a park with a monument at its center. Paths $A$, $B$, and $C$ branch out from the monument forming three equal angles. What is the shortest distance, in meters, along the circular walk from $A$ to $C$?

(A) 465
(B) 620
(C) 930
(D) 1,240
(E) 1,395

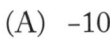
$$5, 10, 15, \ldots, 100$$

13. If each term in the sequence above is 5 more than the previous term, how many times does the digit zero appear in the sequence?

(A) 9
(B) 10
(C) 11
(D) 50
(E) 51

14. Based on the graph in the $xy$-coordinate plane, what is the value of $f(3)$?

(A) −10
(B) −1
(C) 0
(D) 1
(E) 10

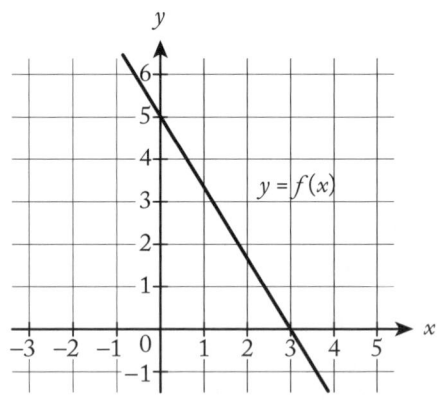

15. A scientist uses exactly three chemicals in the ratio $1 : 5 : n$ by weight. If the third chemical is $\frac{1}{2}$ the total weight, what is the value of $n$?

(A) 1
(B) 3
(C) 5
(D) 6
(E) 12

**GO ON TO THE NEXT PAGE.**

**USE THIS SPACE FOR FIGURING.**

16. Simplify: $2\sqrt{75} - 3\sqrt{27}$

    (A)  $-17\sqrt{3}$
    (B)  $-4\sqrt{3}$
    (C)  $\sqrt{3}$
    (D)  $19\sqrt{3}$
    (E)  $23\sqrt{3}$

17. Which of the following interpretations is supported by the graph?

    (A)  $A$ is increasing in price faster over time than $B$.
    (B)  $B$ is increasing in price faster over time than $A$.
    (C)  $A$ and $B$ are increasing at the same rate.
    (D)  The price of $B$ is always greater than $A$.
    (E)  It is not possible to determine whether the prices of $A$ and $B$ are increasing at different rates.

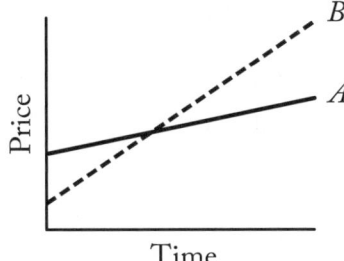

18. In the figure, $X$ and $Y$ are midpoints of two sides of the square as shown. The area of the shaded region is what fraction of the area of the square?

    (A)  $\frac{1}{8}$

    (B)  $\frac{1}{6}$

    (C)  $\frac{1}{4}$

    (D)  $\frac{1}{3}$

    (E)  It cannot be determined from the information given.

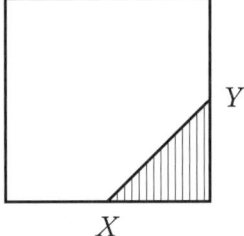

19. Maria contributed $\frac{2}{5}$ of the money needed to buy a certain gift, and Tom contributed $\frac{1}{3}$ of the money. If the remaining $8 was contributed by two other children, how much did Maria contribute?

    (A)  $12.00
    (B)  $10.00
    (C)  $5.87
    (D)  $4.00
    (E)  $3.20

**GO ON TO THE NEXT PAGE.**

**USE THIS SPACE FOR FIGURING.**

20. Which of the following nets folds up into a cube?

    (A)  *a*
    (B)  *b*
    (C)  *c*
    (D)  *d*
    (E)  *e*

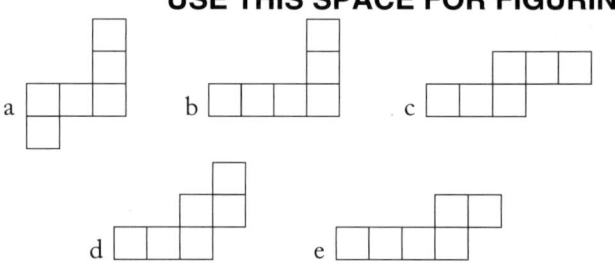

21. Which of the following procedures can be used to find 60% of a number *n* on a hand-held calculator?

    I. Multiply *n* by 0.6.
    II. Multiply *n* by 60 and then divide by 100.
    III. Multiply *n* by 3 and then divide by 5.

    (A)  I only
    (B)  II only
    (C)  I and II only
    (D)  II and III only
    (E)  I, II, and III

22. Substance *S* weighs 3 times as much as substance *T*. A jar filled with *S* weighs 700 grams, and the same jar filled with *T* weighs 400 grams. How many grams does the empty jar weigh?

    (A)  100
    (B)  150
    (C)  200
    (D)  250
    (E)  300

23. The points (5, 1) and (8, –3) lie in the *xy*-coordinate plane. What is the distance between these two points?

    (A)   3 units
    (B)   4 units
    (C)   5 units
    (D)  11 units
    (E)  25 units

**GO ON TO THE NEXT PAGE.**

**USE THIS SPACE FOR FIGURING.**

24. Mike can buy baseball cards at 3 for 25 cents. If he sells the cards at 2 for 25 cents, how many will he have to buy and sell to earn $1.00 in profit?

    (A)  8
    (B)  12
    (C)  20
    (D)  24
    (E)  150

---

$$\frac{(x - 2)(x + 2)}{(x + 1)(x + 3)}$$

25. For which of the following values of $x$ is the expression above undefined?

    (A)  −3 and −1 only
    (B)  −2 and 2 only
    (C)  1 and 3 only
    (D)  −3, −2, −1, and 2
    (E)  −2, 1, 2, and 3

# STOP

**IF YOU FINISH BEFORE TIME IS CALLED, YOU MAY CHECK YOUR WORK ON THIS SECTION ONLY.**
**DO NOT TURN TO ANY OTHER SECTION IN THE TEST.**

## SECTION 2
## 40 Questions

Read each passage carefully and then answer the questions about it. For each question, decide on the basis of the passage which one of the choices best answers the question.

---

In 1742, at the age of 14, James Cook went, or ran away, to sea, shipping at Whitby on board the Freelove, a collier belonging to the brothers Walker. In this hard school Cook learnt his sailor duties. No better training could have been found for his future responsibilities. Here he learnt to endure the utmost rigours of the sea. Constant fighting with North Sea gales, bad food, and
*Line 5* cramped accommodation, taught him to regard with the indifference that afterwards distinguished him, all the hardships that he had to encounter, and led him to endure and persevere where others, less determined or more easily daunted by difficulties, would have hurried on, and left their work incomplete.

Few sailed for the purpose of exploration pure and simple; and even those who started with
10 that view found, when embarked on that vast expanse, that prudence dictated that they should have a moderate certainty of, by a certain time, falling in with a place of sure refreshment. The provisions they carried were bad at starting, and by the time they had fought their way through the Straits of Magellan were already worse; water was limited, and would not hold out more than a given number of days. Every voyage that is pursued tells the same story—short of water, and eagerly looking out
15 for an opportunity of replenishing it.

---

1. Which of the following expressions is used as a metaphor?

   (A) "hard school" (line 2)
   (B) "sailor duties" (line 3)
   (C) "better training" (line 3)
   (D) "utmost rigours" (line 4)
   (E) "North Sea gales"(line 4)

2. The first paragraph implies that in later life Cook gained a reputation for being

   (A) ingenious
   (B) rebellious
   (C) irritable
   (D) generous
   (E) stoic

3. According to the passage, which of the following is true of Cook's experience on board the Freelove?

   (A) It left him disillusioned.
   (B) It prepared him well for later duties.
   (C) It brought him fame as a ship's captain.
   (D) It awakened his interest in exploration.
   (E) It inspired him to reform sailing practices.

4. As used in line 10, "view" most nearly means

   (A) opinion
   (B) angle
   (C) goal
   (D) scene
   (E) glimpse

5. The "story" mentioned in line 14 is one of

   (A) finding glory in adventure
   (B) discovering sources of wealth
   (C) mapping uncharted territories
   (D) seeking means of sustenance
   (E) establishing overseas colonies

**GO ON TO THE NEXT PAGE.**

Becoming Americans did not mean scrubbing away our heritage. The teachers, trying as best they could to sound the Japanese or Italian pronunciation, called us by the names our parents used. None of us ever suffered for speaking our native languages. Matti told the class about his mother's down quilt, which she had made in Italy. Encarnacion acted out how boys learned to

*Line 5* fish in the Philippines. I astounded the class with the story of my travels on a stagecoach, which my classmates had seen only in museums. Miss Hopley herself would express openly her wonder about these matters. For me, becoming an American did not mean forgetting that I was also Mexican.

Getting to be an American, however, was not an entirely smooth matter. I had to
10 fight one lout who doubled up with laughter over one of my translations until I straightened him out with a kick. But it was Homer who gave me the most lasting lesson for a future American.

Homer was an Irishman who dressed as if every day were Sunday. And Homer was smart, as he clearly showed when he and I ran for president of the third grade. Everyone understood that this would be a demonstration of how the American people vote for president.
15 In an election, Miss Hopley explained, the candidates could be generous and vote for each other. We cast our ballots and Homer won by two votes. I polled my supporters and concluded that I had voted for Homer and so had he. He didn't deny it, reminding me that the teacher had said we could vote for each other but didn't have to.

6. In the passage, the author focuses primarily on
(A) evaluating the effects on students of the experience of voting
(B) describing some personal experiences in adapting to life in the United States
(C) explaining how new immigrants become naturalized citizens
(D) arguing the merits of the democratic process
(E) criticizing the school's policy on students speaking their native languages

7. As it is used in line 1, "mean" most nearly means
(A) matter
(B) entail
(C) symbolize
(D) intend
(E) design

8. The description of the "teachers" (line 1) suggests that they were
(A) accommodating
(B) knowledgeable
(C) unsympathetic
(D) frustrated
(E) strict

9. With the word "however" (line 9) the narrator's tone becomes more
(A) somber
(B) desperate
(C) relaxed
(D) enthusiastic
(E) critical

10. The last sentence of the passage (lines 17–18) depicts Homer drawing a distinction between
(A) popularity and competence
(B) generosity and friendship
(C) possibility and necessity
(D) democracy and dictatorship
(E) politics and self-interest

**GO ON TO THE NEXT PAGE.**

> Mostly the captain would not speak when spoken to, only look up sudden and fierce and blow through his nose like a fog-horn; and we and people who came about our house soon learned to let him be. Every day, when he came back from his stroll, he would ask if any seafaring men had gone by along the road. At first we thought it was the want of company of his
>
> *Line 5* own kind that made him ask the question; but at last we began to see he was desirous to avoid them. When a seaman put up at the "Admiral Benbow" (as now and then some did, making by the coast road for Bristol), he would look in at him through the curtained door before he entered the parlour; and he was always sure to be as silent as a mouse when any such was present.

11. In line 1, the word "only" serves to emphasize the captain's

    (A) limited reaction
    (B) solitary achievement
    (C) unique talent
    (D) exceptional status
    (E) singular obsession

12. To describe how the captain would "blow through his nose" (line 2) the narrator uses which literary device?

    (A) Personification
    (B) Onomatopoeia
    (C) Alliteration
    (D) Oxymoron
    (E) Simile

13. The narrator uses "but" in line 5 to

    (A) introduce a new character
    (B) provide an alternative perspective
    (C) correct a mistaken notion
    (D) explain an irregularity
    (E) defend a decision

14. As used in line 6, "put up" most nearly means

    (A) built
    (B) endured
    (C) lodged
    (D) wagered
    (E) displayed

15. In the passage, the captain is portrayed as

    (A) devious
    (B) antisocial
    (C) dejected
    (D) intrusive
    (E) conceited

**GO ON TO THE NEXT PAGE.**

Sir Arthur Conan Doyle said that his character of Sherlock Holmes was inspired by Dr. Joseph Bell, for whom Doyle had worked as a clerk. Like Holmes, Bell was noted for drawing large conclusions from the smallest observations. Sir Henry Littlejohn is also considered a source for Holmes. Littlejohn served as a police surgeon and medical officer, providing for Doyle a link
*Line 5* between medical investigation and the detection of crime.

The primary intellectual detection method used by Holmes is abductive reasoning. "From a drop of water," a logician could detect "the possibility of an Atlantic or a Niagara without having seen or heard of one or the other." Holmes' stories often begin with a bravura display of his talent. "Holmesian" detection often appears to consist of drawing
*10* conclusions based on straightforward practical principles that are the result of careful observation, such as Holmes' study of different kinds of cigar ashes. One quote often used by Holmes is, "When you have eliminated the impossible, whatever remains, however improbable, must be the truth."

In "A Scandal in Bohemia," Holmes deduces that his friend Dr. Watson had got very wet lately and that he had "a most clumsy and careless servant girl." When Watson asks how Holmes
*15* knows this, Holmes answers: "It is simplicity itself. My eyes tell me that on the inside of your left shoe, just where the firelight strikes it, the leather is scored by six almost parallel cuts. Obviously they have been caused by someone who has very carelessly scraped round the edges of the sole in order to remove crusted mud from it. Hence, it is plain to see that you had been out in vile weather."
As is so often the case, Watson is amazed.

16. The passage suggests that the character Sherlock Holmes is

(A) a composite of real people
(B) the invention of several different authors
(C) a fictional representation of Doyle himself
(D) a police surgeon and medical officer
(E) the inventor of abductive reasoning

17. As it is used in line 2 "drawing" most nearly means

(A) attracting
(B) sketching
(C) approaching
(D) inferring
(E) selecting

18. As represented in the third paragraph (lines 13–18), Holmes's demeanor is best described as

(A) sympathetic
(B) tentative
(C) cheerful
(D) arrogant
(E) casual

19. According to the passage, Watson typically reacts to Holmes's deductions with

(A) astonishment
(B) envy
(C) annoyance
(D) ridicule
(E) indifference

20. This passage would most likely be found in which of the following?

(A) A textbook on logic
(B) A journal of literary criticism
(C) A true crime blog
(D) The biography of Dr. Joseph Bell
(E) The autobiography of Sherlock Holmes

**GO ON TO THE NEXT PAGE.**

Around the world, deaf individuals have long used hand gestures to communicate. In 1775, a church leader in France developed a system of finger spelling. One hand gesture stood for each letter of the alphabet. This allowed deaf users of sign language to spell out words by forming shapes with their hands. Americans were introduced to sign language in the early 1800s, when Thomas Hopkins

*Line 5* Gallaudet, a minister, traveled to Europe in search of a way to help his neighbor's deaf child learn to communicate. In Europe, Gallaudet learned about the French system of sign language and began adapting it for Americans. Upon his return to the United States, he started the first school for the deaf in the country. Over time, Gallaudet's system became what we now know as American Sign Language, or ASL.

*10* Sign languages vary across the world, and most cultures have a system of signing. Although they do not use spoken words, sign languages are otherwise much like any other language. Rules of grammar govern the language's use. For instance, in an English sentence, the subject typically goes before the verb. In ASL, however, the order of gestures can vary. In spoken languages, a speaker can use his or her tone of voice to communicate different emotions, but sign languages rely on other

*15* tools, such as facial expressions, to accomplish this. For instance, signers can change the statement "You are hungry" to the question "Are you hungry?" by changing their body language (for instance, by leaning forward) and using their eyebrows.

Over the past two centuries, ASL has grown and become more complex as more people have learned it. Schools for deaf students, including a university named for Thomas Gallaudet, have

*20* been established. American Sign Language is now the fourth most common language used in the United States.

21. It can be inferred from the passage that in the French system of sign language

(A) the subject always followed the verb

(B) facial expressions did not matter

(C) most words required multiple gestures

(D) all signs were made with a single hand

(E) the rules of spelling were inconsistent

22. The passage implies which of the following about Gallaudet?

(A) He has been forgotten.

(B) He failed in his original goal.

(C) He was motivated by a desire to help.

(D) He developed American Sign Language for commercial reasons.

(E) He misinterpreted French sign language.

23. In line 10, the author uses "Although" to

(A) note a singular difference

(B) acknowledge an error

(C) transition to a new topic

(D) contrast opposing ideas

(E) excuse a shortcoming

24. In line 15, "this" refers specifically to

(A) becoming fluent in sign language

(B) conveying one's feelings

(C) inventing new tools

(D) mastering rules of grammar

(E) interpreting ambiguous gestures

25. The primary purpose of the passage is to

(A) sketch a biography of Thomas Gallaudet

(B) advocate the adoption of an international sign language

(C) contrast the French and American systems of sign language

(D) demonstrate that sign language is more expressive than spoken language

(E) present a brief history of American Sign Language

**GO ON TO THE NEXT PAGE.**

During these days of preparation, Queequeg and I often visited the craft, and as often I asked about Captain Ahab and how he was and when he was going to come on board his ship. To these questions they would answer that he was getting better and better and was expected aboard every day; meantime, the two Captains, Peleg and Bildad, could attend to everything necessary to fit the *Line 5* vessel for the voyage. If I had been downright honest with myself, I would have seen very plainly in my heart that I did but half fancy being committed this way to so long a voyage, without once laying my eyes on the man who was to be the absolute dictator of it so soon as the ship sailed out upon the open sea. But when a man suspects any wrong, it sometimes happens that if he be already involved in the matter, he insensibly strives to cover up his suspicions even from himself. And much this way it was with me. I said nothing, and tried to think nothing.

26. The repetition of "and" in lines 1–2 serves to emphasize the narrator's

    (A) enthusiasm
    (B) self-confidence
    (C) weariness
    (D) anger
    (E) inquisitiveness

27. It can be inferred from the passage that Captain Ahab is

    (A) ill
    (B) stern
    (C) crafty
    (D) nervous
    (E) incompetent

28. As it is used in line 4, "fit" most nearly means

    (A) adapt
    (B) belong
    (C) measure
    (D) equip
    (E) match

29. In line 7, "absolute dictator" refers to

    (A) the narrator
    (B) Queequeg
    (C) Captain Ahab
    (D) Captain Peleg
    (E) Captain Bildad

30. In the passage the narrator acknowledges that he has engaged in

    (A) self-deception
    (B) sabotage
    (C) gossip
    (D) mutiny
    (E) piracy

**GO ON TO THE NEXT PAGE.**

It is the strangest yellow, that wallpaper! It makes me think of all the yellow things I ever saw—not beautiful ones like buttercups, but old foul, bad yellow things.

But there is something else about that paper—the smell! I noticed it the moment we came into the room, but with so much air and sun it was not bad. Now we have had a week of fog and rain, and

*Line 5* whether the windows are open or not, the smell is here.

It creeps all over the house.

I find it hovering in the dining-room, skulking in the parlor, hiding in the hall, lying in wait for me on the stairs.

It gets into my hair.

*10* Even when I go to ride, if I turn my head suddenly and surprise it—there is that smell!

Such a peculiar odor, too! I have spent hours in trying to analyze it, to find what it smelled like.

It is not bad—at first, and very gentle, but quite the subtlest, most enduring odor I ever met.

In this damp weather it is awful, I wake up in the night and find it hanging over me.

It used to disturb me at first. I thought seriously of burning the house—to reach the smell.

*15* But now I am used to it. The only thing I can think of that it is like is the COLOR of the paper! A yellow smell.

There is a very funny mark on this wall, low down, near the mopboard. A streak that runs round the room. It goes behind every piece of furniture, except the bed, a long, straight, even SMOOCH, as if it had been rubbed over and over.

*20* I wonder how it was done and who did it, and what they did it for. Round and round and round—round and round and round—it makes me dizzy!

31. It can be inferred from the passage that the narrator's state of mind is one of

(A) anger
(B) agitation
(C) complacency
(D) amusement
(E) optimism

32 In lines 7–8, the author uses which literary device to describe the wallpaper's smell?

(A) Simile
(B) Oxymoron
(C) Personification
(D) Onomatopoeia
(E) Understatement

33. As it is used in line 17, "funny" most nearly means

(A) fraudulent
(B) humorous
(C) ironic
(D) witty
(E) odd

34. The repetition of the word "round" in lines 20–21 serves to emphasize the narrator's

(A) playful attitude
(B) mental obsession
(C) strong work ethic
(D) physical exhaustion
(E) optimistic outlook

35. According to the passage, the narrator is seeking to answer which of the following questions?

(A) How the mark on the wall got there
(B) How the smell got into the room
(C) Who the previous occupant was
(D) What the wallpaper is covering up
(E) How to clean the mark off the wall

**GO ON TO THE NEXT PAGE.**

> I met a traveler from an antique land,
> Who said—"Two vast and trunkless legs of stone
> Stand in the desert. Near them, on the sand,
> Half sunk, a shattered visage lies, whose frown,
>
> *Line 5* And wrinkled lips and sneer of cold command,
> Tell that its sculptor well those passions read
> Which yet survive, stamped on these lifeless things,
> The hand that mocked them, and the heart that fed;
> And on the pedestal these words appear
>
> *10* 'My name is Ozymandias, King of Kings,
> Look on my Works, ye Mighty, and despair!'
> Nothing beside remains. Round the decay
> Of that colossal wreck, boundless and bare,
> The lone and level sands stretch far away."

36. In line 4, "whose" refers to

    (A) the poet
    (B) a face
    (C) the desert
    (D) a sculptor
    (E) a traveler

37. In line 6, the word "passions" refers to feelings of

    (A) loyalty
    (B) determination
    (C) love
    (D) contempt
    (E) inspiration

38. The tone of the inscription quoted in lines 10–11 is best described as

    (A) haughty
    (B) introspective
    (C) irate
    (D) apologetic
    (E) cautious

39. The poem implies that Ozymandias' "Works" (line 11)

    (A) were ridiculed by his followers
    (B) continue to attract travelers
    (C) have vanished without a trace
    (D) influenced later architecture
    (E) caused his own downfall

40. The poem ends on a note of

    (A) regret
    (B) optimism
    (C) triumph
    (D) irony
    (E) envy

# STOP

**IF YOU FINISH BEFORE TIME IS CALLED, YOU MAY CHECK YOUR WORK ON THIS SECTION ONLY.
DO NOT TURN TO ANY OTHER SECTION IN THE TEST.**

## SECTION 3
## 60 Questions

This section consists of two different types of questions: synonyms and analogies. There are directions and a sample question for each type.

**Synonyms**

Each of the following questions consists of one word followed by five words or phrases. You are to select the one word or phrase whose meaning is closest to the word in capital letters.

Sample Question:

CHILLY:

(A) lazy
(B) nice
(C) dry
(D) cold
(E) sunny       Ⓐ Ⓑ Ⓒ ● Ⓔ

---

1. PROGRESS:

   (A) capture
   (B) consult
   (C) advance
   (D) regulate
   (E) nominate

2. ASSORTMENT:

   (A) specialty
   (B) variety
   (C) multitude
   (D) separation
   (E) portion

3. SINISTER:

   (A) familial
   (B) tortured
   (C) menacing
   (D) clever
   (E) skeptical

4. MUSTER:

   (A) require
   (B) increase
   (C) depart
   (D) gather
   (E) decorate

5. DISTRESS:

   (A) shame
   (B) insult
   (C) anxiety
   (D) patience
   (E) emphasis

6. ADVERSARY:

   (A) descendent
   (B) fugitive
   (C) pacifist
   (D) rival
   (E) activist

7. PRY:

   (A) attack secretly
   (B) withdraw hastily
   (C) react angrily
   (D) approach cautiously
   (E) inquire intrusively

8. ABHOR:

   (A) annoy
   (B) detest
   (C) capture
   (D) desert
   (E) obstruct

**GO ON TO THE NEXT PAGE.**

9. VIGILANT:
   (A) organized
   (B) courageous
   (C) insensitive
   (D) infinite
   (E) watchful

10. HILARITY:
    (A) amusement
    (B) sincerity
    (C) caution
    (D) comfort
    (E) boastfulness

11. AMPLE:
    (A) loud
    (B) mobile
    (C) practical
    (D) plentiful
    (E) spotless

12. PINNACLE:
    (A) barrier
    (B) peak
    (C) ornament
    (D) castle
    (E) pyramid

13. MUNDANE:
    (A) ordinary
    (B) obscure
    (C) innocent
    (D) worrisome
    (E) corrupt

14. ENDURE:
    (A) avoid
    (B) perceive
    (C) donate
    (D) confuse
    (E) withstand

15. IMPERATIVE:
    (A) elementary
    (B) dangerous
    (C) necessary
    (D) fortunate
    (E) prominent

16. PARTISAN:
    (A) incomplete
    (B) biased
    (C) explicit
    (D) meager
    (E) intelligent

17. IMPAIR:
    (A) seize
    (B) weigh
    (C) damage
    (D) mislead
    (E) contrast

18. PRECIPICE:
    (A) crest of a wave
    (B) edge of a cliff
    (C) base of a mountain
    (D) curve in a road
    (E) bend in a river

19. FACSIMILE:
    (A) exact copy
    (B) reasonable excuse
    (C) delicate balance
    (D) distinct identity
    (E) literary device

20. FRAUDULENT:
    (A) ridiculous
    (B) impertinent
    (C) deceitful
    (D) greedy
    (E) boastful

**GO ON TO THE NEXT PAGE.**

21. CONDONE:
    (A) explain
    (B) provide
    (C) excuse
    (D) confuse
    (E) perceive

22. EXPENDABLE:
    (A) affordable
    (B) unnecessary
    (C) thrifty
    (D) generous
    (E) promising

23. PORTENT:
    (A) despair
    (B) omen
    (C) burden
    (D) gravity
    (E) gateway

24. PALLID:
    (A) steep
    (B) wan
    (C) frosty
    (D) shy
    (E) uneasy

25. PROFUSION:
    (A) inspiration
    (B) connection
    (C) career
    (D) frankness
    (E) abundance

26. PRISTINE:
    (A) immaculate
    (B) snobbish
    (C) timid
    (D) fragile
    (E) frozen

27. AFFINITY:
    (A) elegance
    (B) multitude
    (C) determination
    (D) kinship
    (E) declaration

28. SALVAGE:
    (A) give
    (B) send
    (C) pray
    (D) wish
    (E) save

29. INCENSED:
    (A) rowdy
    (B) furious
    (C) absurd
    (D) forceful
    (E) doubtful

30. SOLACE:
    (A) seclusion
    (B) bravery
    (C) sunlight
    (D) wealth
    (E) comfort

**GO ON TO THE NEXT PAGE.**

## Analogies

The following questions ask you to find relationships between words. For each question, select the answer choice that best completes the meaning of the sentence.

Sample Question:

> Kitten is to cat as
> (A) fawn is to colt
> (B) puppy is to dog
> (C) cow is to bull
> (D) wolf is to bear
> (E) hen is to rooster     Ⓐ ● Ⓒ Ⓓ Ⓔ

Choice (B) is the best answer because a kitten is a young cat just as a puppy is a young dog. Of all the answer choices, (B) states a relationship that is most like the relationship between <u>kitten</u> and <u>cat</u>.

---

31. Diploma is to graduation as
    (A) recital is to poetry
    (B) trophy is to medal
    (C) agenda is to meeting
    (D) ticket is to event
    (E) crown is to coronation

32. Gill is to fish as
    (A) vein is to blood
    (B) fur is to rodent
    (C) lung is to mammal
    (D) snake is to reptile
    (E) soil is to plant

33. Resident is to dwell as
    (A) beneficiary is to donate
    (B) ancestor is to inherit
    (C) bachelor is to marry
    (D) pedestrian is to walk
    (E) disciple is to teach

34. Actor is to script as
    (A) director is to cast
    (B) musician is to score
    (C) preacher is to pulpit
    (D) voter is to ballot
    (E) novelist is to book

35. Cartographer is to map as
    (A) diarist is to journal
    (B) teacher is to knowledge
    (C) flutist is to flute
    (D) sailor is to ocean
    (E) criminal is to prison

36. Ribcage is to heart as
    (A) habitat is to organism
    (B) disease is to germ
    (C) orbit is to planet
    (D) fence is to yard
    (E) branch is to tree

37. Dental is to tooth as
    (A) ablaze is to fire
    (B) epic is to poetry
    (C) captive is to cage
    (D) trivial is to detail
    (E) floral is to flower

38. Speedometer is to velocity as
    (A) radar is to blip
    (B) thermometer is to fever
    (C) amplifier is to decibel
    (D) odometer is to distance
    (E) prism is to light

**GO ON TO THE NEXT PAGE.**

39. Insomnia is to sleep as

    (A) amnesty is to pardon

    (B) insolence is to anger

    (C) equilibrium is to balance

    (D) phobia is to fear

    (E) amnesia is to memory

40. Nose is to olfactory as

    (A) touch is to tactile

    (B) ear is to auditory

    (C) sight is to blind

    (D) mouth is to edible

    (E) oxygen is to respiratory

41. Revive is to consciousness as

    (A) react is to stimulus

    (B) replace is to damage

    (C) relinquish is to claim

    (D) reassure is to confidence

    (E) relieve is to suffering

42. Procrastinate is to prompt as

    (A) recover is to healthy

    (B) divulge is to public

    (C) prevaricate is to truthful

    (D) intrude is to meddlesome

    (E) remonstrate is to obedient

43. Surgeon is to hospital as

    (A) artist is to studio

    (B) sculpture is to museum

    (C) nurse is to patient

    (D) classroom is to school

    (E) convict is to parole

44. Wrist is to hand as

    (A) knee is to joint

    (B) boat is to lake

    (C) spoke is to wheel

    (D) hinge is to door

    (E) shade is to window

45. Abash is to humiliate as

    (A) annoy is to delight

    (B) capture is to liberate

    (C) dislike is to loathe

    (D) chew is to digest

    (E) broaden is to elevate

46. Hint is to indirect as

    (A) complain is to indifferent

    (B) reason is to inquisitive

    (C) whisper is to quiet

    (D) confess is to innocent

    (E) gossip is to false

47. Avarice is to money as

    (A) wealth is to fortune

    (B) sloth is to sin

    (C) anger is to fury

    (D) gluttony is to food

    (E) notoriety is to fame

48. Brazen is to bold as

    (A) relentless is to fleeting

    (B) illegal is to secretive

    (C) derogatory is to critical

    (D) incompetent is to lazy

    (E) frail is to robust

49. Crack is to chasm as

    (A) gully is to canyon

    (B) mountain is to peak

    (C) street is to road

    (D) cave is to den

    (E) river is to lake

50. Congregation is to worshiper as

    (A) regiment is to soldier

    (B) periodical is to journalist

    (C) traffic is to congestion

    (D) legislature is to law

    (E) clientele is to business

**GO ON TO THE NEXT PAGE.**

51. Bread is to dough as
    (A) window is to pane
    (B) pottery is to clay
    (C) ore is to mine
    (D) ice is to water
    (E) fruit is to tree

52. Diplomatic is to tact as
    (A) ambivalent is to decision
    (B) radical is to tradition
    (C) mundane is to celebration
    (D) punitive is to verdict
    (E) venturesome is to boldness

53. Lively is to vivacity as
    (A) noticeable is to attention
    (B) shallow is to profundity
    (C) luminous is to radiance
    (D) deceptive is to appearance
    (E) curious is to certainty

54. Assailant is to attack as
    (A) escort is to accompany
    (B) fugitive is to surrender
    (C) patient is to operate
    (D) amateur is to compete
    (E) creditor is to borrow

55. Deter is to encourage as
    (A) borrow is to buy
    (B) hoard is to amass
    (C) harass is to complain
    (D) extinguish is to ignite
    (E) remind is to forget

56. Resilient is to spring as
    (A) wooden is to stake
    (B) buoyant is to boat
    (C) level is to ramp
    (D) stripped is to gear
    (E) slow is to pendulum

57. Infamous is to misdeed as
    (A) illustrious is to achievement
    (B) deceitful is to honesty
    (C) respected is to notoriety
    (D) gullible is to trickery
    (E) menial is to labor

58. Building is to dilapidated as
    (A) poem is to hackneyed
    (B) garment is to threadbare
    (C) supply is to depleted
    (D) traffic is to congested
    (E) bridge is to narrow

59. Impulsive is to forethought as
    (A) boorish is to vulgarity
    (B) conciliatory is to compromise
    (C) merciless is to leniency
    (D) easygoing is to geniality
    (E) disciplined is to will

60. Incisor is to tooth as
    (A) hair is to follicle
    (B) finger is to digit
    (C) nostril is to nose
    (D) hand is to fist
    (E) arch is to foot

# STOP

**IF YOU FINISH BEFORE TIME IS CALLED, YOU MAY CHECK YOUR WORK ON THIS SECTION ONLY.
DO NOT TURN TO ANY OTHER SECTION IN THE TEST.**

EMA
SSAT

## SECTION 4
## 25 Questions

Following each problem in this section, there are five suggested answers. Work each problem in your head or in the blank space provided at the right of the page. Then look at the five suggested answers and decide which one is best.

<u>Note:</u> Figures that accompany problems in this section are drawn as accurately as possible EXCEPT when it is stated in a specific problem that its figure is not drawn to scale.

Sample Problem:

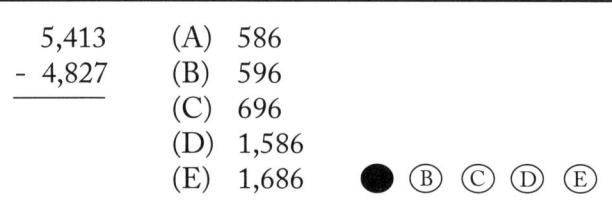

---

1. What is the perimeter of the figure?

    (A) 24
    (B) 40
    (C) 48
    (D) 56
    (E) 68

**USE THIS SPACE FOR FIGURING.**

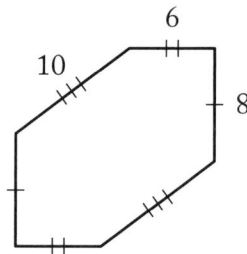

---

2. Rosita and Marc took a math quiz. In their class, Marc had the 8th lowest score, and Rosita had the 9th highest score. If Rosita's score was higher than Marc's and there were three scores between them, how many students took the quiz?

    (A) 20
    (B) 18
    (C) 17
    (D) 15
    (E) 14

---

3, 5, 9, 15, 23, . . .

3. The five numbers above repeat, indefinitely, in the order shown. What is the 30th term of the sequence?

    (A) 3
    (B) 5
    (C) 9
    (D) 15
    (E) 23

**GO ON TO THE NEXT PAGE.**

4. Multiply: $3xy(2x + 4)$
   (A) $6x^2y + 12xy$
   (B) $5x^2y + 7xy$
   (C) $3xy + 6x$
   (D) $12xy$
   (E) $18x^2y$

5. A length was given as 2 meters instead of 2 centimeters. How many times too long was the given length?
   (A) 1
   (B) 4
   (C) 10
   (D) 40
   (E) 100

$$y = -\frac{1}{2}x + 3$$
$$y = 3x - 4$$

6. In the $xy$-coordinate plane, what is the solution to the system of equations above?

   (A) $\left(\frac{1}{2}, -\frac{5}{2}\right)$

   (B) $\left(\frac{1}{2}, \frac{3}{2}\right)$

   (C) $\left(\frac{3}{2}, \frac{1}{2}\right)$

   (D) $(2, -2)$

   (E) $(2, 2)$

**GO ON TO THE NEXT PAGE.**

7. Which graph represents the equation $2y = 4x + 4$ ?

(A)

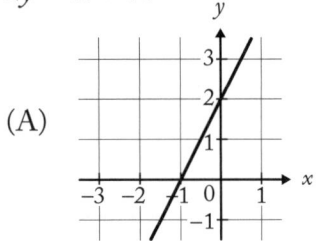

(B)

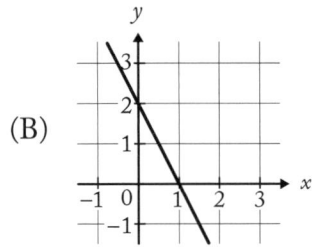

(C)

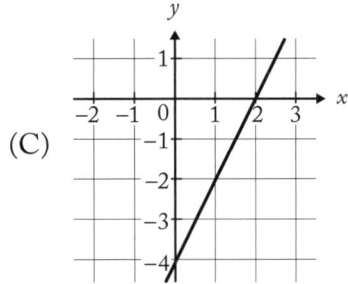

(D)

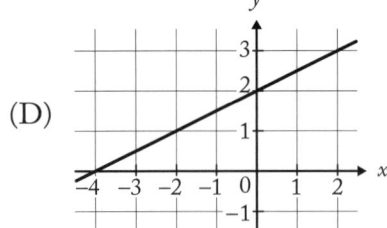

(E)

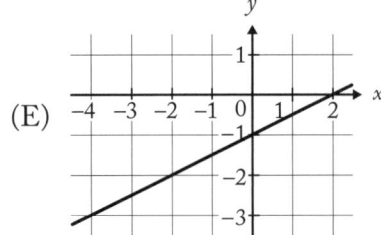

**GO ON TO THE NEXT PAGE.**

**USE THIS SPACE FOR FIGURING.**

8. Given the equation $kx^2 + kx - 5 = 16$, if one solution to this equation is $x = 6$, what is the value of $k$?

    (A) $\frac{11}{42}$

    (B) $\frac{1}{2}$

    (C) $\frac{7}{6}$

    (D) 2

    (E) $\frac{21}{2}$

---

9. The bar graph shows the number of donors at a fund drive who were new donors and the number who were returning donors. Based on the graph, what percent of the donors on Wednesday were new?

    (A) 20%
    (B) 25%
    (C) 40%
    (D) 60%
    (E) 75%

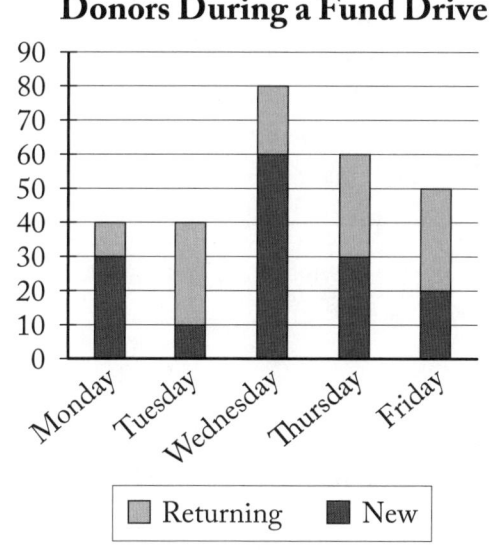

**Donors During a Fund Drive**

---

10. The two legs of a right isosceles triangle each have a length of 5 centimeters. What is the length, in centimeters, of the triangle's hypotenuse?

    (A)  5
    (B)  10
    (C)  15
    (D)  $5\sqrt{2}$
    (E)  $5\sqrt{3}$

**GO ON TO THE NEXT PAGE.**

**USE THIS SPACE FOR FIGURING.**

11. What is the value of $(-1)^7 - (-1)^6$ ?

    (A)   -2

    (B)   -1

    (C)   0

    (D)   1

    (E)   2

---

> A certain copier prints 400 sheets every 5 minutes.
> At that rate, how long will it take the copier to print 11,000 sheets?

12. The answer to the problem above will be

    (A)   less than 1 hour

    (B)   between 1 and 2 hours

    (C)   between 2 and 3 hours

    (D)   between 3 and 4 hours

    (E)   more than 4 hours

---

13. If $x + y = 4$, what must be the value of $x^2 + y^2$ ?

    (A)   2

    (B)   8

    (C)   16

    (D)   32

    (E)   It cannot be determined from the information given.

---

14. Evaluate $9x - 4y - 3z^2$ when $x = \frac{2}{3}$, $y = \frac{3}{4}$, and $z = \sqrt{2}$

    (A)   -15

    (B)   -9

    (C)   -3

    (D)   9

    (E)   21

---

15. Of the following, $48.912 \times (38.7 + 61.4)$ is closest to

    (A)   49,000

    (B)   5,000

    (C)   4,500

    (D)   4,000

    (E)   3,500

**GO ON TO THE NEXT PAGE.**

**USE THIS SPACE FOR FIGURING.**

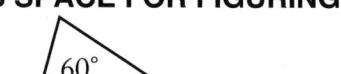

16. In the triangle, what is the value of $x$ ?

    (A)  80
    (B)  50
    (C)  45
    (D)  40
    (E)  30

17. If $n$ is a positive integer greater than 2, then the value of which of the following CANNOT be an integer?

    (A)  $\dfrac{n + 2}{n}$

    (B)  $\dfrac{6n + 8}{2}$

    (C)  $5 - n$

    (D)  $n - 4$

    (E)  $3n - 10$

18. Sam had to read 60 pages a day to finish an assignment on time, but he read an extra 5 pages a day. As a result, for the last 4 days he had only 135 pages left to read. How many days in all did Sam have to finish the assignment?

    (A)  12
    (B)  15
    (C)  25
    (D)  27
    (E)  39

19. Point $G$ bisects the line segment $\overline{FH}$. The length of $\overline{FG}$ is 16 less than 3 times the length of $\overline{GH}$. What is the length of $\overline{FH}$ ?

    (A)   6
    (B)   8
    (C)  10
    (D)  16
    (E)  24

**GO ON TO THE NEXT PAGE.**

EMA
SSAT

20. A spherical balloon has a volume of 36π cubic inches. What is the radius, in inches, of the balloon?

$\left(V = \frac{4}{3}\pi r^3\right)$

(A)  3
(B)  9
(C)  27
(D)  48
(E)  72

---

21. In the multiplication problem ■ 4 × ▲ 6, the symbols ■ and ▲ represent digits. Which of the following could be the product?

(A)   100
(B)   240
(C)   364
(D)   446
(E)  2,446

---

22. A family of five—two parents and three children—are hiking. They come to a narrow path where they must walk in a single file line. They decide to walk with a parent at the beginning of the line, a parent at the end of the line, and the children in the middle. How many different ways can the family arrange themselves in such a line?

(A)    8
(B)   12
(C)   24
(D)  108
(E)  120

---

23. Evaluate: −16 + 2(4 − (6 − 8)²)

(A)  −32
(B)  −16
(C)   0
(D)  16
(E)  32

**GO ON TO THE NEXT PAGE.**

**USE THIS SPACE FOR FIGURING.**

24. There are a total of 19 boys and 14 girls in Fernando's class. The names of each of Fernando's classmates are written on individual slips of paper and placed in a box. Fernando is to select a project partner by drawing the name of one classmate from the box. What are the chances that he will draw a boy's name?

    (A)   1 in 32
    (B)   1 in 19
    (C)   1 in 18
    (D)  18 in 32
    (E)  19 in 33

---

25. If $x$ and $y$ are positive numbers, $\frac{x^8}{y^2} = 180$, and $x^6 = 5$, what is the value of $\frac{x}{y}$?

    (A) $\frac{1}{36}$

    (B) $\frac{1}{6}$

    (C)   6

    (D)  30

    (E)  36

# STOP

**IF YOU FINISH BEFORE TIME IS CALLED, YOU MAY CHECK YOUR WORK ON THIS SECTION ONLY.
DO NOT TURN TO ANY OTHER SECTION IN THE TEST.**

THIS PAGE INTENTIONALLY LEFT BLANK.

# Evaluating Your Upper Level SSAT

# How Did You Do?

When you have completed the practice tests, give yourself a pat on the back, and then take a few moments to think about your performance.

- Did you leave many questions unanswered?

- Did you run out of time?

- Did you read the directions carefully?

Based on your understanding of how well you performed, review the test sections that gave you difficulty.

# Scoring the Practice Tests

In order to calculate your "raw score" (right, wrong, and omitted answers) for each test section, use the answer keys on pages 226–237. *The Official Study Guide for the Upper Level SSAT* contains practice tests, not "retired" forms of the test. They are intended to familiarize you with the format, content, and timing of the test. They do not provide you with a score as if you were taking the actual SSAT.

# Computing Your Raw Score

**1.** Using the Practice Test Answer Keys found on pages 226–237, check your answer sheet against the list of correct answers.

**2.** Look at your answer for each test question in the "Your Answer" column. Next, give yourself a ✓ in the "C" column for each correct answer, a 0 for each wrong answer in the "W" column, and a—for each question omitted in the "O" column.

| Correct Answer | Your Answer | C ✓ | W 0 | O — |
|---|---|---|---|---|
| 1. A | A | ✓ | | |
| 2. B | C | | 0 | |
| 3. C | | | | — |
| 4. C | C | ✓ | | |
| 5. D | D | ✓ | | |

**3.** Add the total number of correct answers and enter the number in the "Total # Correct" box; add the number of 0s and enter in the "Total # Wrong" box. (It is not necessary to add the number of omits. You can use that information to go back and review those questions and to make sure that you understand all answers.)

**4.** Raw scores are calculated by using the following system:

- One point is given for each correct answer.
- No points are added or subtracted for questions omitted.
- One fourth of a point is subtracted for each incorrect answer.

**5.** Divide the number of wrong answers in the "Total # Wrong" box by 4 and enter the number in the "# Wrong ÷ 4" box. For example, if you had 32 right and 19 wrong, then your raw score is 32 minus one fourth of 19, which equals 27¼ (32 - 4¾ = 27¼).

| | |
|---|---|
| Total # Correct: | 1 |
| Total # Wrong: | |
| # Wrong ÷ 4: | 2 |
| Box 1 - Box 2 | 3 |
| Round Box 3 to nearest whole integer: | 4 |
| **Raw Score:** | |

**6.** Round the result in box 3 to the nearest whole integer. Put the integer in Box 4. For example, round 27¼ to 27.

**7.** The integer in Box 4 is the raw score on the section.

**8.** Repeat this procedure for each simulated test section that you have taken.

# Answer Key

## Upper Level Practice Test I : QUANTITATIVE (Sections 1 and 4)

For each question, mark ✓ if correct (C), **0** if wrong (W), or **—** if omitted (O).

| Correct Answer | Your Answer | C ✓ | W 0 | O — |
|---|---|---|---|---|
| Section 1 | | | | |
| 1.  D | | | | |
| 2.  D | | | | |
| 3.  C | | | | |
| 4.  A | | | | |
| 5.  C | | | | |
| 6.  C | | | | |
| 7.  B | | | | |
| 8.  D | | | | |
| 9.  E | | | | |
| 10.  D | | | | |
| 11.  B | | | | |
| 12.  E | | | | |
| 13.  B | | | | |
| 14.  B | | | | |
| 15.  A | | | | |
| 16.  C | | | | |
| 17.  D | | | | |
| 18.  B | | | | |
| 19.  E | | | | |
| 20.  D | | | | |
| 21.  D | | | | |
| 22.  C | | | | |
| 23.  D | | | | |
| 24.  E | | | | |
| 25.  A | | | | |
| Subtotal | | | | |

| Correct Answer | Your Answer | C ✓ | W 0 | O — |
|---|---|---|---|---|
| Section 4 | | | | |
| 1.  C | | | | |
| 2.  D | | | | |
| 3.  B | | | | |
| 4.  E | | | | |
| 5.  C | | | | |
| 6.  B | | | | |
| 7.  A | | | | |
| 8.  B | | | | |
| 9.  B | | | | |
| 10.  C | | | | |
| 11.  E | | | | |
| 12.  A | | | | |
| 13.  D | | | | |
| 14.  D | | | | |
| 15.  D | | | | |
| 16.  B | | | | |
| 17.  E | | | | |
| 18.  A | | | | |
| 19.  C | | | | |
| 20.  C | | | | |
| 21.  E | | | | |
| 22.  E | | | | |
| 23.  B | | | | |
| 24.  C | | | | |
| 25.  D | | | | |
| Subtotal | | | | |

| | |
|---|---|
| Total # Correct: | 1 |
| Total # Wrong: | |
| # Wrong ÷ 4: | 2 |
| Box 1 - Box 2 | 3 |
| Round Box 3 to nearest whole integer: | 4 |

**Quantitative Raw Score:**

*Box 4*

**Quantitative Estimated Scaled Score:**

*See Table on page 238*

# Answer Key

## Upper Level Practice Test I : READING (Section 2)

For each question, mark ✓ if correct (C), **0** if wrong (W), or — if omitted (O).

| Correct Answer | Your Answer | C ✓ | W 0 | O — |
|---|---|---|---|---|
| 1. E | | | | |
| 2. E | | | | |
| 3. B | | | | |
| 4. C | | | | |
| 5. A | | | | |
| 6. B | | | | |
| 7. E | | | | |
| 8. B | | | | |
| 9. D | | | | |
| 10. A | | | | |
| 11. D | | | | |
| 12. C | | | | |
| 13. D | | | | |
| 14. A | | | | |
| 15. E | | | | |
| 16. C | | | | |
| 17. E | | | | |
| 18. A | | | | |
| 19. C | | | | |
| 20. B | | | | |
| Subtotal | | | | |

| Correct Answer | Your Answer | C ✓ | W 0 | O — |
|---|---|---|---|---|
| 21. B | | | | |
| 22. D | | | | |
| 23. C | | | | |
| 24. A | | | | |
| 25. E | | | | |
| 26. C | | | | |
| 27. D | | | | |
| 28. A | | | | |
| 29. E | | | | |
| 30. B | | | | |
| 31. B | | | | |
| 32. D | | | | |
| 33. A | | | | |
| 34. C | | | | |
| 35. E | | | | |
| 36. B | | | | |
| 37. A | | | | |
| 38. D | | | | |
| 39. E | | | | |
| 40. A | | | | |
| Subtotal | | | | |

| | |
|---|---|
| Total # Correct: | 1 |
| Total # Wrong: | |
| # Wrong ÷ 4: | 2 |
| Box 1 - Box 2 | 3 |
| Round Box 3 to nearest whole integer: | 4 |

**Reading Raw Score:**
*Box 4*

**Reading Estimated Scaled Score:**
*See Table on page 238*

**EMA**
SSAT

# Answer Key

## Upper Level Practice Test I : VERBAL (Section 3)

For each question, mark ✓ if correct (C), **0** if wrong (W), or **—** if omitted (O).

| Correct Answer | Your Answer | C ✓ | W 0 | O — |
|---|---|---|---|---|
| 1. B | | | | |
| 2. D | | | | |
| 3. B | | | | |
| 4. C | | | | |
| 5. E | | | | |
| 6. D | | | | |
| 7. A | | | | |
| 8. A | | | | |
| 9. C | | | | |
| 10. B | | | | |
| 11. A | | | | |
| 12. E | | | | |
| 13. D | | | | |
| 14. A | | | | |
| 15. D | | | | |
| 16. C | | | | |
| 17. C | | | | |
| 18. B | | | | |
| 19. D | | | | |
| 20. E | | | | |
| 21. A | | | | |
| 22. E | | | | |
| 23. C | | | | |
| 24. A | | | | |
| 25. B | | | | |
| 26. D | | | | |
| 27. A | | | | |
| 28. B | | | | |
| 29. A | | | | |
| 30. C | | | | |
| Subtotal | | | | |

| Correct Answer | Your Answer | C ✓ | W 0 | O — |
|---|---|---|---|---|
| 31. D | | | | |
| 32. B | | | | |
| 33. C | | | | |
| 34. C | | | | |
| 35. E | | | | |
| 36. E | | | | |
| 37. B | | | | |
| 38. A | | | | |
| 39. D | | | | |
| 40. E | | | | |
| 41. C | | | | |
| 42. B | | | | |
| 43. D | | | | |
| 44. B | | | | |
| 45. B | | | | |
| 46. C | | | | |
| 47. A | | | | |
| 48. C | | | | |
| 49. A | | | | |
| 50. B | | | | |
| 51. A | | | | |
| 52. D | | | | |
| 53. C | | | | |
| 54. E | | | | |
| 55. D | | | | |
| 56. A | | | | |
| 57. B | | | | |
| 58. C | | | | |
| 59. E | | | | |
| 60. B | | | | |
| Subtotal | | | | |

| | |
|---|---|
| Total # Correct: | 1 |
| Total # Wrong: | |
| # Wrong ÷ 4: | 2 |
| Box 1 - Box 2 | 3 |
| Round Box 3 to nearest whole integer: | 4 |

**Verbal Raw Score:**
*Box 4*

**Verbal Estimated Scaled Score:**
*See Table on page 238*

# Answer Key

## Upper Level Practice Test II : QUANTITATIVE (Sections 1 and 4)

For each question, mark ✓ if correct (C), **0** if wrong (W), or — if omitted (O).

| Correct Answer | Your Answer | C ✓ | W 0 | O — |
|---|---|---|---|---|
| Section 1 | | | | |
| 1. E | | | | |
| 2. B | | | | |
| 3. D | | | | |
| 4. A | | | | |
| 5. B | | | | |
| 6. C | | | | |
| 7. A | | | | |
| 8. C | | | | |
| 9. E | | | | |
| 10. D | | | | |
| 11. D | | | | |
| 12. A | | | | |
| 13. B | | | | |
| 14. C | | | | |
| 15. E | | | | |
| 16. C | | | | |
| 17. A | | | | |
| 18. D | | | | |
| 19. C | | | | |
| 20. B | | | | |
| 21. D | | | | |
| 22. C | | | | |
| 23. B | | | | |
| 24. C | | | | |
| 25. D | | | | |
| Subtotal | | | | |

| Correct Answer | Your Answer | C ✓ | W 0 | O — |
|---|---|---|---|---|
| Section 4 | | | | |
| 1. C | | | | |
| 2. A | | | | |
| 3. D | | | | |
| 4. B | | | | |
| 5. A | | | | |
| 6. D | | | | |
| 7. C | | | | |
| 8. E | | | | |
| 9. C | | | | |
| 10. B | | | | |
| 11. D | | | | |
| 12. B | | | | |
| 13. E | | | | |
| 14. C | | | | |
| 15. E | | | | |
| 16. C | | | | |
| 17. B | | | | |
| 18. A | | | | |
| 19. B | | | | |
| 20. C | | | | |
| 21. A | | | | |
| 22. A | | | | |
| 23. A | | | | |
| 24. B | | | | |
| 25. D | | | | |
| Subtotal | | | | |

| | |
|---|---|
| Total # Correct: | 1 |
| Total # Wrong: | |
| # Wrong ÷ 4: | 2 |
| Box 1 - Box 2 | 3 |
| Round Box 3 to nearest whole integer: | 4 |

**Quantitative Raw Score:** 
*Box 4*

**Quantitative Estimated Scaled Score:** 
*See Table on page 238*

# Answer Key

## Upper Level Practice Test II : READING (Section 2)

For each question, mark ✓ if correct (C), **0** if wrong (W), or **—** if omitted (O).

| Correct Answer | Your Answer | C ✓ | W 0 | O — |
|---|---|---|---|---|
| 1. D | | | | |
| 2. E | | | | |
| 3. D | | | | |
| 4. B | | | | |
| 5. A | | | | |
| 6. A | | | | |
| 7. D | | | | |
| 8. C | | | | |
| 9. C | | | | |
| 10. E | | | | |
| 11. B | | | | |
| 12. D | | | | |
| 13. C | | | | |
| 14. A | | | | |
| 15. E | | | | |
| 16. C | | | | |
| 17. A | | | | |
| 18. E | | | | |
| 19. A | | | | |
| 20. D | | | | |
| Subtotal | | | | |

| Correct Answer | Your Answer | C ✓ | W 0 | O — |
|---|---|---|---|---|
| 21. B | | | | |
| 22. D | | | | |
| 23. E | | | | |
| 24. B | | | | |
| 25. C | | | | |
| 26. B | | | | |
| 27. D | | | | |
| 28. A | | | | |
| 29. C | | | | |
| 30. E | | | | |
| 31. D | | | | |
| 32. A | | | | |
| 33. E | | | | |
| 34. B | | | | |
| 35. E | | | | |
| 36. E | | | | |
| 37. B | | | | |
| 38. D | | | | |
| 39. C | | | | |
| 40. E | | | | |
| Subtotal | | | | |

| | |
|---|---|
| Total # Correct: | 1 |
| Total # Wrong: | |
| # Wrong ÷ 4: | 2 |
| Box 1 - Box 2 | 3 |
| Round Box 3 to nearest whole integer: | 4 |

**Reading Raw Score:**
*Box 4*

**Reading Estimated Scaled Score:**
*See Table on page 238*

# Answer Key

## Upper Level Practice Test II : VERBAL (Section 3)

For each question, mark ✓ if correct (C), **0** if wrong (W), or ▬ if omitted (O).

| Correct Answer | Your Answer | C ✓ | W 0 | O ▬ |
|---|---|---|---|---|
| 1. E | | | | |
| 2. A | | | | |
| 3. D | | | | |
| 4. B | | | | |
| 5. B | | | | |
| 6. C | | | | |
| 7. A | | | | |
| 8. E | | | | |
| 9. C | | | | |
| 10. B | | | | |
| 11. A | | | | |
| 12. B | | | | |
| 13. D | | | | |
| 14. B | | | | |
| 15. A | | | | |
| 16. E | | | | |
| 17. D | | | | |
| 18. C | | | | |
| 19. B | | | | |
| 20. A | | | | |
| 21. B | | | | |
| 22. A | | | | |
| 23. E | | | | |
| 24. C | | | | |
| 25. D | | | | |
| 26. A | | | | |
| 27. D | | | | |
| 28. B | | | | |
| 29. C | | | | |
| 30. A | | | | |
| Subtotal | | | | |

| Correct Answer | Your Answer | C ✓ | W 0 | O ▬ |
|---|---|---|---|---|
| 31. C | | | | |
| 32. B | | | | |
| 33. A | | | | |
| 34. E | | | | |
| 35. A | | | | |
| 36. D | | | | |
| 37. D | | | | |
| 38. B | | | | |
| 39. A | | | | |
| 40. E | | | | |
| 41. D | | | | |
| 42. A | | | | |
| 43. C | | | | |
| 44. D | | | | |
| 45. B | | | | |
| 46. A | | | | |
| 47. D | | | | |
| 48. B | | | | |
| 49. B | | | | |
| 50. C | | | | |
| 51. E | | | | |
| 52. C | | | | |
| 53. A | | | | |
| 54. A | | | | |
| 55. B | | | | |
| 56. D | | | | |
| 57. D | | | | |
| 58. B | | | | |
| 59. E | | | | |
| 60. C | | | | |
| Subtotal | | | | |

| | |
|---|---|
| Total # Correct: | 1 |
| Total # Wrong: | |
| # Wrong ÷ 4: | 2 |
| Box 1 - Box 2 | 3 |
| Round Box 3 to nearest whole integer: | 4 |

**Verbal Raw Score:**
*Box 4*

**Verbal Estimated Scaled Score:**
*See Table on page 238*

EMA
SSAT

# Answer Key

## Upper Level Practice Test III : QUANTITATIVE (Sections 1 and 4)

For each question, mark ✓ if correct (C), **0** if wrong (W), or **—** if omitted (O).

| Correct Answer | Your Answer | C ✓ | W 0 | O — |
|---|---|---|---|---|
| Section 1 | | | | |
| 1. E | | | | |
| 2. D | | | | |
| 3. E | | | | |
| 4. B | | | | |
| 5. A | | | | |
| 6. C | | | | |
| 7. C | | | | |
| 8. D | | | | |
| 9. B | | | | |
| 10. E | | | | |
| 11. B | | | | |
| 12. D | | | | |
| 13. E | | | | |
| 14. C | | | | |
| 15. D | | | | |
| 16. E | | | | |
| 17. A | | | | |
| 18. A | | | | |
| 19. A | | | | |
| 20. E | | | | |
| 21. A | | | | |
| 22. E | | | | |
| 23. A | | | | |
| 24. B | | | | |
| 25. C | | | | |
| Subtotal | | | | |

| Correct Answer | Your Answer | C ✓ | W 0 | O — |
|---|---|---|---|---|
| Section 4 | | | | |
| 1. B | | | | |
| 2. C | | | | |
| 3. E | | | | |
| 4. D | | | | |
| 5. C | | | | |
| 6. E | | | | |
| 7. D | | | | |
| 8. D | | | | |
| 9. A | | | | |
| 10. C | | | | |
| 11. B | | | | |
| 12. D | | | | |
| 13. C | | | | |
| 14. A | | | | |
| 15. C | | | | |
| 16. C | | | | |
| 17. B | | | | |
| 18. E | | | | |
| 19. C | | | | |
| 20. E | | | | |
| 21. E | | | | |
| 22. D | | | | |
| 23. A | | | | |
| 24. E | | | | |
| 25. E | | | | |
| Subtotal | | | | |

| | |
|---|---|
| Total # Correct: | 1 |
| Total # Wrong: | |
| # Wrong ÷ 4: | 2 |
| Box 1 - Box 2 | 3 |
| Round Box 3 to nearest whole integer: | 4 |

**Quantitative Raw Score:**
*Box 4*

**Quantitative Estimated Scaled Score:**
*See Table on page 238*

# Answer Key

## Upper Level Practice Test III : READING (Section 2)

For each question, mark ✓ if correct (C), **0** if wrong (W), or **–** if omitted (O).

| Correct Answer | Your Answer | C ✓ | W 0 | O – |
|---|---|---|---|---|
| 1. D | | | | |
| 2. A | | | | |
| 3. D | | | | |
| 4. E | | | | |
| 5. B | | | | |
| 6. C | | | | |
| 7. C | | | | |
| 8. D | | | | |
| 9. E | | | | |
| 10. E | | | | |
| 11. B | | | | |
| 12. C | | | | |
| 13. D | | | | |
| 14. A | | | | |
| 15. D | | | | |
| 16. E | | | | |
| 17. B | | | | |
| 18. A | | | | |
| 19. E | | | | |
| 20. B | | | | |
| Subtotal | | | | |

| Correct Answer | Your Answer | C ✓ | W 0 | O – |
|---|---|---|---|---|
| 21. C | | | | |
| 22. A | | | | |
| 23. B | | | | |
| 24. D | | | | |
| 25. C | | | | |
| 26. B | | | | |
| 27. C | | | | |
| 28. D | | | | |
| 29. B | | | | |
| 30. E | | | | |
| 31. D | | | | |
| 32. D | | | | |
| 33. E | | | | |
| 34. B | | | | |
| 35. B | | | | |
| 36. A | | | | |
| 37. E | | | | |
| 38. C | | | | |
| 39. E | | | | |
| 40. B | | | | |
| Subtotal | | | | |

| | |
|---|---|
| Total # Correct: | 1 |
| Total # Wrong: | |
| # Wrong ÷ 4: | 2 |
| Box 1 - Box 2 | 3 |
| Round Box 3 to nearest whole integer: | 4 |

**Reading Raw Score:**
*Box 4*

**Reading Estimated Scaled Score:**
*See Table on page 238*

# Answer Key

## Upper Level Practice Test III : VERBAL (Section 3)

For each question, mark ✓ if correct (C), **0** if wrong (W), or ▬ if omitted (O).

| Correct Answer | Your Answer | C ✓ | W 0 | O ▬ |
|---|---|---|---|---|
| 1. B | | | | |
| 2. D | | | | |
| 3. E | | | | |
| 4. B | | | | |
| 5. A | | | | |
| 6. C | | | | |
| 7. A | | | | |
| 8. D | | | | |
| 9. D | | | | |
| 10. A | | | | |
| 11. E | | | | |
| 12. A | | | | |
| 13. E | | | | |
| 14. C | | | | |
| 15. C | | | | |
| 16. B | | | | |
| 17. C | | | | |
| 18. E | | | | |
| 19. D | | | | |
| 20. B | | | | |
| 21. B | | | | |
| 22. A | | | | |
| 23. C | | | | |
| 24. A | | | | |
| 25. E | | | | |
| 26. C | | | | |
| 27. A | | | | |
| 28. D | | | | |
| 29. B | | | | |
| 30. B | | | | |
| Subtotal | | | | |

| Correct Answer | Your Answer | C ✓ | W 0 | O ▬ |
|---|---|---|---|---|
| 31. E | | | | |
| 32. C | | | | |
| 33. C | | | | |
| 34. A | | | | |
| 35. E | | | | |
| 36. B | | | | |
| 37. A | | | | |
| 38. C | | | | |
| 39. E | | | | |
| 40. D | | | | |
| 41. C | | | | |
| 42. D | | | | |
| 43. B | | | | |
| 44. C | | | | |
| 45. A | | | | |
| 46. C | | | | |
| 47. E | | | | |
| 48. A | | | | |
| 49. B | | | | |
| 50. D | | | | |
| 51. B | | | | |
| 52. D | | | | |
| 53. A | | | | |
| 54. E | | | | |
| 55. D | | | | |
| 56. A | | | | |
| 57. E | | | | |
| 58. B | | | | |
| 59. C | | | | |
| 60. C | | | | |
| Subtotal | | | | |

| | |
|---|---|
| Total # Correct: | 1 |
| Total # Wrong: | |
| # Wrong ÷ 4: | 2 |
| Box 1 - Box 2 | 3 |
| Round Box 3 to nearest whole integer: | 4 |

**Verbal Raw Score:**
*Box 4*

**Verbal Estimated Scaled Score:**
*See Table on page 238*

# Answer Key

## Upper Level Practice Test IV : QUANTITATIVE (Sections 1 and 4)

For each question, mark ✓ if correct (C), **0** if wrong (W), or **—** if omitted (O).

| Correct Answer | Your Answer | C ✓ | W 0 | O — |
|---|---|---|---|---|
| **Section 1** | | | | |
| 1. D | | | | |
| 2. A | | | | |
| 3. B | | | | |
| 4. E | | | | |
| 5. E | | | | |
| 6. A | | | | |
| 7. E | | | | |
| 8. D | | | | |
| 9. B | | | | |
| 10. A | | | | |
| 11. C | | | | |
| 12. B | | | | |
| 13. C | | | | |
| 14. C | | | | |
| 15. D | | | | |
| 16. C | | | | |
| 17. B | | | | |
| 18. A | | | | |
| 19. A | | | | |
| 20. C | | | | |
| 21. E | | | | |
| 22. D | | | | |
| 23. C | | | | |
| 24. D | | | | |
| 25. A | | | | |
| Subtotal | | | | |

| Correct Answer | Your Answer | C ✓ | W 0 | O — |
|---|---|---|---|---|
| **Section 4** | | | | |
| 1. C | | | | |
| 2. A | | | | |
| 3. E | | | | |
| 4. A | | | | |
| 5. E | | | | |
| 6. E | | | | |
| 7. A | | | | |
| 8. B | | | | |
| 9. E | | | | |
| 10. D | | | | |
| 11. A | | | | |
| 12. C | | | | |
| 13. E | | | | |
| 14. C | | | | |
| 15. B | | | | |
| 16. D | | | | |
| 17. A | | | | |
| 18. C | | | | |
| 19. D | | | | |
| 20. A | | | | |
| 21. C | | | | |
| 22. B | | | | |
| 23. B | | | | |
| 24. D | | | | |
| 25. C | | | | |
| Subtotal | | | | |

| | |
|---|---|
| Total # Correct: | 1 |
| Total # Wrong: | |
| # Wrong ÷ 4: | 2 |
| Box 1 - Box 2 | 3 |
| Round Box 3 to nearest whole integer: | 4 |

**Quantitative Raw Score:**

*Box 4*

**Quantitative Estimated Scaled Score:**

*See Table on page 238*

**EMA
SSAT**

# Answer Key

## Upper Level Practice Test IV : READING (Section 2)

For each question, mark ✓ if correct (C), **0** if wrong (W), or — if omitted (O).

| Correct Answer | Your Answer | C ✓ | W 0 | O — |
|---|---|---|---|---|
| 1. A | | | | |
| 2. E | | | | |
| 3. B | | | | |
| 4. C | | | | |
| 5. D | | | | |
| 6. B | | | | |
| 7. B | | | | |
| 8. A | | | | |
| 9. E | | | | |
| 10. C | | | | |
| 11. A | | | | |
| 12. E | | | | |
| 13. C | | | | |
| 14. C | | | | |
| 15. B | | | | |
| 16. A | | | | |
| 17. D | | | | |
| 18. D | | | | |
| 19. A | | | | |
| 20. B | | | | |
| Subtotal | | | | |

| Correct Answer | Your Answer | C ✓ | W 0 | O — |
|---|---|---|---|---|
| 21. C | | | | |
| 22. C | | | | |
| 23. A | | | | |
| 24. B | | | | |
| 25. E | | | | |
| 26. E | | | | |
| 27. A | | | | |
| 28. D | | | | |
| 29. C | | | | |
| 30. A | | | | |
| 31. B | | | | |
| 32. C | | | | |
| 33. E | | | | |
| 34. B | | | | |
| 35. A | | | | |
| 36. B | | | | |
| 37. D | | | | |
| 38. A | | | | |
| 39. C | | | | |
| 40. D | | | | |
| Subtotal | | | | |

| | |
|---|---|
| Total # Correct: | 1 |
| Total # Wrong: | |
| # Wrong ÷ 4: | 2 |
| Box 1 - Box 2 | 3 |
| Round Box 3 to nearest whole integer: | 4 |

**Reading Raw Score:**

*Box 4*

**Reading Estimated Scaled Score:**

*See Table on page 238*

# Answer Key

## Upper Level Practice Test IV : VERBAL (Section 3)

For each question, mark ✓ if correct (C), **0** if wrong (W), or **–** if omitted (O).

| Correct Answer | Your Answer | C ✓ | W 0 | O – |
|---|---|---|---|---|
| 1. C | | | | |
| 2. B | | | | |
| 3. C | | | | |
| 4. D | | | | |
| 5. C | | | | |
| 6. D | | | | |
| 7. E | | | | |
| 8. B | | | | |
| 9. E | | | | |
| 10. A | | | | |
| 11. D | | | | |
| 12. B | | | | |
| 13. A | | | | |
| 14. E | | | | |
| 15. C | | | | |
| 16. B | | | | |
| 17. C | | | | |
| 18. B | | | | |
| 19. A | | | | |
| 20. C | | | | |
| 21. C | | | | |
| 22. B | | | | |
| 23. B | | | | |
| 24. B | | | | |
| 25. E | | | | |
| 26. A | | | | |
| 27. D | | | | |
| 28. E | | | | |
| 29. B | | | | |
| 30. E | | | | |
| Subtotal | | | | |

| Correct Answer | Your Answer | C ✓ | W 0 | O – |
|---|---|---|---|---|
| 31. E | | | | |
| 32. C | | | | |
| 33. D | | | | |
| 34. B | | | | |
| 35. A | | | | |
| 36. D | | | | |
| 37. E | | | | |
| 38. D | | | | |
| 39. E | | | | |
| 40. B | | | | |
| 41. D | | | | |
| 42. C | | | | |
| 43. A | | | | |
| 44. D | | | | |
| 45. C | | | | |
| 46. C | | | | |
| 47. D | | | | |
| 48. C | | | | |
| 49. A | | | | |
| 50. A | | | | |
| 51. B | | | | |
| 52. E | | | | |
| 53. C | | | | |
| 54. A | | | | |
| 55. D | | | | |
| 56. B | | | | |
| 57. A | | | | |
| 58. B | | | | |
| 59. C | | | | |
| 60. B | | | | |
| Subtotal | | | | |

| | 1 |
|---|---|
| Total # Correct: | |
| Total # Wrong: | |
| # Wrong ÷ 4: | 2 |
| Box 1 - Box 2 | 3 |
| Round Box 3 to nearest whole integer: | 4 |

**Verbal Raw Score:**

*Box 4*

**Verbal Estimated Scaled Score:**

*See Table on page 238*

# Equating Raw Scores to Scaled Scores

Raw scores are calculated by awarding one point for each correct answer and subtracting one quarter of one point for each incorrect answer. Raw scores can vary from one edition of the test to another due to differences in difficulty among editions. *Score equating* is used to adjust for these differences. Even after these adjustments, no single test score provides a perfectly accurate estimate of your proficiency.

Because *The Official Study Guide for the Upper Level SSAT* contains practice tests and not "retired" forms of the test, there are no norm-group data associated with these forms, and calculations of exact scaled scores or specific percentile rankings are not possible. But the following chart will give you an estimate of where your scaled scores might fall within each of the three scored sections: verbal, quantitative/math, and reading.

| Table: Upper Level Estimated SSAT Scaled Scores | | | |
|---|---|---|---|
| Raw Score | Estimated Verbal Scaled Score | Estimated Quantitative Scaled Score | Estimated Reading Scaled Score |
| 60 | 800 | | |
| 55 | 800 | | |
| 50 | 791 | 800 | |
| 45 | 767 | 791 | |
| 40 | 740 | 764 | 800 |
| 35 | 716 | 740 | 746 |
| 30 | 692 | 716 | 710 |
| 25 | 668 | 692 | 680 |
| 20 | 641 | 668 | 650 |
| 15 | 614 | 641 | 620 |
| 10 | 587 | 611 | 587 |
| 5 | 557 | 578 | 554 |
| 0 | 524 | 545 | 521 |
| -5 | 500 | 512 | 503 |

*These are estimated scaled scores based on the raw-to-scaled conversion of many forms, and a student's score will vary when taking the test.*

# Notes

# Notes